Modern China and International Economic Law

This book series offers an essential forum for Chinese economic law scholars, as well as international scholars interested in China's practice in the context of international economic law. It is thus the aim of this book series to publish essential monographs/compilations in the field of international economic law that focus on China, or on uniquely Chinese characteristics. This book series above all focuses on research that closely relates current practices with past history, and future policies with current circumstances, pursuing a philosophy of understanding legal practices by combining the past and present. Accordingly, top scholars in China and beyond its borders will be invited to contribute to this project from their respective areas of focus, which can cover broad topics related to international law in the current context of China's peaceful rise, such as China's economic policy with various countries, its participation in the WTO legal system and bilateral investment treaty practices, etc.; as well as more specific topics such as China's domestic legislation regarding foreign business, its unique "one country, two systems" policy and its implications on external economic interactions between different "systems" within China.

Bingyu Liu

China's Green Investment in Africa: A State-Centric Corporate Social Responsibility Perspective

中国国际经济法学会
Chinese Society of International Economic Law, CSIEL

Springer

Bingyu Liu
School of International Law
China University of Political
Science and Law
Beijing, China

ISSN 2364-8317 ISSN 2364-8325 (electronic)
Modern China and International Economic Law
ISBN 978-981-95-2156-2 ISBN 978-981-95-2157-9 (eBook)
https://doi.org/10.1007/978-981-95-2157-9

This Springer imprint is published by the registered company Springer Nature Singapore Pte Ltd.
The registered company address is: 152 Beach Road, #21-01/04 Gateway East, Singapore 189721, Singapore

Preface

This book is an original intellectual product of the author, including the identification and design of this book, performance of the various parts of this book, and analysis of the book data.

Portions of the findings have been published in *Transnational Environmental Law* in a single-authored article titled "China's State-Centric Approach to Corporate Social Responsibility Overseas: A Case Study in Africa".

Portions of the findings have been published in *Review of European, Comparative & International Environmental Law* in a co-authored article titled "Establishing Binding Climate-Change-Related Investor Obligation Clauses in International Investment Agreements: Obstacles and Pathways".

Portions of the findings have been published in *The Cambridge Handbook of China and International Law* in a co-authored article titled "China and Global Climate Change Governance: A Union of Top-Down Governance and Multistakeholder Engagement".

Beijing, China   Bingyu Liu

Acknowledgements The journey of completing this book has been one of the most transformative chapters of my life. This book stands as a testament to my journey from a doctoral student to a young scholar, encapsulating the intellectual growth, challenges, and discoveries that defined my Ph.D. years. This endeavor, both exhilarating and demanding, would not have been possible without the unwavering support, guidance, and encouragement of countless individuals and institutions. To all who have walked this path with me, I offer my sincerest gratitude.

First and foremost, I extend my deepest gratitude to my Ph.D. supervisors, Professor Li-Wen Lin and Professor Pitman Potter. Your patience, wisdom, and steadfast guidance have been a beacon of inspiration for this project. You have not only shaped my academic pursuits but also profoundly influenced my personal growth. Your rigorous engagement, and invaluable insights have elevated this work to heights I could not have achieved alone.

I am also profoundly grateful to Professors Victor V. Ramraj, Timothy Cheek, Tianbao Qin, and Yongmin Bian, whose meticulous review and thoughtful feedback enriched this book. To Professors Paul Evans, Karin Mickelson, Ljiljana Biuković, Natasha Affolder, and Galit Sarfaty, thank you for your encouragement and intellectual inspiration at various stages of this project. Your contributions, whether through a kind word or a critical insight, have left an indelible mark on this book.

The financial support of the Doctoral Scholarship from the University of British Columbia (UBC)-China Scholarship Council made this journey possible, and for that, I am deeply thankful. To the faculty, staff, and friends at the Peter A. Allard School of Law, St. John's College, and the Institute of Asian Research, your generosity and support have been instrumental in my academic and personal life at UBC. I am particularly grateful to my dear friends at the UBC, whose passion and shared experiences have been a constant source of motivation and insight.

This book would not have been possible without the contributions of the interviewees in China and Kenya, whose voices and stories have enriched its narrative. My heartfelt thanks also go to my colleagues and friends at UN Environment in Kenya, who guided and supported my empirical research during my fieldwork between September 2016 and February 2017. Your kindness and expertise were invaluable to this project.

As I embark on a new chapter of my career, I am filled with gratitude for my colleagues and the platform that China University of Political Science and Law has given me. Your support and collaboration have already begun to shape my work in meaningful ways, and I am excited to continue this journey alongside such inspiring individuals, to inspire the next generation of thinkers and to explore more fascinating and meaningful questions.

Above all, I owe my deepest thanks to my family. Your love, patience, and unwavering belief in me have been my anchor through every challenge and triumph. To my parents, thank you for being my life models and for instilling in me the values that guide me every day. To my husband and my daughter, thank you for being my companions, my confidants, and my greatest source of strength. I am truly blessed to have you in my life.

Competing Interests The author has no competing interests to declare that are relevant to the content of this manuscript.

Contents

Abbreviations

ABC	Agricultural Bank of China
ADB	Asian Development Bank
AfDB	African Development Bank
AIIB	Asian Infrastructure Investment Bank
BRI	Belt and Road Initiative
CAO	Compliance Advisor Ombudsman
CBD	Convention on Biological Diversity
CBIRC	China Banking and Insurance Regulatory Commission
CCCC	China's Communications Construction Company
CCCMC	China Chamber of Commerce of Metals, Minerals and Chemicals Importers and Exporters
CCP	Chinese Communist Party
CDB	China Development Bank
China Exim Bank	China Export-Import Bank
CPC	Committee of the Communist party of China
CRBC	China Road and Bridge Corporation
CSFM	Community with a Shared Future for Mankind
CSR	Corporate Social Responsibility
ECCO	Economic and Commercial Counselor's Office
ESG	Environmental, Social and Governance
ESIA	Environmental and Social Impact Assessment
FDI	Foreign Direct Investment
FOCAC	The Forum on China-Africa Cooperation
GH	Greenhouse Gas Emissions
GRI	Global Reporting Initiative
HSBC	Hong Kong and ShangHai Banking Corporation
ICBC	Industrial and Commercial Bank of China
IFC	International Finance Corporation
IIA	International Investment Agreement
ISO	International Organization for Standardization
KCETA	Kenya China Economic and Trade Association

KWS	Kenya Wildlife Service
MEE	Ministry of Ecology and Environment
MOFCOM	Ministry of Commerce
NDB	New Development Bank
NDC	Nationally Determined Contribution
NDRC	National Development and Reform Commission
NLC	National Land Commission
PPP	Public Private Partnerships
PRB	Principle for Responsible Banking
PRI	Principles for Responsible Investment
RTI	Railway Training Institute
SACE	Sino-African Centre of Excellence Foundation
SASAC	State-owned Assets Supervision and Administration Commission
SDGs	Sustainable Development Goals
SOE	State-Owned Enterprise
SRI	Socially Responsible Investing
SSCCF	South–South Climate Cooperation Fund
SSTC	South-South and Triangular Cooperation
UNCTAD	The United Nations Conference on Trade and Development
UNDP	United Nations Development Programme
UNEP	United Nations Environmental Programme
UNFCCC	United Nations Framework Convention on Climate Change

List of Figures

List of Tables

Chapter 1
Introduction

The green investment cooperation between China and African countries is of far-reaching significance within the framework of global sustainable development. The cooperation not only contributes to environmental protection and economic development, but also provides important support for the realization of the global sustainable development goals, and has extensive social, economic, and environmental significance. This comprehensive cooperation not only serves the long-term interests of both China and Africa, but also provides an important reference for the cooperation of the international community. However, after more than 70 years cooperation between China and Africa, has the green investment cooperation lived up to its expectations? Moreover, in the context of the evolving concept of green investment, the international community has also added new requirements for the international investment policy framework. Has the Chinese sustainable investment regime adapted, or should it adapt to, the changes therein?

With the rapid growth of Chinese state-owned enterprises (SOEs)' overseas investment, it is of great significance to study the state-centric corporate social responsibility (CSR) approach to promote the development of Chinese SOEs and financial institutions' overseas investment. Corporate social responsibility (CSR) is often understood as voluntary corporate action that goes beyond minimum regulatory compliance.[1] The traditional understanding of CSR is that it is market-based and driven by non-governmental actors. This traditional understanding is mainly based on the study of CSR in Western countries. However, many developing countries do not have similar institutional qualities. How could CSR be promoted in a context where socioeconomic institutions are non-market-based and where there is a lack of active non-governmental actors? This suggests the need to rethink the traditional CSR approach and explore possible alternatives. A possible alternative is the "state-centric" approach practiced in China, where the government and its affiliated institutions are the primary actors in driving and framing CSR initiatives. Ho observes

---

[1] Vogel (2006). See also, Ribstein (2006).

B. Liu, *China's Green Investment in Africa: A State-Centric Corporate Social Responsibility Perspective*, Modern China and International Economic Law,
https://doi.org/10.1007/978-981-95-2157-9_1

the emergence of state-centric CSR in China, showing that Chinese national and subnational government actors are not only regulators but also important corporate stakeholders in advancing CSR.[2] Under this state-centric CSR paradigm, the Chinese government has made efforts to raise awareness of, facilitate, and mandate the practice of CSR in China. The state-centric CSR framework was originally proposed to explain Chinese companies' *domestic* CSR behavior. With the rapid increase of China's outward foreign investment under the high-profile "Belt and Road" (BRI) initiative, it is important to examine how the state-centric approach can also be applied to the CSR behavior of Chinese companies *overseas*.

Africa is a central destination of China's BRI. Chinese investment in Africa has increased significantly in the last 10 years and it is expected that Chinese state-owned enterprises (SOEs) and financial institutions will continue to drive this under the BRI. Infrastructure investment is a main focus under the BRI and Kenya is a major location of infrastructure projects undertaken by Chinese SOEs. As infrastructure projects are large in scale and have great impact on the local environment and local communities, there are many risks and challenges that these Chinese SOEs have to face in the implementation stage, such as how to secure social acceptance, how to ensure adequate labor and working conditions, and how to protect the environment and indigenous peoples' land and property rights.

Moreover, green finance has the potential to shape borrowing companies' CSR behavior, which in turn may lead to more socially acceptable business practices.[3] Companies that have better environmental conservation practices for their operations may have better chances of acquiring capital from private and multilateral financial institutions.[4] As most countries in Africa have limited domestic financial resources to fill infrastructure gaps and energy shortages, since its announcement of the BRI, China has urged the banks under its control to provide financial support to the BRI construction projects in Africa.[5] With dramatic increase of Chinese companies going abroad and the rise of socially responsible investment, there is need to promote socially responsible investment under BRI. However, as many of large infrastructure projects are supported through debt-based finance, questions are raised over its sustainability and the rising debt levels of African economies.[6] There are some criticisms that China's loans to African countries just sink them into financial traps.[7] Moreover, as China adopts lower environmental standards for its aid and investment projects than multilateral institutions or Western companies, investment recipient countries may lower their environmental and social requirements for Chinese companies.[8] Improper management of the environmental and social impact of Chinese infrastructure projects and financial institutions may result in conflicts

---

[2] Ho (2013).

[3] Clark and Wójcik (2007).

[4] Hu et al. (2014).

[5] Foster (2009).

[6] Chen (2018).

[7] Beattie and Callan (2006). See also Fernholz (2018).

[8] Shinn (2016). See also Munson and Zheng (2011).

with local communities and/or direct economic losses that affect Chinese investors' overseas long-term interests. Handling these issues is an urgent task for Chinese companies when they engage in investment in Africa. To ensure the sustainable and green investment of Chinese foreign investment and address the criticism from the international community, there is a need to improve the sustainable and green finance from Chinese financial institutions under the BRI.

China's state-centric CSR approach offers a unique opportunity to consider the potential and limitations for the state in monitoring and driving Chinese sustainable investment overseas. This book, therefore, theoretically analyzes the similarities and differences between China's state-centric CSR approach and Western-led marked-based CSR approach, and specifically examines the advantages and limitations of the state-centric approach to CSR in promoting China's sustainable investment in Africa. Moreover, the findings of the book are based on in-depth interviews, an extensive review of publicly available documents, and field visits to project sites. This book first summarizes and analyzes the development of the Chinese government's policies with regard to foreign investment, CSR practices, and green financing in connection with sustainable investment overseas. In recent years, the Chinese government has become more sensitive to criticisms of Chinese companies' overseas investments and has made a concerted effort to improve its environmental and social regulations and guidelines. Under the Chinese government's direction, Chinese companies and financial institutions are increasingly adopting socially responsible business measures and practices to respond to the environmental and social protection needs of host countries.

In particular, the book uses a case study of a major Chinese investment project in Kenya, i.e., the Standard Gauge Railway (SGR) project, to analyze the potential utility of the state-centric approach in promoting China's sustainable investment in Africa. China intends to use the SGR project as part of China's BRI to open up the Eastern Africa for trade and investment. Like other Chinese infrastructure projects in Africa, the SGR has sparked controversy for its community and environmental impact, contracting practices, and financing arrangements. This book analyzes how the state-centric CSR approach influences China Road and Bridge Corporation (CRBC)'s CSR practices in the Standard Gauge Railway (SGR) project in Kenya. The case study is in order to understand more thoroughly the strengths and limitations of the state-centric CSR approach in advancing Chinese companies' overseas CSR practices. Specifically, by examining the roles of different stakeholders—the Kenyan government, the Chinese government, China Export–Import Bank (China Exim Bank), CRBC, and NGOs and the media in Kenya—the case study shows how CRBC has tried to tackle environmental and social pressures, comply with Kenya's domestic and international environmental standards, and fulfill its CSR practices during the construction project. The SGR case demonstrates the role of the state-centric approach in advancing CRBC's CSR practices. This case also reflects the limitations of the state-centric approach and provides a deeper understanding of China's state-centric CSR policy.

In addition, the book uses China's green finance cooperation with Africa a case study to further examine the application of the state-centric CSR approach. As

Chinese financial institutions, serving as a major financing vehicle for Chinese companies' investment overseas, play a significant role in minimizing the environmental and social risks of Chinese financed infrastructure projects in Africa, the book analyzes the feature and development of China's state-led green finance in Africa. This chapter explores the formation and development of China's green finance overseas (in Africa)—development that overwhelmingly revolve under the state-led approach. It compiles and analyzes legal documents on the promotion of green finance by the Chinese government and its affiliated state-controlled financial institutions (including Chinese policy banks and state-controlled commercial banks) in Africa. It further highlights the promises and limitations of for the state-centric CSR approach to promote the development of green finance in Africa.

Taking together, the empirical case study and the legal analysis provide a deeper understanding of the promises and limitations of China's state-centric CSR approach in advancing Chinese SOEs and financial institutions' behavior overseas. By examining the limitations of the existing Chinese SOEs and financial institutions' investment in Africa, the book provides regulatory lessons for future Chinese infrastructure investment in Africa and beyond.

1.1 Problem Statement and Research Questions

CSR is typically a self-regulated and market-driven attempt in advancing corporate social and environmental behavior. Considering the potential limitations and ineffectiveness of the traditional CSR approach, Ho proposes a state-centric CSR approach in the context of China.[9] Under the state-centric approach, Ho claims that Chinese national and subnational government actors are not only regulators but also companies' most important stakeholders in advancing CSR. While some studies in China have noted the state-centric approach, these have focused on its application to Chinese domestic rather than overseas CSR practices.[10] China has rapidly become one of the world's biggest overseas investors, particularly with investments heavily concentrated in infrastructure projects.[11] Its grand infrastructure projects in Africa, for instance, have sparked controversies given their community and environmental impact. A series of pollution incidents has not only caused ecological degradation but also harmed China's international image. Considering the mounting international scrutiny and criticism of Chinese companies' environmental and social performance, it is important to examine how the state-centric approach applies to advancing Chinese investors' CSR overseas.

This book aims to enrich the knowledge of China's state-centric CSR by contextualizing Chinese investment in Africa and addresses the following questions. This book addresses the following questions: How has the state-centric approach been

---

[9] Ho (2013).

[10] Ibid. See also, Lin (2010) and Zhao (2014).

[11] For more discussion, see Chapter 3.

applied to promote Chinese sustainable investment overseas? What are the features, strengths, and limitations of the state-centric approach in advancing the CSR practices of Chinese SOEs and financial institutions in Africa? What are the policy implications that could further promote Chinese sustainable investment framework? The book sheds lights on how Chinese SOEs and financial institutions conducted green investment in Africa under the state-centric CSR approach in the context of international sustainable investment regime.

To these questions, this book has developed the following propositions: Close institutional, relational, and bureaucratic ties between the state and the business community give the Chinese government the power to influence Chinese companies' (especially SOEs') and financial institutions' behavior overseas. Under the state-centric approach of CSR, the Chinese government can facilitate Chinese state-owned companies and financial institutions' overseas CSR practices through mandating, facilitating, endorsing, and partnering to minimize the negative externalities of Chinese investors' overseas activities. However, the state-centric CSR approach limits the space for the engagement of civil society. The effectiveness of the state-centric approach to CSR abroad is constrained by different institutional contexts and ownership types of Chinese companies and financial institutions. The strengths and limitations of the state-centric approach illuminated through the SGR project and China's green finance in Africa could provide regulatory lessons for future Chinese infrastructure investment.

1.2 Research Methodology

1.2.1 Qualitative and Quantitative Analysis of Legal Instruments

This book compiles and examines legal documents on the promotion of sustainable investments by the Chinese government and its affiliated entities (including state-owned industrial companies and state-controlled financial institutions) from 2007 to 2024. Taken together, these documents provide a framework to reveal how the Chinese state intends to shape the social and environmental performance of Chinese companies and financial institutions overseas as a whole.

1.2.2 Case Study

In the current international context, due to different social and cultural environments, environmental governance varies from nation to nation. Legal strategies must be consistent and congruent with empirical realities in each cultural context. Detailed and localized field research should help to design a better regulatory framework for companies' environmental and social behavior. The case study of CRBC's CSR practices in the SGR project in Kenya is used here to investigate and analyze the role and utility of the state-centric approach. The case selection was based on whether the company was willing to provide and verify relevant information and whether the project has triggered considerable environmental and social controversy at the local level. In this case, the SGR project is the largest infrastructure project in Kenya in the past century. It is also the flagship project of Kenya's "Vision 2030".[12] The contractor for the SGR project is a Chinese SOE, with 85% of the project's funding coming from China's Exim Bank, one of China's major policy banks. Since its commencement, the SGR project has received great attention from the Kenyan government and people. It has sparked controversy due to its community and environmental impact, contracting practices, and financing arrangements. Hence, the SGR project in Kenya is a good case study to illuminate and examine the strengths and weaknesses of the state-centric approach in regulating Chinese companies' environmental and social behavior overseas.

1.2.3 Interviews and Fieldwork

A stakeholder analysis is used to analyze the roles of different actors related to development projects. The main goals of the stakeholder analysis are to: (1) identify the stakeholders; (2) assess how stakeholders affect/are affected by projects; (3) examine the relations among stakeholders; and (4) assess the stakeholders' participation during project construction and implementation. The stakeholders involved in the SGR project are listed in Fig. 1.1.

In the context of Chinese overseas investment, the environmental and social behavior of Chinese companies is influenced by the governments of the host and home countries as well as their respective financial institutions, media, and non-governmental organizations (NGOs). Under the state-centric approach, China's government and state-controlled financial institutions are crucial actors that considerably influence the environmental and social behavior of Chinese companies.[13] By conducting semi-structured interviews with the different stakeholders indicated in Fig. 1.1, this book aims to examine the strengths and weaknesses of the state-centric CSR approach in addressing the environmental and social impact of the SGR project in Kenya.

Given resource constraints and lack of access to comprehensive surveys or in-depth interviews with large samples, this book uses small but representative in-depth interviews and gathers further insights from experts. A total of 39 interviewees were interviewed for this book (see Appendix 1). These included government officials, staff members of environmental NGOs, and media personnel in Kenya and China; officers of UN Environment in Kenya; (project) managers and officers at Kenyan

[12] Kenya "Vision 2030". http://www.vision2030.go.ke/.

[13] Hu and Wang (2015).

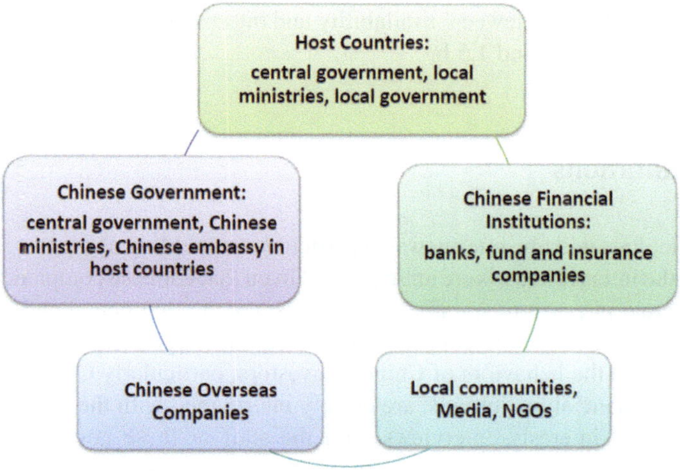

Fig. 1.1 Stakeholders involved in Chinese investment projects overseas. Author's diagram

branches of Chinese companies; project managers of Chinese policy banks; and elected government officials of affected Kenyan counties. The detailed explanation of the interview design is included in Chapter 4. The interview questions were given to all respondents and are listed in Appendix 2–5. In general, the interviews looked at the interviewees' perception of Chinese infrastructure's impact at the local level and their opinions on what effective regulatory mechanisms can be adopted to promote sustainable Chinese investment. Open-ended questions were designed for the interviewees to investigate their alternative livelihoods and basic attitudes toward the SGR project and to explore whether and to what extent the construction of the SGR project would affect their livelihoods.

The interviewees were contacted through personal contacts and email correspondence. Four of the interviewees were known from prior personal contact before arriving in Kenya. The snowballing technique was used to solicit more interviews by asking interviewees to refer other potential interviewees. Thirteen interviewees were contacted through introductions provided by the four previous contacts in Kenya. Many interviewees were contacted through conferences and social activities, including China's Ecological Civilization Cooperation under the South-South Cooperation Conference held at UN Environment in Kenya in September 2016, training programs for project managers of Chinese SOEs operating in Kenya held by the Chinese embassy in Kenya, the 2016 Nairobi Conference on Earth System Governance, and one local NGO protest against the SGR project outside the Chinese embassy in Kenya in 2016. These events provided unique and valuable opportunities to network with 20 Chinese infrastructure companies, policy makers, government officials, and researchers working for NGOs. Two colleagues from UN Environment were also invited to participate in the interviews. Each of the eight interviewees contacted via email, who indicated a willingness to be interviewed, was sent a copy of the consent form and was informed on how the interviews would be conducted.

Depending on the interviewees' availability and interest in the topic, each interview lasted between 45 min and 1.5 h.

1.3 Limitations

Some difficulties with the interviews, in particular the building of rapport and mutual trust with the interviewees, were anticipated. Given that Chinese companies overseas mostly operate in environmentally fragile areas, the environmental and social risks caused during infrastructure construction are sensitive topics for Chinese investors. Furthermore, as the behaviors of Chinese investors, particularly Chinese SOEs and state-owned financial institutions, are closely intertwined with the Chinese government's political interests, interviews with the staff of these companies may not provide reliable information. Interviewees, especially officials from the Chinese government and managers of Chinese infrastructure SOEs and state-owned financial institutions, may be unwilling to provide objective evaluations or accounts of Chinese investors' environmental and social behavior in Africa. In addition, different cultures and habits made it difficult to interact and communicate with local environmental NGOs and communities. There were limited opportunities to build trust with interviewees, leading to potential issues of low trust and inconsistency in the interview sets.

Furthermore, it should be noted that the case selected in this book is mainly intended to present some specific CSR aspects of one Chinese SOE engaged in infrastructure construction in Kenya. It does not intend to examine all aspects of corporate behavior of the SOE in the case or broadly in other SOEs. In addition, although the interview sample covers a wide range of interviewees, the small number of interviewees means that the book cannot fully represent the complex landscape of Chinese companies' operations in Kenya. There are various types of Chinese companies operating in Kenya from SOEs to privately-owned companies. The state-centric approach to CSR may not be equally effective to influence privately-owned Chinese companies' CSR considering the diverse political and business cultures of different ownership types of Chinese companies. Lastly, the economic and social conditions in African countries also vary from one country to another. Whether the state-centric approach could also be applied to other Chinese infrastructure companies in other African countries requires further examination. This book serves only as a starting point for further research and lays a foundation for future empirical work to analyze the strengths and limitations of the state-centric approach in promoting Chinese sustainable overseas investment.

1.4 Research Contribution

The book will have an impact from two perspectives: from the academic literature (as a gap-filler) and from the China-Africa relationship (as a response to political, economic, and environmental protection cooperation demand). This book is an original interdisciplinary study of international environmental law, international investment law, and international politics. It aims to fill this gap in the academic literature with an examination of the application of China's state-centric CSR approach oversees (Africa). It contributes to an innovative analysis of China's SOEs and financial institutions' sustainable investment in Africa in the context of the latest international investment sustainable investment reform, and helps the international community correctly understand China's investment environment and social impact on Africa. It also provides innovative and detailed proposals on reforms of China's sustainable investment framework and an outlook for reforms of China's sustainable investment framework in Africa and beyond.

This book provides a better understanding of the promises and limitations of the state-centric approach in advancing Chinese infrastructure SOEs' environmental and social protection activities overseas. The existing literature on China's state-centric approach focuses on its application on domestic CSR practices; few scholars have empirically examined the role of state-centric approach in promoting China's sustainable investment overseas. This book expands the application of Ho's state-centric CSR framework by analyzing its utility and limitations for the regulation of Chinese SOEs' environmental and social behavior overseas. This book provides a valuable academic study that gives a comprehensive analysis of China's SOEs and financial institutions' sustainable investment in Africa in the context of the reform of international sustainable investment regime, and theoretically examines the application of the state-centric CSR approach in promoting China's investment in Africa. This book demonstrates that the Chinese government is an important force in promoting positive CSR behavior of its affiliated companies and financial institutions. This book also shows the limitations of the state-centric approach, such as the lack of engagement with the civil society and its limited role in influencing and directing Chinese privately-owned companies and financial institutions' CSR overseas. A better understanding of China's state-centric CSR approach is helpful in designing effective regulatory methods to promote sustainable investments by Chinese companies and financial institutions.

In addition, the bulk of the literature focuses on the impact of Chinese foreign investment on host countries generally but rarely focuses on specific countries.[14] This book analyzes the most recent and influential infrastructure project of Chinese investment in Kenya, Kenya's SGR project. This book conducts the first academic study that examines the environmental and social impact of the project from a legal perspective. It also interrogates the widespread assumption that China is responsible for ignoring many of the environmental and social problems in the SGR case in Kenya. The SGR project presented in this book can provide as a regulatory lesson for

---

[14] Shinn (2016). See also, Alden and Davies (2006), Arewa (2016), Mol (2011) and Tull (2006).

future Chinese infrastructure investment in African countries. CRBC's CSR practices in the SGR project, which stem from the direct governing and monitoring power of the Chinese government and China Exim Bank, is a good example of the implementation of the state-centric CSR approach overseas. This experience could be applied to advance other Chinese infrastructure companies' CSR in Kenya and possibly elsewhere. Meanwhile, given the deficiencies of the state-centric approach revealed in the SGR Project, other Chinese infrastructure companies overseas could learn how to facilitate large-scale development projects sustainably such as through having close engagement with local NGOs and improving information disclosure by Chinese financial institutions.

Beyond scholarly contributions, this book has practical policy implications. It provides a representative empirical study of China's green investment in Africa and systematically designs a feasible roadmap to promote China's investment in Africa and beyond. It proposes suggestions on how to improve sustainable investment of Chinese SOEs in Kenya and possibly in other African countries. The practical policy recommendations include the following: (1) improve the implementation of vague guidelines by providing host country specific guidelines and platforms for sharing practical experiences; (2) improve Chinese companies' and financial institutions' performance capacity by hiring qualified personnel and implementing internal governance rules; (3) enhance supervision and transparency mechanisms; (4) improve Chinese institutions' engagement with local NGOs and media in host countries; (5) provides useful guidance for Chinese SOEs and financial institutions to make sustainable investment in Africa and beyond; (6) helps governments and institutions to formulate and revise sustainable investment framework. The policy suggestions may help Chinese overseas companies and financial institutions more effectively reduce investment risks and achieve the long-term financial success of investment projects. The improvement of environmental and social behavior of Chinese companies and financial institutions may also help sustainable development in host states. As China continues to expand its overseas investment, the policy recommendations could help Chinese investment make greater contributions to host societies.

1.5 Book Overview

Starting with the Chapter 1, which introduces this book question and methodology, this book mainly addresses the following questions: How has the state-centric approach been applied to promote Chinese sustainable investment overseas? What are the features, strengths, and limitations of the state-centric approach in advancing Chinese investors' overseas CSR practices? What are the policy implications emerging from the SGR case and green finance cooperation in Kenya? Chapter 2 first reviews the CSR literature and introduces the theoretical development of the state-centric approach. Against this theoretical framework, this book examines the development of the Chinese government's sustainable investment policies from 2007 to 2024.

As Africa is one of China's major investment destinations, Chapter 3 applies the state-centric approach to the African context. It examines the economic, community and environmental concerns of Chinese investment in Africa under China's BRI. The African context enriches the theoretical understanding of the strengths and weaknesses of the state-centric approach to CSR. Moreover, the general assessment of China's CSR implications in Africa is helpful to understanding the empirical case study on the SGR case in Chapter 4.

Chapter 4 uses the SGR project in Kenya as an empirical case study to more concretely examine the strengths and limitations of the state-centric approach. The chapter first provides a general background of Kenya's institutional environments and China's infrastructure investment in Kenya. It then examines the roles of key actors in addressing the environmental and social concerns of the SGR project. In particular, the chapter focuses on how the Chinese government and China Exim Bank directed and supervised CRBC's CSR behavior in the SGR project. Finally, this chapter analyzes the limitations of the state-centric approach revealed in the project.

Chapter 5 uses China's green finance cooperation with Africa as a case study. Financial institutions, serving as a major financing vehicle for Chinese companies' investment overseas, play a significant role in minimizing the environmental and social risks of Chinese financed infrastructure projects in Africa. This chapter analyzes the feature and development of China's state-led green finance in Africa. It highlights the promises and limitations of China's state-centricity for the development of green finance overseas.

With the problems revealed in the existing regulatory framework discussed in Chapter 2, the SGR case in Chapter 4 and China's green finance cooperation in Chapter 5, Chapter 6 presents policy recommendations on how to improve Chinese sustainable investment in the future. Chapter 7 summarizes the key findings of the study and offers suggestions for future research.

References

Alden C, Davies M (2006) A profile of the operations of Chinese companies in Africa. S Afr J Int Aff 13(1):83–96

Arewa O (2016) Constructing Africa: Chinese investment, infrastructure deficits, and development. Cornell Int Law J 49:101–139

Beattie A, Callan E (2006) 'China loans create 'new wave of Africa debt'. Financial Times, December 8.

Chen Y (2018) Silk road to the Sahel: African ambitions in China's belt and road initiative. Johns Hopkins SAIS-CARI Policy Brief No. 23

Clark G, Wójcik D (2007) The geography of finance: corporate governance in the global marketplace. Oxford University Press, Oxford

Fernholz T (2018) Eight countries in danger of falling into China's 'debt trap". Quartz, March 8

Foster V (2009) Building bridges: China's growing role as infrastructure financier for Sub-Saharan Africa. World Bank, Washington

Ho V (2013) Beyond regulation: a comparative look at state-centric corporate social responsibility and the law in China. Vanderbilt J Transnatl Law 46:375–442

Hu T et al (2014) Managing environmental impact: international experience and lessons in risk management for overseas investments. World Resources Institute, Washington

Hu T, Wang Y (2015) Environmental and social risk management of Chinese transnational corporations. Yale School of Forestry and Environmental Studies and WWF. http://www.wwfchina.org/content/press/publication/2015/Yale-WWF_final.pdf

Lin L (2010) Corporate social responsibility in China: window dressing or structural change. Berkeley Int Law J 28:64–100

Mol A (2011) China's ascent and Africa's environment. Glob Environ Chang 21(3):785–794

Munson P, Zheng R (2011) Feeding the dragon: managing Chinese resource acquisition in Africa. Seattle J Environ Law 2:373–376

Ribstein L (2006) Accountability and responsibility in corporate governance. Notre Dame Law Rev 81:1444–1447

Shinn D (2016) The environmental impact of China's investment in Africa. Cornell Int Law J 25:25–65

Tull D (2006) China's engagement in Africa: scope, significance and consequences. J Mod Afr Stud 44(3):459–479

Vogel D (2006) The market for virtue: the potential and limits of corporate social responsibility. Brookings Institution Press, Washington

Zhao J (2014) Corporate social responsibility in contemporary China. Edward Elgar, Cheltenham

Chapter 2
State-Centric Corporate Social Responsibility (CSR) and China's Policy Framework

The chapter begins with an introduction to the theoretical development of CSR, highlighting the strengths and limitations of the conventional market-based CSR approach. It then transitions to the state-centric CSR approach that has emerged in China. The Chinese government plays a pivotal role in promoting CSR by mandating, facilitating, and endorsing CSR practices among Chinese companies. This state-centric approach is realized through numerous policies and regulations issued by the Chinese government. The chapter specifically analyzes the selective legal instruments used by the Chinese government to promote overseas CSR and green finance from 2007 to 2021. The analysis of China's policies and regulations reveals the potential advantages and challenges of the state-centric approach.

2.1 The Conventional Approach to CSR: Market-Based and Non-Governmental Actors Driven

There is a large body of literature on the concept and practice of CSR.[1] The rise of CSR can be understood as an attempt to seek for a more socially embedded form of economic governance.[2] CSR emerges as a network governance structure of international organizations, civil society, and private business actors that tries to address institutional weaknesses and compensate for the failures of market liberalism, such as information asymmetry and the insufficient provision of public goods.[3] The development of CSR theory reflects a paradigm shift from one that protects shareholders' economic interests to one that increasingly takes stakeholders' interests as well as

[1] Garriga and Melé (2004).

[2] Levy and Kaplan (2008a).

[3] Scherer et al. (2013).

B. Liu, *China's Green Investment in Africa: A State-Centric Corporate Social Responsibility Perspective*, Modern China and International Economic Law,
https://doi.org/10.1007/978-981-95-2157-9_2

global social welfare into consideration.[4] The emerging stakeholders in the CSR framework can be viewed in the context of the "emergence of global civil society and the diffusion of state authority to more decentralized networks of actors".[5] The definition, which places the company at the center of analysis, describes stakeholders as "any group or individual who can affect or is affected by the achievement of the organization's objectives",[6] such as suppliers, consumers, clients, and financial institutions.[7] In the context of environmental and social protection, CSR essentially suggests that companies should pay more attention to environmental protection, human rights, anti-corruption measures, and the interests of non-traditional stakeholders such as employees, consumers, and local communities.[8] With attention to CSR, multinational companies not only focus on the economic benefits of investment, but also try to contribute to the public interest, social justice, local development, and environmental concerns in their host countries.[9]

CSR is often regarded as a self-regulated and market-driven attempt that companies take to move toward and beyond minimum regulatory requirements.[10] Under the conventional marked-based approach, companies voluntarily engage in more socially responsible activities because of various considerations, such as reputation and long-term profitability, and pressure from shareholders and consumers.[11] Under this approach, corporate practices are driven mostly by civil society organizations and in response to market pressures from investors and consumers.[12] Although governments may adopt incentives to motivate companies to conform to legal requirements, much of the impetus toward responsible business practice depends on companies' self-regulation and their engagement with investors and other stakeholders.[13]

The conventional market-based approach has some strengths, such as adopting firm-specific CSR strategies to gain business reputation and market shares.[14] This approach also enables civil society to influence and shape companies' CSR practices through consumption choices, urging companies to emphasize the integration of social and environmental protection demands in daily business.[15] Under the market-based approach, civil society and the media are often decisive in influencing market reactions and public perception, and play significant roles in pressuring companies to behave socially and environmentally responsible. As Vogel puts it, a more responsibly managed company "will be more likely to avoid consumer boycotts, be better able

---

[4] Carroll (2008).

[5] Levy and Kaplan (2008b). See also, Kanie and Haas (2004).

[6] Freeman (1984).

[7] Garriga and Melé (2004).

[8] Carroll (2008).

[9] Mele (2008). See also, Carroll (2008).

[10] Vogel (2006a).

[11] Ibid.

[12] Ribstein (2006).

[13] Ho (2013a).

[14] Vogel (2006a).

[15] Mele (2008).

to obtain capital at a lower cost, and be in a better position to attract and retain committed employees and loyal customers".[16] Optimal CSR performances usually have positive correlations with economic benefits.[17]

However, the conventional market-based approach has limitations in protecting stakeholders' interests in practice. As CSR is voluntary and market driven, companies engage in CSR "only to the extent that it makes business sense for them to do so".[18] Unlike government regulation, a voluntary CSR framework cannot force companies to make unprofitable but socially beneficial decisions. With an increasing number of multinational companies' ethical, environmental, and social scandals around the world, scholars have questioned the capacity and willingness of companies to tackle with social and environmental problems under the conventional market-based approach.[19] In addition, CSR cannot deal with all market failures. It often cannot effectively address opportunistic behaviors, such as free riding, which can undermine the effectiveness of CSR.[20]

The market-based approach is more doable in developed countries with mature markets and strong civil society. In other words, the market-based approach requires institutional qualities. Unfortunately, many countries do not have such institutional conditions. Without strong market forces and civil society pressures, companies' CSR performance is at best simply window-dressing or at worst not responsive at all. Existing literature has shown that companies operating in less developed countries including Latin America, sub-Saharan Africa, and Asia have terrible CSR performance under the market-based approach.[21] In less developing countries, CSR programs are usually pursued only for public relations and are "driven by short-term expediency rather than the long-term development needs of a community".[22]

The institutional constraints in developing countries suggest alternative approaches to market-based CSR. Scholars have revisited the role of government in promoting CSR.[23] The role of government in driving CSR has been proposed as a complementary way to promote CSR.[24] Zadek, for instance, highlights the incorporation of governments into CSR frameworks as a new and crucial stage in the development of CSR.[25] Over the last decade, governments have joined other stakeholders in strengthening CSR in different fields, such as public warfare and environmental protection.[26] As McBarnet describes, CSR is a field where market forces, voluntary

16 Vogel (2006b).

17 Ong (2001).

18 Vogel (2006c).

19 Zerk (2006).

20 Vogel (2006a).

21 Visser (2008). See also, Hilson (2013).

22 Frynas (2005).

23 McBarnet (2009).

24 Albareda et al. (2008).

25 Zadek (2001).

26 Moon (2002). See also, Fox et al. (2002), Albareda et al. (2008).

action and legal obligation intertwine.[27] On the one hand, companies' CSR practices are enforced by civil society and consumer activism[28]; on the other hand, regulation, policymaking, standard setting, and other forms of governmental facilitation of CSR also influence companies' voluntary adoption of responsible business practices.[29]

2.2 The Emergence of State-Centric CSR in China

2.2.1 Definition and Characteristics of State-Centric CSR

Ho was among the first to propose the framework of state-centric CSR to understand the practice of CSR in China's context. Ho claims that in a state-centric CSR framework, Chinese national and subnational government actors are not only regulators but also companies' most important stakeholders in advancing CSR. Instead of leaving CSR in the hand of companies and non-governmental organizations, the government takes the lead in driving CSR. It can be understood as a complementary regulatory approach to address the above-mentioned flaws of a fully market-based approach of CSR.[30]

China is a leading practitioner of the state-centric CSR approach. By examining domestic CSR regulatory measures in China, Ho shows that the Chinese government has a vital role in promoting CSR, reflecting broader governance trends that embrace "quasi-voluntary standards" and other novel incentives to "move companies toward and beyond minimum regulatory goals".[31] The development of the state-centric approach is closely related to China's authoritarian political system and the Chinese Communist Party's (CCP) broad roles "as intermediary, as sponsor or patron of civil society and business organizations, and as controlling shareholder of state enterprise".[32] In this context, the Chinese government is able to advance CSR directly by using its capacity as "legislator, regulators, enforcers, and market players".[33] Furthermore, as Chinese SOEs are linked to state organs through institutionalized channels and political practices, their performance and behavior are closely intertwined with the political interests of the government. Lin and Milhaupt demonstrate that the Chinese central government exercises great powers over the selection and compensation of top managers of the SOEs.[34] As top managers of Chinese SOEs usually hold important positions in the government concurrently, the CCP is also

---

27 McBarnet (2009).

28 Verdier (2009). See also, Zerk (2006).

29 Parker (2002).

30 Ho (2013a).

31 Ibid., 375.

32 Ibid., 427.

33 Ibid., 381.

34 Lin and Milhaupt (2013a).

functionally well-situated to monitor personnel in the SOEs.[35] Close institutional, relational, and bureaucratic ties between the state and the business community give the Chinese government the power to influence the CSR programs of Chinese SOEs.

Under the state-centric CSR approach, the key roles of the Chinese government include mandating, facilitating, and endorsing Chinese companies' practice of CSR.[36] The Chinese government can endorse and raise awareness of CSR through direct policy statements, information dissemination, training, and educational programs. The Chinese government can facilitate companies' CSR practices through capacity building, drafting voluntary guidelines and certification systems, auditing and monitoring, standard setting, establishing financial and reputational incentives, and providing government-coordinated services. The Chinese government can also facilitate CSR by enacting regulations to implement multilateral conventions and guidelines. The Chinese government can mandate and promote CSR adoption through legislative and regulatory enforcement to advance Chinese companies' CSR practices. For example, the government could require mandatory sustainability reporting of companies' codes of conduct. Finally, the Chinese government can partner with businesses and civil society in designing, implementing, and monitoring programs to advance CSR practices. This would require Chinese government's direct collaboration with companies, participation in international organizations, and involvement in dialogues about CSR with other stakeholders to promote CSR. A detailed summary of the role of the Chinese government can play in advancing CSR under the state-centric approach is presented in Table 2.1.

2.2.2 *Why Does the Chinese Government Have Incentives to Promote CSR?*

2.2.2.1 At the Domestic Level

An important question arising from the state-centric approach is why the Chinese state has incentives to advocate for CSR. The Chinese government has political, social and economic motivations to promote CSR and develop a more environmentally and socially sustainable framework.[37] At the domestic level, the consequences of Chinse companies and foreign multinationals' irresponsible CSR behaviors have caused significant outrages within China and posed threats to the ruling legitimacy of the Chinese Community Party.[38] CSR is consistent with "social harmony", a political doctrine formally adopted by the Chinese Communist Party in 2006.[39] The

[35] Ibid.

[36] Ho (2013a). See also, Fox et al. (2002).

[37] Lin (2010a).

[38] Ibid., 93.

[39] The Sixth General Meeting of the Sixteenth Central Commission of the Chinese Communist Party (2016).

Table 2.1 The Chinese government's roles in advancing CSR under the state-centric approach

Government roles	Instruments
Endorsing/raising awareness	•Identify and promote companies leading in CSR through websites, publications, and public surveys •Undertake public surveys and communication campaigns •Advocate CSR as part of international trade and investment policy
Facilitating	•Form institutions to develop and implement CSR policy and initiatives •Develop CSR guidelines, monitoring and audit programs •Offer incentives for voluntary CSR performance, and adoption of international CSR standards •Provide technical assistance and training to enhance capacity building •Promote standardization of CSR management models, standards, reports, indicators and auditing systems •Enact enabling legislation to promote environmentally socially responsible investment •Finance CSR research and innovation programs
Mandating	•Require mandatory CSR reports or similar disclosures •Include CSR measures within public procurement requirements and state fiscal policy •Establish minimum compliance standards and enforcement mechanisms •Implement international agreements and guidelines through national legislation and binding standards •Standardize or require CSR management models, reports, indicators, and auditing system •Mandate disclosures regarding socially responsible investment
Partnering	•Facilitate business networks around CSR •Establish public–private partnerships with business and/or civil society organizations

Adapted from Ho (2013a, b, c, d)'s Framework.[40]

Party declared that a number of social concerns including wealth inequality, corruption, pollution, and unequal access to education and health care should have equal importance of economic growth.[41] The promotion of CSR helps the Party deal with the mounting environmental and social pressure and achieve its political goal of a harmonious society.[42] It can also pressure foreign companies operating in China to improve their CSR behaviors and contribute to the welfare of Chinese society.[43] As the performance and behavior of Chinese companies, particularly SOEs, are closely

[40] Ho (2013a).

[41] Lin (2010a).

[42] Potter (2009). See also, Lin (2010a) and Zhao (2014).

[43] Lin (2010b).

intertwined with the Chinese government's political interests, the Chinese government's promotion of CSR is also meant to build domestic support for state capitalism and to justify the legitimacy of the SOEs.[44]

2.2.2.2 At the International Level

(1) The Increasing Demand of Holding Investors' Climate Responsibility

Multinational companies, also known as multinational companies or multinational companies, are groups of companies linked by capital, formed by a collection of legal or unincorporated organizations scattered in several countries.[45] Under the wave of economic globalization and investment and trade liberalization, multinational companies are driving their own and global economic development, while the negative impact of climate change caused by their production and operation activities is gradually becoming a global issue. The 25 largest high-carbon emission fossil fuel companies have accounted for 51% of the total global greenhouse gas (GHG) emissions since 1988.[46] Therefore, it is important to hold multinational companies legally responsible for their climate change mitigation obligations. A small but significant proportion of cases have been initiated to sue against multinational companies, in order to advance climate policy or change the behavior of industrial actors.[47]In particular, the pressure on large companies engaging in the fossil fuel and cement industries to take action in addressing climate change is increasing.[48] The focus of climate litigation has already begun to extend from governments to private actors, primarily the large fossil fuel and cement multinationals known as the "Carbon Majors",[49] which have received much attention for their particularly significant impact on the climate system.[50] In 2019, Milieudefensie et al. v. Royal Dutch Shell decision was the first time that a court has imposed specific climate mitigation obligations on private companies beyond the emission reduction targets set by existing cap-and-trade regulations and/or governmental climate change mitigation policies.[51]

---

[44] Ibid., 86–93.

[45] Yu (2020).

[46] Paul (2017).

[47] Joana and Catherine (2021).

[48] Marc-Philippe and Mai-Lan (2022).

[49] Isabella (2021).

[50] Between 1751 and 2010, 90 companies accounted for 63% of global emissions of carbon dioxide, including methane, from fuel and cement production. See Richard Heede, Carbon Majors: Accounting for carbon and methane emissions 1854–2010 Methods & Results Report, commissioned by Climate Justice Programme (Sydney) & Greenpeace International (Amsterdam), Climate Mitigation Services, Snowmass, CO, 5 and Ivano et al. (2021).

[51] District Court of The Hague, Milieudefensie et al. v Royal Dutch Shell PLC (26 May 2021) C/09/571932/HA ZA 19–379, English Version (Milieudefensie v RDS), para 4.4.46.

Moreover, the Paris Agreement recognizes that the achievement of its temperature targets will require action by the private sector,[52] noting that climate change is a global responsibility that requires the involvement of governments and a variety of actors, including multinational companies.[53] Multinational companies are gradually becoming one of the key subjects in realizing Nationally Determined Contribution Targets (NDC). In the most representative case is Milieudefensie et al. v. Royal Dutch Shell, the Dutch court extended the Paris Agreement's autonomous national contribution commitment to GHG emissions reduction to private companies, stating that GHG emissions reduction and global warming mitigation cannot be achieved by states alone, and arguing that companies should also work toward achieving the autonomous national contribution commitment, with all participants jointly pursuing the goal of net zero emissions by 2050 should be achieved by all participants.[54] The third revised draft of the Legally Binding Instrument to Regulate, in International Human Rights Law, the Activities of Transnational Companies, and Other Business Enterprise also stipulates that business entities should develop while respecting the climate and the environment.[55] Parties should ensure that companies conduct regular climate change impact assessments in the course of their operations, publish policies and risks related to climate change standards, and provide for legal liability in their domestic law for human rights abuses committed by natural or legal persons whom they "control, manages or supervises".[56] While it remains to be seen whether these provisions will be changed into binding national laws or regulatory instruments, they do provide direction for the promotion of national legislation on the traceability of transnational companies' climate responsibility.

In addition to avoiding litigations, the Chinese government expressly recognizes that CSR helps Chinese companies' international competitiveness.[57] As note, CSR has become an important ticket to the international market. Moreover, empirical evidence shows that CSR helps long-term financial performance.[58] The government seeks to encourage CSR to help Chinese companies to grow internationally and sustainably.

(2) Sustainable Investment Regime Requires Investors to Conduct Sustainable Investment

The international community has reached a clear consensus that transnational companies are key targets and participants in climate governance, and the role of

---

[52] UNFCCC, "Decision 1/CP.21, Adoption of the Paris Agreement", UN Doc CCC/CP/2015/10/Add.1 (29 January 2016), paras 117, 133 and 134.

[53] Paris Agreement, opened for signature 16 February 2016, UNTS I-54113 (entered into force 4 November 2016), preamble.

[54] District Court of The Hague, Milieudefensie et al. v Royal Dutch Shell PLC (26 May 2021) C/09/571932/HA ZA 19–379, English Version (Milieudefensie v RDS) paras 4.4.26, 4.4.34, 4.4.52.

[55] The UN Human Rights Council (2021).

[56] Ibid., Art. 6(4), 8(6).

[57] The State-Council Information Office (2011). See also, Xi (2017).

[58] Orlitzky et al. (2003).

private capital flows in financing and technology transfers is a fundamental determinant of the fulfillment of government commitments under the Paris Agreement,[59] which explicitly cites the importance of capital flows for climate governance objectives and the necessity of regulating investments with a focus on climate governance and establishes the obligation to regulate investments for the contracting parties.[60] To provide clear support for investors' climate action, numerous international nonbinding instruments have established specific requirements and standards for investors to meet their climate obligations. For example, the Principles for Responsible Investment (PRI) require investors to incorporate ESG (environmental, social, and governance) factors into their investment analysis and decision-making processes, actively supporting and promoting climate action through risk management and information disclosure.[61] Multiple international organizations focused on climate change have also joined forces to develop the Investor Climate Action Plans Expectations Ladder, which aims to consolidate existing best practices and guidelines for investor climate action to help investors gradually enhance the depth and breadth of their climate-related activities.[62]

In the context of the evolving concept of green investment, the international community has added new requirements for the international investment policy framework, calling for the balance between the rights of the host state and foreign investors to be given close attention in international investment agreements (IIAs) in order to promote the sustainable development of the host state.[63] As the international community increasingly recognizes the responsibility of investors in driving the transition to a low-carbon economy, a new generation of international investment agreements are beginning to incorporate investor codes of conduct such as corporate social responsibility standards, standards of responsible business conduct, and codes for multinational companies. Investor obligation clauses in the new generation of IIAs related to climate governance, environmental protection, human rights protection, represent a gradual evolution of IIAs in terms of their function and value orientation and marking a shift from a focus solely on protecting the private rights and interests of foreign investors to balancing and reconciling the interests of both host states and investors. The United Nations Conference on Trade and Development (UNCTAD) is now actively encouraging states to reform and redraft IIAs to incorporate more investor obligations related to sustainable development.[64]

Moreover, the development of state-led CSR is driven by the state's interest in improving China's international power and reputation. The Chinese government

---

59 The Investor Agenda (2022).

60 Wei (2021).

61 PRI, "Principles for Responsible Investment: Investor Initiative in Collaboration with the United Nations Environment Programme Finance Initiative and the United Nations Global Compact" (2021). https://www.unpri.org/download?ac=10968.

62 The Investor Agenda, "Investor Climate Action Plan (ICAPS) Ladder of Expectations" (2021). https://www.aigcc.net/wp-content/uploads/2021/11/expectations-ladder-english-1.pdf.

63 Xiao (2015).

64 UNCTAD (2015).

actively uses Chinese companies to gain "soft power" in the international politics and economy. As CSR has become a popular norm of international business, it would be difficult to gain access to the international market if not following the norm. Moreover, with the development of international legal instruments such as the UN Sustainable Development Goals (SDGs)[65] and the Paris Climate Agreement, investment recipient countries have linked market access with CSR. CSR is an important strategy for China's international political and economic expansion. Furthermore, Chinese companies that actively engage in international investment are usually SOEs that have close ties with the state.[66] Any criticisms against such state-affiliated companies may ultimately harm the Chinese state's reputation. In particular, as China's global expansion has encountered the allegation of "neo-colonialism", the state has incentives to use CSR as a political strategy to alleviate the international concern.

Hence, to guarantee stability and long-term financial success in overseas investment projects and to improve its international reputation in environmental and social protection overseas, the Chinese government has motivations to develop overseas environmental and social protection policies, and other guidelines to guide and regulate the environmental and social behaviors of Chinese companies.

2.2.3 Strengths and Limitations of State-Centric CSR

The state-centric approach to CSR has some strengths. It fosters and enhances positive communication between the Chinese government and business community. It may also improve Chinese companies' compliance with CSR policies initiatives in practice. Like formal regulation, state-backed CSR instruments "signal the government's endorsement of CSR practices", which can have a stronger indirect effect on the social norms than the CSR policies made by companies themselves.[67] In addition, the government's all-encompassing control over the economy and society has advantages in nation-wide policy formation and implementation. This may help "regulatory convergence" across companies.[68] This is impossible under the traditional CSR approach where CSR policy scope is only company-based.

Moreover, as the Chinese government can influence many dimensions of companies and state-owned financial institutions' operations through administrative control over issuing operation licenses, it can effectively motivate companies to adopt relevant CSR guidelines that it issues.[69] The Chinese government can mobilize various

[65] Sustainable Development Knowledge Platform, "Transforming Our World: the 2030 Agenda for Sustainable Development". https://sustainabledevelopment.un.org/post2015/transformingourworld.

[66] Ministry of Commerce of China (2017).

[67] Ho (2013b).

[68] Ibid., 428.

[69] Ibid., 431.

institutional, managerial, and financial resources to protect its political image when negative social and environmental accidents occur overseas. Close institutional, relational, and bureaucratic ties between the state and the business community give the Chinese government the power to endorse CSR practices of SOEs and state-owned financial institutions. In this way, the Chinese government can more effectively monitor and advance CSR directly and enhance the implementation of CSR initiatives. The state-centric approach thus fills some important gaps in addressing companies and financial institutions' incapacity and unwillingness to genuinely tackle social and environmental problem under the conventional market-based CSR approach.

In addition, the state-centric approach may strengthen companies and financial institutions' positive relationships with regulators and fill communication gaps. By supporting the governmental CSR programs and initiatives, Chinese companies and financial institutions may strengthen their legitimacy in the eye of regulators. They also may enhance their social legitimacy by gaining better reputations, broadening their access to customers and business partners.[70]

However, there are limitations in the state-centric CSR approach. The effectiveness of the state-centric approach depends on the continued commitment, resources, and influence of the Chinese government. It requires extensive governmental resources and financial input to develop, administer and enforce CSR programs. The viability of state-centric voluntary tools also depends on the capacity and will of state agencies and government officials. Corruption, the lack of transparency and capacities of government officials could all undermine the legitimacy of the Chinese government as an advocate of CSR.[71]

In addition, as Ho points out, this approach "weakens the potentially reinforcing and balancing role of stakeholders and of market forces by limiting the space for independent civil society and voluntary firm initiative" and "constrains the space for public participation and civil society leadership in CSR".[72] The state-centric approach is more likely to the adopted by a government which is "unwilling to cede control over CSR initiatives and policymaking to other actors and is not an impartial partner with business or mediator of firm–stakeholder engagement".[73]

Civil society plays major a role in influencing western companies' behavior.[74] Unlike Western companies' CSR practices, which are driven almost entirely by robust civil organizations and companies themselves, the CSR practices of Chinese SOEs and state-owned financial institutions' are mainly driven by the Chinese government through strong governmental control over civil organizations and by the companies and state-owned financial institution' close political and economic connections with the Chinese government.[75] Civil society and media in China are strictly controlled by the government and have far less power in influencing public opinion. Even though

[70] Ibid., 431.

[71] Ibid., 434.

[72] Ibid., 437.

[73] Ibid., 425.

[74] Ribstein (2006).

[75] Watson (2008).

the Chinese government also sees "harnessing the influence of international standard-setting organizations, economic institutions, trading partners, internal management, and civil society"[76] as important mechanisms of informal social control, the country's state-centric CSR approach toward civil society remains conservative compared to democratic countries.

Finally, an important limitation of the state-centric approach may arise from the demands of financial performance. While SOEs and state-owned financial institutions are probably the most responsive group to the state-centric CSR approach, they are also the group that strive for good financial returns in the face of common criticisms of their poor financial performance. How to resolve the conflict between the financial interest and the CSR mission? The state's performance evaluation scheme hints an answer: financial performance accounts for the major part of performance evaluation while CSR are only minor performance indicators. It suggests that when SOE and state-owned financial institution managers do not see any (especially short-term) economic interests in relation to a given CSR activity, they prefer to pursue financial returns and take such CSR activity superficially. It suggests that the state itself must fully embrace CSR in order to make the state-led CSR approach take effect profoundly.

2.3 Extending the State-Centric Approach Beyond Chinese Borders

The state-centric CSR framework was originally proposed to explain Chinese companies and financial institutions' *domestic* CSR behavior. With more and more Chinese companies and financial institutions invest overseas with corresponding impacts to local communities in host countries, there is a necessity to examine how the state-centric CSR approach influences Chinese companies and financial institutions' overseas behavior. Unfortunately, there is scarce understanding about how China's state-centric approach has been applied outside China. The government's continued dominance in the political, economic, and societal spheres in China creates conditions conducive for the emergence of the state-centric approach to CSR. However, the application of the state-centric approach in other national or geographical contexts presents many challenges and opportunities due to the different cultural, economic, political, and legal dynamics of host countries.

First, the institutional environment of the host country is an important variable in the effectiveness of the state-centric approach, as the Chinese central government has little control over the political, economic, social, and legal conditions in the host country. On the one hand, China's state-centric approach may be welcomed by host countries that share similar institutional qualities. On the other hand, China's state-centric approach may encounter suspicion in host countries with democratic institutions and a tradition of active civil society. As noted, an important limitation of

[76] Ho (2013c). See also, Gunningham (2008).

the state-centric approach is the lack of engagement with civil society. This limitation is salient within China as the social sphere is tightly controlled by the state. However, the civil society weakness of the state-centric approach may be alleviated when applied overseas, particularly in host countries of active civil monitoring. Active civil society in host countries might help the effectiveness of the state-centric approach.

In addition, the environmental and social policies of host countries—as well as the political will and capacity of the institutions that enforce and implement these policies—are significant factors in interacting with China's state-centric approach.[77] As CSR is intended to fill the traditional regulatory gaps, if host countries have mature regulatory institutions and strong legal governance in social and environmental protection, CSR may be less important, regardless of the state-centric or market-driven approach.

Second, geographical distance may loosen state control over Chinese investors overseas and the loosening effect may vary with ownership types. The Chinese government probably may not exercise control over Chinese overseas companies and financial institutions to the same level as it does over Chinese domestic companies and financial institutions. This loosening of control is more salient in privately-owned companies. While the Chinese government does not exercise control over privately-owned companies and financial institutions through ownership ties, it can influence many dimensions of the domestic operations of Chinese private companies and financial institutions through various regulatory measures such as licensing and inspections.[78] However, Chinese privately-owned companies and financial institutions have even weaker ties with Chinese government bodies in host countries compared to Chinese SOEs.[79] Since Chinese private companies and financial institutions have much less contact with Chinese government bodies and rarely receive government-linked financial support, there are substantial challenges toward holding these private companies and financial institutions accountable and orienting them toward more responsible business practices.

This section offers a brief analysis of the potential challenges and opportunities of applying China's state-centric CSR approach overseas and the differences between the domestic and overseas implementation of the approach. The following section will provide an overview of the regulatory framework of China's state-centric approach to CSR overseas.

---

[77] Hu and Wang (2015). See also, Leung and Zhao (2013).

[78] Ho (2013a).

[79] Interview with official of Chinese embassy in Kenya and official of National Development and Reform Commission.

2.4 A Regulatory Overview of China's State-Centric Approach to CSR Abroad

China's "Going Out" policy provides the context and legitimacy for Chinese companies' investment overseas. The "Going Out" policy involves different procedures, administrative approval, outflows of funds, and inflows of capital.[80] It shows that among all stakeholders, the Chinese government and state-controlled financial institutions are the major actors in influencing the process of Chinese companies' investment overseas. In addition to its "Going Out" policy, which establishes the fundamental regulatory background, the Chinese government has promulgated various regulations and policies from 2007 to 2021 on promoting sustainable overseas investment by the Chinese government, companies, and financial institutions.

2.4.1 The Regulatory Framework of China's "Going Out" Policy

The "Going Out" policy is part of China's proactive diplomacy strategy. It aims to encourage and support Chinese companies to invest overseas to solve the problems of over-capacity in production within the Chinese economy and to facilitate industrial structural adjustments.[81] Before a Chinese company "goes out", it usually needs to get administrative approval from the Chinese government and obtain capital from a financial institution. In most cases, the financial institution is a state-owned bank, such as China Exim Bank. The Chinese government uses a wide range of substantial state finance to facilitate Chinese companies' foreign investment activities. Hence, the Chinese government and Chinese state-controlled financial institutions are vital stakeholders in ensuring Chinese companies' operation overseas. Usually, Chinese companies must obtain approval of at least three governmental departments, including the National Development and Reform Commission (NDRC), the Ministry of Commerce, and the State Administration of Foreign Exchange.[82] In 2014, the NDRC and the Ministry of Commerce promulgated new management measures, which simplified the flow of overseas investment and significantly reduced the approval time.[83] These interactions are shown in the Fig. 2.1.

For both Chinese companies and financial institutions, ownership structure asserts a huge influence over the governance practices. China is regarded as the world's

[80] Leung and Zhao (2013).

[81] Gu et al. (2016).

[82] Their powers are as follows: NRDC: Supervisor: planning, supervising and coordinating China's economic development and industrial policies; approving and approving foreign investment projects; Ministry of Commerce: approving specific overseas investment matters and issuing overseas investment certificates for Chinese companies; the State Administration of Foreign Exchange: Foreign exchange registration and filing of overseas investment.

[83] NDRC and the Ministry of Finance (2014).

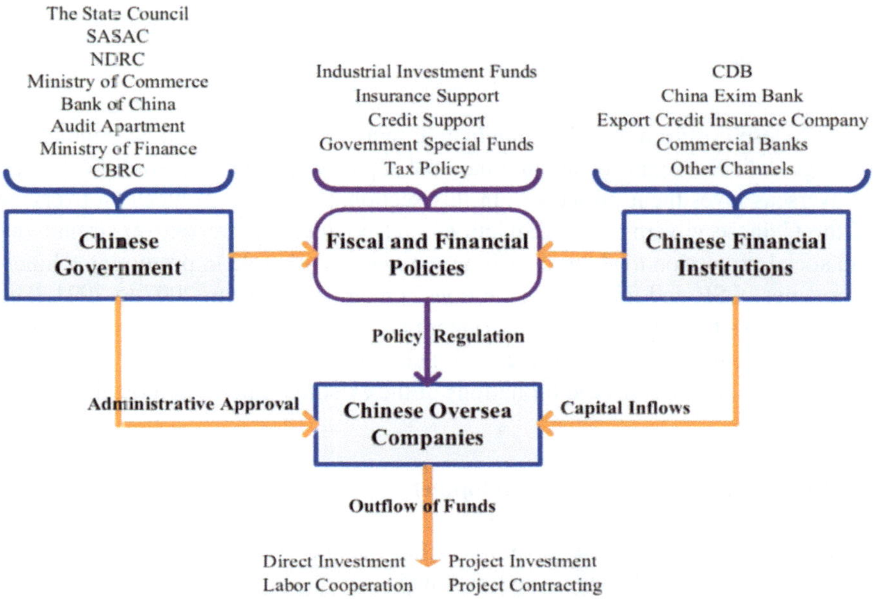

Fig. 2.1 Stakeholders involved in Chinese companies' "Going Out" process. Author's diagram

leading practitioner of "state capitalism", where important overseas companies, especially in "critical industries such as steel, telecom, and transportation", have a close relationship with the state.[84] Most Chinese companies engaging in large-scale overseas infrastructure projects are SOEs, and the financial institutions providing support for the projects are state-owned policy banks. As Chinese SOEs are organized as "networked hierarchies", they are linked through institutionalized personnel channels and political practices to state organs.[85] As discussed before, the Chinese government exercises direct and indirect control over SOEs, "not only as controlling shareholder, but also through personnel management, cross-shareholdings, and direct bureaucratic oversight" by the State-Owned Assets Supervision and Administration Commission (SASAC).[86] The Chinese government plays a large role in the supervision and governance of the state-owned banks, including its lending practices to SOEs. Therefore, the interaction among the Chinese government, Chinese overseas SOEs, and state-owned banks provide the condition for the implementation of the state-centric approach.

[84] Lin and Milhaupt (2013b).

[85] Ibid., See also, Lin and Milhaupt (2017).

[86] Ho (2013d).

2.4.2 Recent Developments of China's Sustainable Investment Policies

The Chinese government has promulgated many overseas sustainable policies and CSR guidelines to gain better international reputations and to ensure the success of overseas investment projects.[87] In this section, this book provides an overview of the Chinese government's regulations and policies on overseas environmental and social protection to show the Chinese government's role in promoting Chinese companies' CSR and financial institutions' green finance from 2007 to 2021. This section shows that the Chinese government has made a concerted effort to improve its environmental and social protection regulations and guidelines. This section also summarizes and analyzes the limitations of the existing policies and regulations.

2.4.2.1 China's CSR Policy Development

In recent years, the Chinese government has become more sensitive to criticisms of Chinese corporate behavior and has made efforts to promote the development of Chinese CSR policies. The Chinese government demonstrates a clear interest in promoting CSR and actively pursues CSR as a strategy to promote the implementation of "scientific development" and a "harmonious society".[88] The SASAC defines CSR as actions to implement the philosophy of scientific development and requires SOEs to not only develop in a people-centered way and make profits, but also " be responsible to stakeholders and environment, so as to achieve well-balance among the growth of companies, social benefit and environment protection".[89] These specific requirements include resource conservation and environmental protection, promoting innovation and technological progress, protecting production safety, participating in social welfare undertakings, honesty and trust, sustainable development, and so on.[90] In 2008, SASAC issued "Guidelines on Fulfilling Corporate Social Responsibilities of the State-owned Overseas Companies Directly Managed under the Central Government", which mandated that all SOEs under its management set up CSR mechanisms within their governance structures. This policy, and the subsequent momentum it generated, led to "the release of more than 1,600 Chinese sustainability reports".[91] SASAC is now exploring ways to build an internal system to evaluate companies' CSR performance, which may take corporate social and environmental impact as part of the assessment of corporate leaders' remuneration.[92] In addition,

[87] Bernasconi-Osterwalder et al. (2013). See also, Dolzer and Schreuer (2008) and Leung and Zhao (2013).

[88] Potter (2009).

[89] SASAC (2008a).

[90] Ibid.

[91] Liu (2015).

[92] Interview with deputy director of Institute of International Development Cooperation at the Chinese Academy of International Trade and Economic Corporation, MOFCOM.

the Chinese government has also promoted the development of CSR through the establishment of industrial associations and organizations aimed at publicizing the best practices of business behavior.[93] Dialogues with industrial associations, such as the China Chamber of Commerce of Metals, Minerals & Chemicals Importers & Exporters, help to publicize and disseminate CSR policies and guidelines and enhance communications between governments and companies.[94]

Echoing the Chinese government's expansion of its CSR policies and regulatory frameworks, some Chinese companies have introduced CSR over the years.[95] A growing number of Chinese companies are embracing CSR as part of their corporate strategy.[96] In terms of China's implementation of CSR, Lin proposes that even though the enforcement and effectiveness of CSR in China still faces many challenges, the achievement of China's CSR development should not be seen as simply window dressing.[97] According to the 2017 Golden Bees Chinese Companies' Corporate Social Responsibility Report, the level of Chinese companies' CSR performance has reached its highest in history, especially in the areas of information disclosure and engagement with communities, employees, suppliers, and stakeholders.[98] The top CSR performers in China are usually SOEs rather than private companies.[99]

Chinese CSR policies have joined the trend of referring to international standards, such as the "UN Global Compact",[100] the "OECD Guidelines for Multinational Overseas Companies",[101] the "Equator Principles", the "UN Principles for Responsible Investment", the "UN Norms on the Responsibilities of Transnational Companies

---

[93] China WTO Tribune (2017).

[94] China Chamber of Commerce of Metals, Minerals and Chemicals Importers and Exporters. http://www.cccmc.org.cn.

[95] Lin (2010c).

[96] Ho (2013a).

[97] Lin (2010a).

[98] Since the beginning of 2016, the Golden Bees index has accessed Chinese companies' CSR performance domestically and overseas. In the 10 years, the Golden Bees assessment has received a total of 3088 feedbacks and 976 cases. The "Golden Bee China CSR Index Report 2016" shows the latest development of China's CSR programs. China WTO Tribune (2017), "The 2017 Golden Bees Chinese Companies' Corporate Social Responsibility Report". http://images.mofcom.gov.cn/csr/201712/20171219174229375.pdf.

[99] Ibid.

[100] The "United Nations Global Compact" is a voluntary corporate responsibility initiative that commits businesses to align their operations and strategies with ten universally accepted principles to support and respect internationally recognized human rights, avoid complicity in human rights abuses, uphold freedom of association and collective bargaining, eliminate forced and compulsory labor, eliminate child labor, eliminate all forms of discrimination in employment, support a precautionary approach to environmental challenges, promote greater environmental responsibility, encourage the development of environmentally friendly technologies, and work against corruption in all its forms, including extortion and bribery. See more, The United Nations Global Compact. https://www.unglobalcompact.org/.

[101] The "OECD Guidelines for Multinational Overseas Companies" is one of the most comprehensive international agreements in this space covering labor rights, human rights, the environment, information disclosure, bribery, consumer interests, competition, taxation, and intellectual property rights. The OECD Guidelines for Multinational Companies' ten chapters cover a broad range of

and other Business Overseas Companies with Regard to Human Rights", and the "IFC Performance Standards on Environmental and Social Sustainability". As of the end of 2008, nearly 200 Chinese companies joined the UN Global Compact, which is an initiative that commits companies to 10 principles in the areas of labor, environment, human rights, and anti-corruption.[102] Over 100,000 Chinese overseas companies have become ISO 14001 certified, which signifies that the companies have started to enhance their environmental management systems.[103] Besides, some Chinese companies operating in developing countries have voluntarily worked with and adopted Extractive Industries Transparency Initiative (EITI) standards and Global Reporting Initiative (GRI) Sustainability Reporting Guidelines. As of 2016, at least 130 Chinese companies are involved in EITI reporting showing an increase in Chinese companies reporting to EITI.[104] As of 2015, more than 75 percent of China's top 100 companies and financial institutions produce sustainability reports based on the GRI's standards.[105] Study show that, Chinese companies no longer have fundamental differences from Western companies regarding the recognition of international environmental sustainability criteria.[106]

2.4.2.2 CSR Measures in Outward Foreign Investment

As China has rapidly evolved into one of the world's largest overseas investors, CSR is an important topic for Chinese companies operating overseas. Since 2006, the Chinese government has issued a series of guidelines and recommendations calling on companies to respect the environment, community interests, and workers' rights when investing abroad. In 2007, the Ministry of Commerce issued a circular on "Enhancing Environmental Supervision on Export Companies" to restrict socially irresponsible overseas companies from conducting foreign trade.[107] SASAC also issued the CSR guidelines to strengthen SOEs' overseas CSR performance.[108] Over 80 official policies and regulations regarding Chinese foreign investment have been issued since 2005.[109] Different agencies, including China's State Council, the NDRC, the Ministries of Commerce and Foreign Affairs, and other state entities, such as the China Export–Import Bank, have been involved in the regulation-making process.

Monumentally, the 18th National Congress of the CCP adopted "Ecological Civilization" as one of its guiding principles in 2012, making green growth and

---

corporate activities, and one of the chapters deals specifically with environmental issues. OECD (2011).

102 Tan-Mullins and Mohan (2013).

103 McGuire (2016). See also, Hohnen (2007).

104 EITI International Secretariat (2016).

105 KPMG (2015).

106 Farrell (2016).

107 U.S. Chamber of Commerce (2012).

108 SASAC (2008b).

109 Bernasconi-Osterwalder et al. (2013).

green development an essential part of its national development and overseas investments.[110] Ecological protection gained importance comparable to economic development. This reflects the CCP's determination to promote a harmonious relationship between people and nature as well as to advance China's sustainable development in the future.[111] This pledge to environmental protection has been translated into not only domestic environmental policies but also foreign sustainable investment measures.[112] The "Vision and Action to Promote the Silk Road Economic Belt and the 21st Century Maritime Silk Road" published in 2015 also highlights the importance of ecological civilization, biodiversity, and climate change cooperation to build the green Silk Road.[113] In December 2016, the Ecological Conservation Dialogue Conference released the "Initiative on Fulfilling Corporate Environmental Responsibility to Build Green One Belt One Road".[114] In April 2017, The Ministry of Commerce and four other ministries jointly issued the "Guidance on Promoting Green One Belt One Road" to further advocate the building of a green BRI.[115] Under the Chinese government's existing policies and guidelines, some Chinese overseas companies have started to realize the importance of CSR in reducing friction and operational risks, obtaining local trust, and achieving sustainable development in host countries.[116]

As a large part of China's foreign investment involves infrastructure contracts, the Chinese government has particularly issued CSR guidelines in this area. For instance, in 2008 the State Council issued the "Regulation on Management of Foreign Contracted Project".[117] Consistent with the State Council's regulatory move, the China International Contractors Association in 2012 issued the "Guidance on Social Responsibility for Chinse International Contractors", which recommends suppliers and subcontractors to incorporate "ethics and environmental protection into procurement and subcontracting contracts".[118] Accordingly, Chinese companies started to issue internal rules for suppliers and contractors based on the abovementioned regulations. For example, China Petrochemical Corporation issued the "Notice on Further Strengthening Contractor Management Work", which requires project contractors to

[110] China Council for International Cooperation on Environment and Development (2016a). See also, UNEP (2016) and China Council for International Cooperation on Environment and Development (2016b).

[111] Geall (2015).

[112] China Council for International Cooperation on Environment and Development (2016b).

[113] NDRC, Ministry of Foreign Affairs and Ministry of Commerce of China (2015).

[114] Foreign Affairs Department of Shenzhen Government (2016).

[115] Guidance on Promoting Green One Belt One Road (关于推进绿色"一带一路"建设的指导意见). http://www.mep.gov.cn/gkml/hbb/bwj/201705/t20170505_413602.htm.

[116] China WTO Tribune (2017). See also, Guo (2008) and UNDP China (2017).

[117] The State Council (2012).

[118] China International Contactors Association (2012).

comply with relevant laws and regulations, and meet relevant qualification requirements.[119] Subsequently, the Chinese government put addressing climate change as an important element during Chinese companies foreign investment, including mobilizing more funds to the field of climate change and deepening international cooperation in climate investment and financing in 2020 and 2021. The following table shows China's main policy development in enhancing environmental and social protection regulations for Chinese companies overseas (Table 2.2).

2.4.2.3 China's Policy Supports to Green Finance

Green finance refers to financial services provided for project investment, project financing, project operations, and risk management in the fields of environmental protection, energy conservation, emission reduction, and green technology.[120] It has become a critical issue in financial innovation, global economic development, and environmental governance. Under green finance, financial institutions allocate resources to attract and guide social capital into new low-emission and low-pollution technologies and industries to achieve economic transformation and development.[121] Green finance requires financial institutions to integrate consideration of environmental and social protection into lending decisions, to ensure the transparency of environmental information and measures, and to facilitate oversight and accountability in the lending process.[122] Financial institutions should consider external systemic risks arising from political, economic, and social security environments. With the rise of socially responsible investment, companies that have better environmental conservation practices for their operations may have better chances of acquiring capital from private and multilateral financial institutions.[123] Green finance has the potential to shape borrowing companies' CSR behavior.

The Chinese government is an advocator for green finance. A series of measures have been introduced to support the development of green finance, including the sustainable credit principle and the responsibility investment principle; the promotion of environmental information disclosure and governance requirements; and the introduction of green loans, green infrastructure investment trusts, and green index funds.[124] The Hangzhou G20 Summit led by China passed the first "G20 Green

[119] The notice requires that contractor shall be qualified to carry out the safety disclosure and risk informing, carry on the on-the-spot guardianship system, and strengthen the contractor's safety training, etc.

[120] Lindenberg (2014).

[121] Ecological Finance Research Centre of Renmin University of China (2017a).

[122] Ma (2017a, b).

[123] Hu (2014).

[124] Ecological Finance Research Centre of Renmin University of China (2017b).

Table 2.2 Selected state-led initiatives on Chinese companies' overseas CSR performance

Time	Issue agency	Policy name	Main contents
August 2007	State Forestry Administration	Guidance on Sustainable Overseas Silviculture by Chinese Overseas Companies[125]	Requires Chinese overseas companies engaging in logging/silviculture to preserve high-value forests and endangered species, sets up monitoring systems, and consults with local communities
January 2008	SASAC	Guidelines to the State-owned Companies Directly under the Central Government on Fulfilling Corporate Social Responsibilities[126]	Emphasizes the importance of CSR for Chinese SOEs and requires SOEs to take measures for making sustainable profits. Social responsibility is defined broadly as product safety, resource conservation, technological innovation, employee rights, and public welfare. SOEs are asked to establish a communication mechanism to engage stakeholders, disclose CSR activities, and publish CSR report on a regular basis

(continued)

[125] "Guidance on Sustainable Overseas Silviculture by Chinese Overseas Companies" (中国企业境外可持续森林培育指南). http://www.mofcom.gov.cn/aarticle/b/g/200712/20071205265858.html.

[126] "Guidelines to the State-owned Companies Directly under the Central Government on Fulfilling Corporate Social Responsibilities" (关于中央企业履行社会责任的指导意见). http://www.sasac.gov.cn/n103/n85881/n85921/c969197/content.html.

Table 2.2 (continued)

Time	Issue agency	Policy name	Main contents
July 2008	The State Council	Regulation on Management of Foreign Contracted Projects[127]	Regulates overseas contracted companies in the fields of safety production and unfair competition. Although the object of the regulation is limited to the domestic parent company of the contracted engineering company, it is also binding on its overseas subsidiary
April 2009	State Forestry Administration and Ministry of Commerce	A Guide on Sustainable Management and Utilization of Overseas Forest by Chinese Companies[128]	Guides Chinese companies to rationally manage, utilize, and protect overseas forests in order to play a positive role in sustainable development of global forest resources. Further standardizes the management of forest resources as well as the wood processing and utilization activities of Chinese companies in foreign countries, and enhances self-regulation within the industry. Promotes the legitimate, sustainable management and utilization of global forest resources and related trade activities
June 2011	SASAC	Interim Measure on Supervision and Administration of the Assets of Central State-Owned Overseas Companies[129]	Requires Chinese SOEs to strengthen the administrative assessment, supervision, and evaluation of Chinese overseas subsidies. SASAC shall regularly supervise, audit and inspect the operation and management of Chinese overseas companies

(continued)

[127] "Regulation on Management of Foreign Contracted Projects" (对外承包工程管理条例). http://www.gov.cn/gongbao/content/2017/content_5219165.htm.

[128] "A Guide on Sustainable Management and Utilization of Overseas Forest by Chinese Companies" (中国企业境外森林可持续经营利用指南). http://www.mofcom.gov.cn/aarticle/b/g/200904/20090406191363.html.

[129] "Interim Measure on Supervision and Administration of the Assets of Central State-Owned Overseas Companies" (中央企业境外国有资产监督管理暂行办法). http://www.gov.cn/flfg/2011-06/24/content_1891821.htm.

Table 2.2 (continued)

Time	Issue agency	Policy name	Main contents
September 2012	China International Contractors Association and International Cooperation Department of Ministry of Commerce	Guidance on Social Responsibility for Chinese International Contractors[130]	Aims at seven core issues of quality and safety, employee development, owner's rights and interests, supply chain management, fair competition, environmental protection and community development, to request Chinese companies to fulfill CSR, and clear the main points of social responsibility management. The guideline refers to international practices such as the United Nations Global Compact and the ISO 26000 Guide
February 2013	Ministry of Commerce and Ministry of Environmental Protection	Guidance on Environmental Protection in Foreign Investment and Cooperation[131]	Encourages all Chinese companies operating overseas to conduct environmental impact assessments, develop mitigation measures, and work with local communities to identify potential negative impact of the investment
September 2013	Ministry of Commerce	Norms on Foreign Investment Cooperation in the Field of Competition[132]	Proposes to establish relevant departments such as foreign investment bad credit record system. In case of unfair competition behavior, companies shall not enjoy national support policies for 3 years; requires Chinese overseas companies to adhere to the principle of mutual benefit and common development, establish and improve the scientific and standardized project decision-making mechanism and quality management system; attach importance to environmental protection, safeguard local labor rights, and actively participate in local public welfare undertakings

(continued)

130 "Guidance on Social Responsibility for Chinese International Contractors" (对外承包工程行业社会责任指引). http://www.mofcom.gov.cn/article/b/bf/201302/20130200039930.shtml.

131 "Guidance on Environmental Protection in Foreign Investment and Cooperation" (对外投资合作环境保护指南). http://www.mofcom.gov.cn/article/b/bf/201302/20130200039930.shtml.

132 "Norms on Foreign Investment Cooperation in the Field of Competition" (规范对外投资合作领域竞争行为的规定). http://www.mofcom.gov.cn/article/b/g/201309/20130900322914.shtml.

Table 2.2 (continued)

Time	Issue agency	Policy name	Main contents
December 2015	The China Chamber of Commerce of Metals, Minerals and Chemicals Importers and Exporters	Guidelines for Social Responsibility in Outbound Mining Investments[133]	Regulates CSR activities of Chinese parent companies that joins the CCCMC during mining investment; doesn't cover overseas legal entities that are registered in the host country in the form of joint ventures, shares, or acquisitions. Encourages Chinese companies that invest overseas to pay careful attention to labor issues, environmental protection, supply chain due diligence, and human rights concerns
June 2016	Ministry of Commerce	Guidance on Safety Risk Prevention for Chinese Overseas Companies[134]	Encourages to build risk and responsibility awareness of Chinese overseas companies, improve the quality of expats, improve local employment, respect local culture to avoid conflicts with local communities, and avoid bribery activities, etc
April 2017	Ministry of Environmental Protection, Ministry of Foreign Affairs, NDRC and Ministry of Commerce	Guidance on Promoting Green One Belt One Road[135]	Makes detailed arrangements from the aspects of strengthening exchanges and publicity, safeguarding the ecological environment of investment activities, establishing a green cooperation platform, improving policy measures

(continued)

133 "Guidelines for Social Responsibility in Outbound Mining Investments" (中国对外矿业投资行业社会责任指引). http://www.csr.gov.cn/article/policies/ind/201709/20170902652964.shtml.

134 "Guidance on Safety Risk Prevention for Chinese Overseas Companies" (中国企业海外安全风险防范指南). http://www.mofcom.gov.cn/article/i/dxfw/gzzd/201606/20160601345155.shtml.

135 "Guidance on Promoting Green One Belt One Road" (关于推进绿色"一带一路"建设的指导意见). http://www.mep.gov.cn/gkml/hbb/bwj/201705/t20170505_413602.htm.

Table 2.2 (continued)

Time	Issue agency	Policy name	Main contents
October 2020	Ministry of Ecology and Environment, the National Development and Reform Commission, the People's Bank of China, the China Banking and Insurance Regulatory Commission and the China Securities Regulatory Commission	Guidelines on Promoting Investment and Financing in Response to Climate Change[136]	Proposes 15 measures in five areas to mobilizing more funds to the field of climate change and deepen international cooperation in climate investment and financing
July 2021	Ministry of Commerce and the Ministry of Ecology and Environment	Guidelines on Green Development in Overseas Investment Cooperation[137]	Requires Chinese companies to strictly and conscientiously abide by a series of international norms such as the UNFCCC, and expand foreign cooperation with a higher quality and level. There are ten priorities of the new guidelines, covering climate, biodiversity and pollution, encourage companies to promote green development-related activities during foreign investment, and fulfill environmental responsibilities, which sets higher and more detailed requirements for environmental protection

Author's Compilation

[136] "Guiding Opinions on Promoting Investment and Financing in Response to Climate Change" (关于促进应对气候变化投融资的指导意见). https://www.mee.gov.cn/xxgk2018/xxgk/xxgk03/202010/t20201026_804792.html.

[137] "Guidelines on Green Development in Overseas Investment Cooperation" (对外投资合作绿色发展工作指引). http://images.policy.mofcom.gov.cn/file/20220711/50791657527087450.pdf.

Finance General Report" and urged multilateral banks to incorporate social and environmental impact into their infrastructure investment considerations.[138] As the investment projects under the BRI are capital intensive, financial institutions (including Chinese policy banks and state-controlled commercial banks) play a particularly important role in influencing the CSR behavior of Chinese companies that engage in overseas investment. It raises questions whether Chinese financial institutions are properly incorporating social and environmental risk into their investments overseas and monitoring borrowing institutions' CSR performance. International observers, environmental groups, and civil organizations have warned that the lack of environmental and social protection standards adopted by China's financial institutions has contributed to increases in carbon emissions in host countries.[139] Western financiers and scholars are concerned that Chinese competitors are using lower environmental and social protection standards as a strategy to gain a larger share of international infrastructure sectors.[140]

In general, the Chinese government's policy on green finance has gone through two stages. The development of green finance policies involves the powers and responsibilities of multiple parties, including the People's Bank of China, the China Banking Regulatory Commission (CBRC), the China Securities Regulatory Commission, the China Insurance Regulatory Commission, and the NDRC.[141] In the initial construction of its green finance policy, a key mission of the Chinese government was to launch green credit policies after realizing the importance of promoting sustainable activities and recognizing potential risks to the financial system. The Chinese government started to promote the development of green finance from a national strategic perspective, especially after the release of the 2012 "Guidance on Green Finance". Between 2012 and 2017, there was a rapid development of their green finance policy to support sustainable financial development. During this stage, the construction of a more comprehensive green finance system was proposed.[142] Particularly, in 2015, the Central Committee of the Communist party of China (CPC) and The State Council issued "Integrated Reform Plan for Promoting Ecological Progress", which first proposed to build China's green finance system.[143] Subsequently, the "The 13th Five-year Plan for Economic and Social Development of the PRC" elevated green finance as a national strategy.[144] On March 2019, National

---

138 G20 Green Finance Study Group (2017).

139 Ibid.

140 Ma (2017a, b). See also, Chan-Fishel (2017).

141 Leung and Zhao (2013).

142 'Guidance on Building Green Finance System'(关于构建绿色金融体系的指导意见). http://www.mep.gov.cn/gkml/hbb/gwy/201611/t20161124_368163.htm. For more details regarding China's green finance policy development, see Liu (2019), 'China's Approach to Corporate Social Responsibility (CSR) Abroad: A Case Study in Africa', PhD diss., University of British Columbia, 34-37.

143 "Integrated Reform Plan for Promoting Ecological Progress". http://english.www.gov.cn/policies/latest_releases/2015/09/22/content_281475195492066.htm.

144 "The 13th Five-year Plan for Economic and Social Development of the People's Republic of China (2016–2020). http://en.ndrc.gov.cn/newsrelease/201612/P020161207645765233498.pdf.

Development and Reform Commission and other seven ministries issued "Green Industry Guidance Catalogue".[145] It is China's most detailed guideline for defining green industries by far. Other standards including green credit standard, green bond standard, and green enterprise standard therefore have a general reference. Under the guidance of the policies and initiatives, the green credit balance of 21 Chinese major banks had exceeded 10 trillion RMB by June 2019.[146] Table 2.3 introduces the efforts of the Chinese government in promoting green finance to better address overseas investment risks from 2007 to 2021.

2.4.3 Limitations of Current Policies and Regulations

Although the Chinese government has developed a series of ostensibly regulatory measures to regulate Chinese companies' overseas behavior, many of these administrative regulations and departmental rules are simply guidelines without enforcement power. This means that compliance is essentially voluntary. Only a few of these new regulations take the form of prescriptive regulations or compulsory standards for foreign operations.[147] The language of the guidelines is also broad and general, essentially taking the form of a rhetoric statement of objectives—for example, Chinese companies should "adhere to the law to operate honest and trustworthy", "establish and deepen the sense of social responsibility", "actively participate in local public welfare activities", and "encourage overseas companies to regularly publish companies' environment information".[148] Concrete details on how to make companies achieve these objectives, such as specific constraints, assessments, or follow-up measures, are absent. The government's documents often set ostensibly high standards for Chinese businesses operating overseas while lacking any implementation and enforcement details.[149] In addition, even if the headquarters or head offices of Chinese companies adopt the guidelines and principles, their supervision over the implementation of the principles at subsidiaries in host countries remains questionable.

Due to the voluntary nature of the government's guidelines, different types of Chinese companies hold different attitudes toward the guidelines. It appears that Chinese SOEs and state-owned financial institutions pay more attention to socio-environmental issues urged by the government's initiatives, whereas smaller private

---

[145] "Green Industry Guidance Catalogue" (绿色产业指导目录). http://www.ndrc.gov.cn/gzdt/201903/W020190306355285868217.pdf.

[146] International Institute of Green Finance, CUFE, "21 Chinese Major Banks had Exceeded 10 Trillion RMB", July 17, 2019. http://iigf.cufe.edu.cn/article/content.html?id=1468.

[147] Interview with director of WWF-China.

[148] Interview with program officer of China House.

[149] Interview with project manager of Sino Hydro Corporation Limited (Kenya), and staff of China Council for International Cooperation on Environment and Development.

Table 2.3 Selective Chinese government's green finance initiatives

Issue time	Name of regulation and policy	Issuing agents	Main contents
May 2007	Guidelines on Compliance Risk Management of Commercial Banks[150]	China Banking Regulatory Commission	Requires commercial banks to take into consideration the interrelatedness between compliance risk and credit risk, market risk, operational risk, and other risks, to ensure the consistency of different risk management policies and procedures
July 2007	Opinions on Implementing Environmental Protection Policies and Regulations to Prevent Credit Risks[151]	People's Bank of China and China Banking Regulatory Commission	Requires environmental protection bureaus and financial institutions at all levels to fully understand the significance of credit policies as tools for environmental protection, and to strengthen environmental monitoring and credit management of construction projects and companies
January 2009	Guidance on Social Responsibility of Chinese Banking Financial Institutions[152]	China Banking Association	Proposes to establish a green financial system and stress the importance of financial institutions in fulfilling corporate social and environmental responsibility goals

(continued)

150 "Guidelines on Compliance Risk Management of Commercial Banks" (商业银行合规风险管理指引). http://www.cbrc.gov.cn/chinese/home/docDOC_ReadView/2835.html.

151 "Opinions on Implementing Environmental Protection Policies and Regulations to Prevent Credit Risks" (关于落实环保政策法规防范信贷风险的意见). http://www.cbrc.gov.cn/chinese/home/docView/20080129C3FA6D993AC4AEF7FFE133D6E2AD0D00.html.

152 "Guidance on Social Responsibility of Chinese Banking Financial Institutions" (中国银行业金融机构企业社会责任指引). http://www.china-cba.net/bencandy.php?fid=44&id=6901.

Table 2.3 (continued)

Issue time	Name of regulation and policy	Issuing agents	Main contents
June 2009	Circular on Full Implementation of Green Credit Policies and Further Improvement of Information Sharing[153]	Ministry Environmental Protection and People's Bank of China	Requires environmental protection authorities and financial institutions at all levels to fully understand the importance of establishing a mechanism for sharing information on green credit and make use of the Credit Reference Center of the People's Bank of China as a platform to share environmental information and prescribe as well as the respective responsibilities of environmental protection authorities and financial institutions
February 2012	Guidance on Green Loans[154]	China Banking Regulatory Commission	Defines the meaning and scope of environmental and social risks to promote financial institutions to adjust credit structure through green credit to prevent investment risks stipulating that banking financial institutions shall increase their support to the green, low-carbon economy and adopt stronger environmental and social risk management for clients
February 2013	Guidance on Environmental Protection during Foreign Investment and Corporation[155]	Ministry of Commerce and Ministry Environmental Protection	Guides Chinese companies to standardize environmental protection behavior in foreign investment, and to fulfill CSR to promote the sustainable development of foreign investment
December 2014	The Critical Assessment Criteria on Green Loan Implementation[156]	China Banking Regulatory Commission	Prescribes environmental and social assessment criteria for overseas projects

(continued)

153 "Circular on Full Implementation of Green Credit Policies and Further Improvement of Information Sharing" (关于全面落实绿色信贷政策进一步完善信息共享工作的通知). http://zfs.mep.gov.cn/hjjj/gjfbdjjzcx/lsxdzc/201507/t20150716_306758.shtml.

154 "Guidance on Green Loans" (绿色信贷指引). http://www.cbrc.gov.cn/chinese/home/docView/127DE230BC31468B9329EFB01AF78BD4.html.

155 "Guidance on Environmental Protection during Foreign Investment and Corporation" (对外投资合作环境保护指南). http://www.mofcom.gov.cn/article/b/bf/201302/20130200039930.shtml.

156 "The Critical Assessment Criteria on Green Loan Implementation" (绿色信贷实施情况关键评价指标). http://www.cbrc.gov.cn/chinese/home/docDOC_ReadView/FC5E38D62BE54E3D836E441D6FC2442F.html.

Table 2.3 (continued)

Issue time	Name of regulation and policy	Issuing agents	Main contents
August 2016	Guidance on Building Green Finance System[157]	People's Bank of China, Ministry of Finance, National Development and Reform Commission, Ministry Environmental Protection, China Banking Regulatory Commission, China Securities Regulatory Commission, China Insurance Commission	Consists of 35 Articles which outline the future of China's green financial system. It expresses the official definition of green finance for the first time. It supports Chinese financial institutions and companies to issue green bonds abroad, and guides international funds to invest in our green bonds, green stocks and other green financial assets, and encourages the establishment of joint venture green development fund
November 2016	The 13th Five-Year Plan on Eco-Environmental Protection[158]	China State Council	Overall plan for the reform of ecological civilization system with a clear proposal to develop green finance
April 2017	Guidance on Promoting Green One Belt One Road[159]	China Foreign Affairs Agency, Ministry Environmental Protection, National Development and Reform Commission, Ministry of Commerce	General guidance on promoting a green BRI. Promotes the development of green finance and regards green finance cooperation as one of the five core principles
May 2017	BRI Eco-Environmental Protection Cooperation Planning[160]	Ministry Environmental Protection	Proposes a green financial policy formulation which explores the establishment of green investment, financing management standards, a green development fund, and environmental risk management tools

(continued)

157 "Guidance on Building Green Finance System" (关于构建绿色金融体系的指导意见). http://www.mep.gov.cn/gkml/hbb/gwy/201611/t20161124_368163.htm.

158 "The 13th Five-Year Plan on Eco-Environmental Protection" ("十三五"生态环境保护规划). http://www.gov.cn/zhengce/content/2016-12/05/content_5143290.htm.

159 "Guidance on Promoting Green One Belt One Road" (关于推进绿色"一带一路"建设的指导意见). http://www.mep.gov.cn/gkml/hbb/bwj/201705/t20170505_413602.htm.

160 "BRI Eco-Environmental Protection Cooperation Planning" ("一带一路"生态环境保护合作规划). http://www.mep.gov.cn/gkml/hbb/bwj/201705/t20170516_414102.htm.

Table 2.3 (continued)

Issue time	Name of regulation and policy	Issuing agents	Main contents
September 2017	Environmental Risk Management Initiative for China's Overseas Investment[161]	The Green Finance Committee of China Society for Finance and Banking, Investment Association of China, China Banking Association, Asset Management Association of China, Insurance Asset Management Association of China, China Trustee Association, and the Foreign Economic Cooperation Office of the Ministry of Environment Protection	Consists of 12 Articles on the disclosure of environmental and social governance information, green finance, and environmental and social protection standards overseas to improve institutions and companies' capacity for environmental risk management overseas. The regulation especially emphasizes the importance of financial institutions in complying with regulations in China and host countries, with prevailing international standards, and with the adoption of the highest standards where possible
September 2018	Code of Governance for Listed Companies[162]	China Securities Regulatory Commission	Listed companies should disclose environmental information in accordance with laws and regulations and the requirements of the relevant authorities
June 2017	Plan for the Implementation of the Guidance on Building Green Financial System[163]	Bank of China, the Ministry of Finance, the Development and Reform Commission, Ministry of Environmental Protection, the China Banking Regulatory Commission, the China Securities Regulatory Commission and the China Insurance Regulatory Commission	Establishing a mandatory environmental information disclosure system for listed companies step by step: the first step is to revise the guidelines on the content and format of periodic reports for listed companies by the end of 2017 and require voluntary disclosure; the second step is to make it mandatory for key emission units to disclose environmental information in March 2018; the third step is to make environmental information disclosure mandatory for all listed companies by December 2020

(continued)

161 "Environmental Risk Management Initiative for China's Overseas Investment" (中国对外投资环境风险管理倡议). http://www.greenfinance.org.cn/displaynews.php?id=1472.

162 "Code of Governance for Listed Companies" (上市公司治理准则). http://www.csrc.gov.cn/csrc/c101864/c1024585/content.shtml.

163 "Plan for the Implementation of the Guidance on Building Green Financial System" (落实《关于构建绿色金融体系的指导意见》的分工方案). https://www.mee.gov.cn/gkml/hbb/gwy/201611/t20161124_368163.htm.

Table 2.3 (continued)

Issue time	Name of regulation and policy	Issuing agents	Main contents
October 2020	Guidance on Promoting Investment and Financing to Address Climate Change[164]	Ministry of Ecology and Environment, National Development and Reform Commission, People's Bank of China, Banking and Insurance Regulatory Commission and Securities Regulatory Commission	Proposing to improve the information disclosure standards for climate investment and finance, further strengthening the "climate attributes" of the information disclosure system. This includes accelerating the development of information disclosure standards for climate investment and financing projects, entities and funds, and promoting the establishment of a climate information disclosure system in which companies make public commitments, information is made public in accordance with the law and is widely monitored by society
May 2021	Programme for the Reform of the Legal Disclosure System for Environmental Information[165]	Ministry of Ecology and Environment	The People's Bank of China and the securities supervision administration authorities have implemented a system of legal disclosure of environmental information. However, there are no mandatory requirements on what kind of climate information is to be disclosed and in what form

(continued)

[164] "Guidance on Promoting Investment and Financing to Address Climate Change" (关于促进应对气候变化投融资的指导意见) https://www.mee.gov.cn/xxgk2018/xxgk/xxgk03/202010/t20201026_804792.html.

[165] "Programme for the Reform of the Legal Disclosure System for Environmental Information" (环境信息依法披露制度改革方案). https://www.mee.gov.cn/xxgk2018/xxgk/xxgk03/202105/W020210525651775162451.pdf.

Table 2.3 (continued)

Issue time	Name of regulation and policy	Issuing agents	Main contents
December 2021	Pilot Work Plan on Climate Investment and Finance[166]	Ministry of Ecology and Environment	Strengthen carbon accounting and information disclosure: guide pilot places to strengthen the supervision and management of enterprise carbon accounting, explore the development of enterprise carbon accounting system, conduct regular enterprise carbon audits, and strictly prevent companies from falsifying carbon data. Guide pilots to establish a climate information disclosure system. Encourage pilots to establish environmental information sharing platforms to facilitate financial institutions to carry out carbon accounting and climate information disclosure for financial institutions

Author's Compilation

166 "Pilot Work Programme on Climate Investment and Finance" (气候投融资试点工作方案). https://www.gov.cn/zhengce/zhengceku/2021-12/25/5664524/files/10bf58f69f4d40269e07f3b84a47bb78.pdf.

businesses often take them lightly.[167] Compared to Chinese private companies, Chinese SOEs tend to have rather long-term investment horizons and have better capacity and awareness to engage in CSR.[168] Their foreign investment and environmental policy decisions reflect the organizational realities in China, where corporate decisions are partly influenced and directed by national interests. It seems that Chinese SOEs tend to think the CSR guidelines helpful to guide their daily business operations.[169] One SOE project manager claimed that "as an SOE, we must follow the instructions", and "it's helpful for the long-term development of our company".[170] However, privately-owned Chinese companies have a vague understanding of these documents and think the contents too broad to be useful in solving problems.[171]

Explicit monitoring and enforcement mechanisms are a straightforward way to regulate Chinese companies' overseas performance. Converting Chinese soft CSR policies into hard laws may be desirable. However, there are challenges regarding the implementation of home countries' and international environmental standards at the local level in host countries based on the current jurisdiction theory. Given the regionalized characteristics of rules and laws, localized contextual conditions, and the specificity of the sociocultural contexts of various countries, the implementation of extraterritorial legislation is difficult to realize.[172] Under the traditional jurisdiction theory, if companies operate outside of their home state's jurisdiction, the application and extension of the home country's laws and standards could be considered extraterritorial interference in the host country, thus infringing on its sovereignty.[173] The selective and institutional capacity theory also points out the difficulty of local adaptations of extraterritorial laws and standards due to the relationship between rule regimes and the underlying norms and functions of regulatory institutions at the local level.[174]

In addition, the legal and social environments in host countries affect the performance of Chinese CSR initiatives. Chinese CSR initiatives are implemented differently in overseas projects due to varying local conditions.[175] In countries with weak governance and law enforcement, the gap between policy and practice remains a major challenge for Chinese companies' operations in host countries.[176] A range of "unwritten" factors such as political connections, low governance capacity, weak law enforcement, and corruption also strongly affect Chinese overseas companies' operations. As the central government has little control over Chinese overseas companies'

167 Interview with project manager of China-Africa Excellency Foundation.

168 Beyer et al. (2014).

169 Interview the project managers of CRBC, China Wu Yi Co., Ltd. (Kenya Branch), and China Gezhouba Group Company Limited (Kenya).

170 Interview with project manager of China Wu Yi Co., Ltd. (Kenya Branch).

171 Interview with program officer of China House.

172 Bourdieu (1987). See also, Friedman (2006).

173 Judy (1986).

174 Potter (2011).

175 Tan-Mullins and Mohan (2013).

176 Interview with official from National Development and Reform Commission of PRC.

daily operations, the enforcement of CSR programs falls almost entirely on companies without sufficient supervision by the central government. In such cases, Chinese companies can easily take advantage of various kinds of regulatory loopholes, which may lead to non-compliance with environmental and social standards.[177]

Existing evidence has shown the gap between CSR policies and practices adopted by Chinese overseas companies. Some Chinese overseas companies have interpreted CSR as being only about corporate philanthropy.[178] Surveys of CSR among Chinese companies in Africa, for example, have found that the most common approach to CSR issues is through philanthropic support focusing on education, health, and the environment.[179] The majority of Chinese companies' donations are for health and medical provisions, and donations are also directed toward education and training, medical treatment, agriculture and food security, etc.[180] The relatively short history of Chinese foreign investment and the lack of overseas operation experience of Chinese companies further increase the difficulties to promote Chinese overseas companies' green operations.[181] Although some Chinese overseas companies have begun to pay attention to environmental and social management practices, at present, most of them still do not understand CSR in depth and lack experience in green overseas operations.[182] Many Chinese overseas companies have not established overseas environmental and social protection departments with technical experts to carry out green operations.[183]

2.5 Conclusion

By comparing the state-centric approach with the conventional market-based approach, this chapter presents the promises and limitations of the state-centric CSR approach. This chapter surveys the development of the state-centric CSR approach in China through examining the role of the Chinese government in advancing Chinese companies' CSR practices overseas. There are both domestic and international incentives for the Chinese government promote CSR. As the performance and behavior of Chinese state-owned companies and financial, are closely intertwined with the Chinese government's political interests, the Chinese government's promotion of CSR is also meant to build domestic support for state capitalism and to justify the

[177] Mol (2011).

[178] Forstater et al. (2010).

[179] Ibid., 15.

[180] Kenya China Economic and Trade Association (2017).

[181] As the director of WWF-China noted, "Chinese companies have a relatively short history of foreign investment, with fast development. The accumulation of experience cannot keep up with the speed of investment." Interview with director of WWF-China.

[182] Interview with counselor of Economic and Commercial Counselor's Office of the Chinese Government in Kenya. See also, Forstater et al. (2010).

[183] Interview with Interview with official from National Development and Reform Commission.

legitimacy of the SOEs. Additionally, due to increasing demand of holding investors' climate responsibility and development of the sustainable investment regime, all the factors require investors to conduct sustainable investment. The chapter demonstrates that in recent years, the Chinese government has made efforts to promulgate numerous CSR guidelines to promote Chinese companies' overseas CSR behavior. Under the guidance of the state, Chinese companies (especially SOEs) and state-controlled financial institutions have been increasingly adopting CSR measures in response to the environmental and social protection needs of their host countries.

However, there are limitations to China's state-centric approach to sustainable investment governance. Many guidelines are voluntary in nature without enforcement and assessment measures. In addition, Chinese financial institutions are still in the initial stage of integrating environmental and social considerations into their lending policies without comprehensive environmental and social protection frameworks. Overall, the survey of the government's CSR policies and the financial institutions' internal rules tells very little about the implementation in practice. The following chapters will put the formal rules in a more concrete setting to see how the policies and rules have been possibly reflected in actual practice.

References

Albareda L et al (2008) The changing role of governments in corporate social responsibility: drivers and responses. Bus Ethics 17:347–363

Bernasconi-Osterwalder N et al (eds) (2013) Chinese outward investment: an emerging policy framework. International Institute for Sustainable Development

Beyer A et al (2014) Study on how investment horizon and expectations of shareholder base impact corporate decision-making. National Investor Relations Institute and The Rock Center for Corporate Governance. https://www.gsb.stanford.edu/sites/default/files/2014_Investment-Horizon-Final_0.pdf

Bourdieu P (1987) The force of law: toward a sociology of the juridical field. Hastings Law J 38:805–853

Carroll A (2008) A history of corporate social responsibility: concepts and practice. The Oxford handbook of corporate social responsibility. Oxford University Press, Oxford, pp 19–46

Chan-Fishel M (2017) Time to Go Green: Environmental Responsibility in the Chinese Banking Sector. Friends of the Earth–US and Bank Track. https://www.banktrack.org/download/time_to_go_green_environmental_responsibility_in_the_chinese_banking_sector/0_0_070509_chinese_bank_public_report_final.pdf

China Council for International Cooperation on Environment and Development (2016a) South-South Cooperation for Ecological Civilization (Draft). http://www.cciced.net/cciceden/POLICY/rr/prr/2016/201612/P020161214521504952840.pdf

China Council for International Cooperation on Environment and Development (2016b) China's Ecological Civilization and the World. Issues Paper. http://www.cciced.net/cciceden/POLICY/rr/Issuespaper/201612/P020161214521507778827.pdf

China International Contactors Association (2012) Guidance on social responsibility for Chinse international contractors 中国对外承包工程行业社会指引. http://www.mofcom.gov.cn/aarticle/ae/ai/201209/20120908364916.html

China WTO Tribune (2017) The 2017 Golden Bees Chinese Companies' Corporate Social Responsibility Report. http://images.mofcom.gov.cn/csr/201712/20171219174229375.pdf

Dolzer R, Schreuer C (2008) Principles of International Investment Law. Oxford University Press, Oxford, pp 352–385
Ecological Finance Research Centre of Renmin University of China (2017a) Green finance for the belt and road initiative. China Financial Publication House, p 48
Ecological Finance Research Centre of Renmin University of China (2017b) Green finance for the belt and road initiative. China Financial Publication House, pp 122–136
EITI International Secretariat (2016) Chinese companies reporting in EITI countries, 4. https://eiti.org/document/eiti-brief-chinese-companies-reporting-in-eiti-implementing-countries.
Farrell J (2016) How do Chinese contractors perform in Africa? Evidence from World Bank Projects. Johns Hopkins SAIS-CARI Working Paper 3. https://static1.squarespace.com/static/5652847de4b033f56d2bdc29/t/573c970bf8baf3591b05253f/1463588620386/Working+Paper_Jamie+Farrell.pdf
Foreign Affairs Department of Shenzhen Government (2016) Ecological conservation dialogue conference on the BRI. http://www.sz.gov.cn/wsbgs/xxgkml/gzdt/201612/t20161212_5669488.htm
Forstater M et al (2010) Corporate responsibility in African development: insights from an emerging dialogue. The Institute of West-Asian Studies of the Chinese Academy of Social Science. https://sites.hks.harvard.edu/m-rcbg/CSRI/publications/workingpaper_60.pdf
Fox T et al (2002) Public sector roles in strengthening corporate social responsibility: a baseline study. The World Bank. http://documents.worldbank.org/curated/en/284431468340215496/Public-sector-roles-in-strengthening-corporate-social-responsibility-a-baseline-study.
Freeman E (1984) Strategic management: a stakeholder approach. Pitman, Boston, p 46
Friedman L (2006) The place of legal culture in the sociology of law. In: Freeman L (ed) Law and Sociology: current legal issues. Oxford University Press, Oxford. Chapters 11–12
Frynas J (2005) The false developmental promise of corporate social responsibility: evidence from multinational oil companies. Int Aff 81(3):585
G20 Green Finance Study Group (2017) 2017 G20 Green Finance Synthesis Report. http://unepinquiry.org/wp-content/uploads/2017/07/2017_GFSG_Synthesis_Report_EN.pdf. The 2nd session of the Group of 20 Ministers of Energy (G20) formally adopted the G20 Voluntary Action Plan on Renewable Energy to encourage countries to accelerate the development of renewable energy.
Garriga E, Melé D (2004) Corporate social responsibility theories: mapping the territory. J Bus Ethics 53:51–71
Geall S (2015) Interpreting ecological civilization (China Dialogue). https://www.chinadialogue.net/article/show/single/en/8018-Interpreting-ecological-civilisation-part-one
Gu J et al (2016) Chinese state capitalism? Rethinking the role of the state and business in Chinese development cooperation in Africa. World Dev 81:24–34
Gunningham N (2008) Environmental regulation and non-state law. In: Schooten H, Verschuuren J (eds) International governance and law: state regulation and non-state law. Edward Elgar, Cheltenham
Guo P (2008) Socially responsible investment emerges in China (China Dialogue). https://www.ChinaDialogue.net/article/2020-Socially-responsible-investment-emerges-in-China
Hilson G (2013) Corporate social responsibility in the extractive industries: experiences from developing countries. Resour Policy 37(2):131–137
Ho V (2013a) Beyond regulation: a comparative look at state-centric corporate social responsibility and the law in China. Vanderbilt J Transnatl Law 46:375–442
Ho V (2013b) Beyond regulation: a comparative look at state-centric corporate social responsibility and the law in China. Vanderbilt J Transnatl Law 46:434
Ho V (2013c) Beyond regulation: a comparative look at state-centric corporate social responsibility and the law in China. Vanderbilt J Transnatl Law 46:425
Ho V (2013d) Beyond regulation: a comparative look at state-centric corporate social responsibility and the law in China. Vanderbilt J Transnatl Law 46:408

Hohnen P (2007) Corporate social responsibility an implementation guide for business, International Institute for Sustainable Development. http://www.iisd.org/pdf/2007/csr_guide.pdf

Hu T, Wang Y (2015) Environmental and social risk management of Chinese transnational companies. Yale School of Forestry and Environmental Studies and WWF. http://www.wwfchina.org/content/press/publication/2015/Yale-WWF_final.pdf

Hu T et al (2014) Managing environmental impact: international experience and lessons in risk management for overseas investments. World Resources Institute. www.wri.org/managing-environmental-impact-international-experience-and-lessons-in-risk-management-for-overseas-investments

Isabella K (2021) Climate Litigation up in 2021, with Private Sector now Exposed, China Dialogue, December 21. https://chinadialogue.net/en/climate/climate-litigation-up-in-2021-with-private-sector-now-exposed/

Ivano A et al (2021) Climate change litigation: comparative and international perspectives, British institute of international and perspectives. British Institute of International and Comparative Law May 2021, 2

Joana S, Catherine H (2021) Global trends in climate change litigation: 2021 snapshot, July 2021, 5

Judy D (1986) Hazardous substances in developing countries: who should regulate foreign companies? Virginia J Nat Resour Law 6:143–177

Kanie N, Haas P (eds) (2004) Emerging forces in environmental governance. United Nations University Press, New York

Kenya China Economic and Trade Association (2017) 2017 Chinese Overseas Companies in Kenya Social Responsibility Report. http://ke2.mofcom.gov.cn/17en.pdf

KPMG (2015) Currents of change: the KPMG survey of corporate responsibility reporting 2015, 33. https://assets.kpmg.com/content/dam/kpmg/pdf/2016/02/kpmg-international-survey-of-corporate-responsibility-reporting-2015.pdf

Leung D, Zhao Y (2013) Environmental and social policies in overseas investments: progress and challenges for China. World Resources Institute, Washington

Levy D, Kaplan R (2008a) Corporate social responsibility and theories of global governance. In: Crane A et al (eds) The Oxford handbook of corporate social responsibility. Oxford University Press, Oxford, pp 432–451

Levy D, Kaplan R (2008b) Corporate social responsibility and theories of global governance. In: Crane A et al (eds) The Oxford handbook of corporate social responsibility. Oxford University Press, Oxford, p 439

Lin L (2010a) Corporate social responsibility in China: window dressing or structural change. Berkeley Int Law J 28:64–100

Lin L (2010b) Corporate social responsibility in china: window dressing or structural change. Berkeley Int Law J 28:94

Lin L (2010c) Corporate social responsibility in China: window dressing or structural change. Berkeley Int Law J 28:84

Lin L, Milhaupt C (2013a) We are the (national) champions: understanding the mechanisms of state capitalism in China. Stanford Law Rev 65:697–759

Lin L, Milhaupt C (2013b) We are the (national) champions: understanding the mechanisms of state capitalism in China. Stanford Law Rev 65:699

Lin L, Milhaupt C (2017) Bonded to the state: a network perspective on China's corporate debt market. J Financ Regul 3(10):1–39

Lindenberg N (2014) Definition of Green Finance. German Development Institute. https://www.cbd.int/financial/gcf/definition-greenfinance.pdf

Liu M (2015) Is corporate social responsibility China's secret weapon?. Eco-Business. https://www.weforum.org/agenda/2015/03/is-corporate-social-responsibility-chinas-secret-weapon/

Liu B (2019) China's approach to Corporate Social Responsibility (CSR) abroad: a case study in Africa, PhD diss., University of British Columbia, pp 34–37

Ma J (2017a) Green finance leads green one belt one road initiative. China Financial Publication House

Ma J (2017b) Establishing China's green financial system. China Financial Publication House

Marc-Philippe W, Mai-Lan T (2022) Climate litigation against companies. Clim Action 14(1):1

McBarnet D (2009) Corporate social responsibility beyond law, through law, for law: the new corporate accountability. In: McBarnet D et al (eds) The New corporate accountability: corporate social responsibility and the law. Cambridge University Press, Cambridge

McGuire W (2016) The role of ISO 14001 in China's environmental crisis. https://aede.osu.edu/sites/aede/files/!import/McGuire-The%20Role%20of%20ISO%2014001%20in%20China's%20Environmental%20Crisis.pdf

Mele D (2008) Corporate social responsibility theories. The Oxford handbook of corporate social responsibility. Oxford University Press, Oxford, pp 47–82

Ministry of Commerce of China (2017) Report on Development of China's Outward Investment and Economic Cooperation. 中国对外投资合作发展报告. http://fec.mofcom.gov.cn/article/tzhzcj/tzhz/upload/zgdwtzhzfzbg2017.pdf

Mol A (2011) China's ascent and Africa's environment. Glob Environ Chang 21(3):785–794

Moon J (2002) Business social responsibility and new governance. Gov Oppos 37(3):385–408

NDRC and the Ministry of Finance (2014) OFDI Project Verification and Registration Management Plan. 境外投资项目核准和管理办法. http://www.sdpc.gov.cn/zcfb/zcfbl/201404/W020140410560098013507.pdf

NDRC, Ministry of Foreign Affairs and Ministry of Commerce of China (2015) Vision and action on joint building silk road economic belt and 21st-century maritime silk road. https://reconasia-production.s3.amazonaws.com/media/filer_public/e0/22/e0228017-7463-46fc-9094-0465a6f1ca23/vision_and_actions_on_jointly_building_silk_road_economic_belt_and_21st-century_maritime_silk_road.pdf

OECD (2011) The OECD Guidelines for Multinational Companies. http://www.oecd.org/daf/inv/mne/48004323.pdf

Ong D (2001) The impact of environmental law on corporate governance: international and comparative perspectives. Euro J Int Law 12(4):685–726

Orlitzky M et al (2003) Corporate social and financial performance: a meta-analysis. Organ Stud 24:403–441

Parker C (2002) The open corporation: effective self-regulation and democracy. Cambridge University Press, Cambridge

Paul G (2017) The carbon majors database CDP Carbon Majors Report 2017, Climate Accountability Institute, p 8

Potter P (2009) Coordinating corporate governance and corporate social responsibility. Hong Kong Law J 39:675–695

Potter P (2011) Introduction: selective adaptation, institutional capacity, and the reception of international law under conditions. In: Potter P, Biuković L (eds) Globalization and local adaptation in International Trade Law. University of British Columbia Press, Vancouver, pp 3–20

Ribstein L (2006) Accountability and responsibility in corporate governance. Notre Dame Law Rev 81:1444–1447

SASAC (2008a) Guidelines on fulfilling corporate social responsibilities of the state-owned overseas companies directly managed under the Central Government. http://en.sasac.gov.cn/2011/12/06/c_313.htm

SASAC (2008b) Guidelines to the state-owned companies directly under the central government on fulfilling corporate social responsibilities. 关于中央企业履行社会责任的指导意见. http://www.sasac.gov.cn/n103/n85881/n85921/c969197/content.html

Scherer A et al (2013) Democratizing corporate governance: compensating for the democratic deficit of corporate political activity and corporate citizenship. Bus Soc 52(3):473–514

Tan-Mullins M, Mohan G (2013) The potential of corporate environmental responsibility of Chinese state-owned companies in Africa. Environ Dev Sustain 15(2):265–284

The Investor Agenda (2022) 2022 Global investor statement to governments on the climate crisis. https://www.capdyn.com/Customer-Content/www/news/PDFs/2022-Global-Investor-Statement-.pdf
The Sixth General Meeting of the Sixteenth Central Commission of the Chinese Communist Party (2016) Several important resolutions on the construction of Socialist Harmonious Society by the Central Commission of the Chinese Communist Party. 中共中央关于构建社会主义和谐社会若干重大问题的决定. http://www.gov.cn/govweb/gongbao/content/2006/content_453176.htm.
The State Council (2012) Regulation on Management of Foreign Contracted Projects 对外承包工程管理条例. http://www.gov.cn/gongbao/content/2017/content_5219165.htm
The State-Council Information Office (2011) General Approach to Reform Central State-owned Companies during the 12th Five-Year Plan Period. "十二五"时期中央企业改革发展的总体思路. http://www.scio.gov.cn/xwfbh/yg/2/Document/860921/860921.htm
The UN Human Rights Council (2021) Legally binding instrument to regulate, in International Human Rights Law, the Activities of Transnational Companies and Other Business Companies, OEIGWG Chairmanship Third Revised Draft, preamble
UNCTAD (2015) Investment Policy Framework for Sustainable Development, pp 77–78. https://unctad.org/system/files/official-document/diaepcb2015d5_en.pdf
UNDP China (2017) 2017 Report on the sustainable development of Chinese companies overseas supporting—the belt and road regions to achieve the 2030 agenda for sustainable development. http://www.cn.undp.org/content/china/en/home/library/south-south-cooperation/2017-report-on-the-sustainable-development-of-chinese-enterprise.html
UNEP (2016) Green is gold. The strategy and actions of China's ecological civilization. https://reliefweb.int/sites/reliefweb.int/files/resources/greenisgold_en_20160519.pdf
U.S. Chamber of Commerce (2012) Corporate responsibility and sustainable economic development in China: Implications for Business. https://www.uschamber.com/sites/default/files/legacy/international/files17296_China%20Corp%20Social%20Responsibility_Opt.pdf
Verdier P-H (2009) Transnational regulatory networks and their limits. Yale J Int Law 34(1):114–171
Visser W (2008) Corporate social responsibility in developing countries. In: Crane A, McWilliams A, Matten D, Moon J, Siegel DS (eds) The Oxford handbook of corporate social responsibility. Oxford University Press, Oxford, pp 473–499
Vogel D (2006a) The market for virtue: the potential and limits of corporate social responsibility. Brookings Institution Press, Washington
Vogel D (2006b) The market for virtue: the potential and limits of corporate social responsibility. Brookings Institution Press, Washington, p 16
Vogel D (2006c) The market for virtue: the potential and limits of corporate social responsibility. Brookings Institution Press, Washington, p 4
Watson A (2008) Civil society in a transitional state: the rise of associations in China. In: Unger J (ed) Associations and the Chinese state: contested spaces. Routledge, Oxon, pp 14–47
Wei YR (2021) Climate governance from the perspective of international investment agreements. Jiangxi Soc Sci 41(193):194
Xi J (2017) Report to the 19th National Congress of the Communist Party of China. http://www.gov.cn/zhuanti/2017-10/27/content_5234876.htm.
Xiao J (2015) How can a prospective China–EU BIT contribute to sustainable investment: in light of the UNCTAD Investment Policy Framework for Sustainable Development. J World Energy Law Bus 8(521):523
Yu L (2020) The human rights obligations of multinational companies' home countries. Law Press, p 2
Zadek S (2001) The civil corporation: the new economy of corporate citizenship. Earthscan, London
Zerk J (2006) Multinationals and corporate social responsibility: limitations and opportunities in international law. Cambridge University Press, Cambridge, pp 69–72
Zhao J (2014) Corporate social responsibility in contemporary China. Edward Elgar, Cheltenham

Chapter 3
China's Foreign Investment in Africa and Its CSR Implications

After examining the recent development of the Chinese government's guidelines and policies to promote sustainable overseas investment, this chapter examines the application of China's state-centric approach to CSR in a particular geographic region—Africa. Africa is a central destination of China's BRI and hence is an important illuminating context for the consideration of the impact of Chinese investment overseas. This chapter first traces the growth of investment by Chinese SOEs and state-controlled financial institutions in Africa under China's BRI. It then analyzes China's investment impact to show the need to promote responsible behavior of Chinese companies in Africa. The government-led investment indicates the importance of the state in influencing social and environmental impact arising from the investment in Africa. This chapter therefore discusses the implications of the state-centric approach to advance Chinese companies and financial institutions' CSR in African countries. This chapter hence also sets the background for the empirical case study of the SGR project in Kenya in Chapter 4 and the case study of China's green finance cooperation with Africa in Chapter 5.

3.1 China's Foreign Investment in Africa Under the BRI

3.1.1 The BRI

China's entry into the World Trade Organization in 2001 heralded a high level of economic growth for the country. China now is not only a major recipient of foreign direct investment but also an important investor of foreign investment around the world.[1] In 2013, Chinese President Xi Jinping announced China's intention to develop "The Silk Road Economic Belt and the 21st Century Maritime Silk Road",

---

[1] Gallagher and Shan (2009).

B. Liu, *China's Green Investment in Africa: A State-Centric Corporate Social Responsibility Perspective*, Modern China and International Economic Law,
https://doi.org/10.1007/978-981-95-2157-9_3

commonly known as the BRI. According to the government, the BRI will enhance inter-regional connectivity worldwide by focusing on five areas: "policy coordination, facility connectivity, unimpeded trade, financial integration, and people-to-people bonds".[2] The BRI aims at facilitating efficient allocation of economic resources, integrating and coordinating regional economies in order to create an open and inclusive regional, social, and economic cooperation framework to benefit involved stakeholders.[3] The Chinese government expects that the initiative will help the countries along the route "improve the connectivity of their infrastructure construction plans and technical standard systems"[4]; promote coordinated construction of international highways; and form an infrastructure network of sub-regions in Asia, Europe, and Africa. Specific actions include expanding the scope and scale of financial cooperation and integration with countries along the BRI routes, such as by working together to operationalize the Asian Infrastructure Investment Bank (AIIB), the New Development Bank (NDB), and the Silk Road Fund to strengthen practical, bilateral, and multilateral financial cooperation.[5]

The BRI routes will connect over 60 countries, accounting for 60% of the world's population and a collective GDP equivalent to 33% of the world's wealth.[6] The influence of the BRI is already evident in China's overseas investment flows, which rose 16.3% in the first 10 months of 2015 to $92.5 billion, with BRI-related investment rising 36.7% to $13.7 billion.[7] Accordingly, China has now rapidly become one of the world's largest overseas investors and has increasingly encouraged more companies to go abroad. As of the end of 2017, China's non-financial outward direct investment amounted to USD $120 billion in 6236 overseas companies in 174 countries and regions.[8] Figure 3.1 shows the map of the BRI.

According to the Chinese government, as China has accumulated rich experience in manufacturing, infrastructure construction, and fund mobilization, it can share the experience with countries along the BRI routes to promote their economic development and industrialization.[9] According to the 2017 United Nations Development Programme (UNDP) report undertaken by a research team affiliated with the Chinese government, the implementation of the BRI is expected to bring unprecedented opportunities for infrastructure construction, industrial transformation and upgrades, and trade and investment facilitation.[10] It expects that the investment cooperation of Chinese overseas companies along the BRI routes will effectively enhance

---

2 UNDP China (2017a).

3 Gu (2015). See also, Chhibber (2017).

4 NDRC, Ministry of Foreign Affairs and Ministry of Commerce of China (2015).

5 Cheng (2018).

6 NDRC, Ministry of Foreign Affairs and Ministry of Commerce of China (2015).

7 Ibid.

8 National Development and Reform Commission, Ministry of Foreign Affairs, and Ministry of Commerce (2015). See also, Database of Commerce of the People's Republic of China. http://www.mofcom.gov.cn/article/tongjiziliao.

9 Gu (2015).

10 UNDP China (2017b).

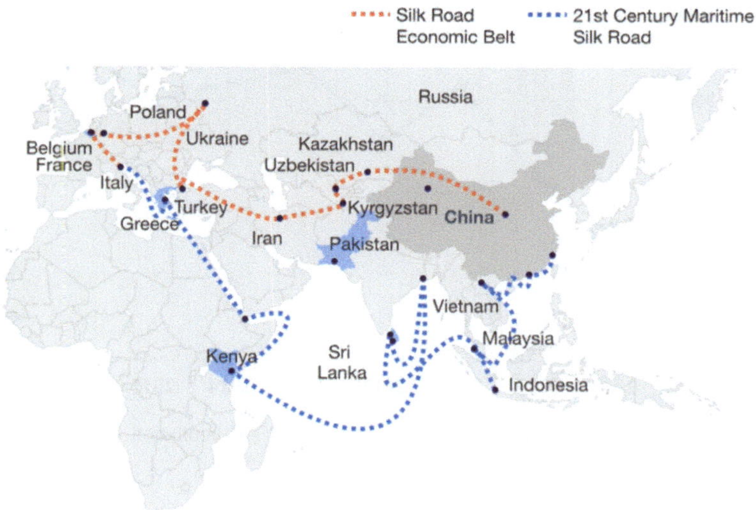

Fig. 3.1 The map of the BRI initiative. *Source* McKinsey & Co. (2016)[11]

infrastructure construction in these countries and provide strong support for local economic and social development.[12]

Africa is a major focus of the BRI.[13] Chinese companies may make significant contributions to the economic and social development of African countries, especially in improving infrastructure, upgrading industries, creating jobs, transferring technology, and contributing to social well-being.[14] China's foreign direct investment (FDI) in Africa has grown "even faster over the past decade, with a breakneck annual growth rate of 40 percent".[15] China's investment in Africa is likely to expand in the future given China's surging need to boost external demand by taking advantage of its excess manufacturing capacity.[16] Figure 3.2 shows that Chinese FDI flows to Africa continued to grow at a steady rate, reaching $US 3610 million in 2016, from previous levels of $US 1439 million in 2009.[17]

Chinese companies operate in many sectors of the African economy. Table 3.1 shows the diverse sectors in which Chinese companies have invested in Africa—with concentrations in trade, manufacturing, construction, mining, and agriculture. Chinese companies have rapidly achieved a sizeable market share, especially in manufacturing, construction, and real estate. Moreover, Chinese companies account

[11] Tian (2016).

[12] Ibid. See also, Global Markets-EY Knowledge (2015).

[13] Chen (2016).

[14] Chen (2018). See also, Jian (2017) and Blue Book of Outbound Investment and Risks (2017).

[15] Omoruyi (2018). See also, Ministry of Commerce (2016).

[16] Yu et al. (2016). See also, Chen (2018).

[17] Eom et al. (2016), UN Conference on Trade and Development (2016) and Kazeemm (2017).

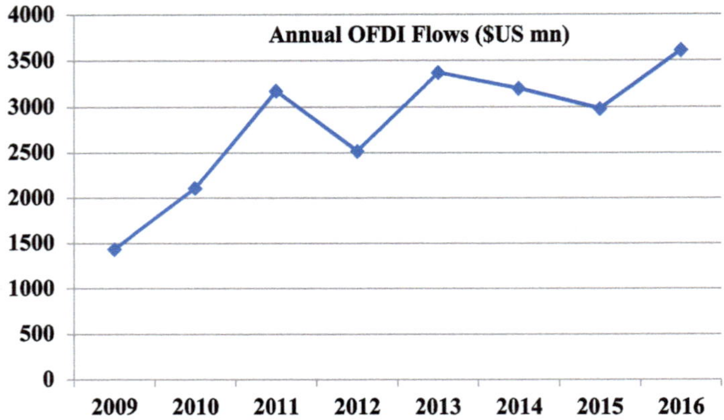

Fig. 3.2 Chinese OFDI flows to Africa ($US mn). Author's Compilation Based on Data from McKinsey & Co. (2017a)[18]

Table 3.1 Chinese companies' investment in diverse sectors in Africa

Investment by sector	Market share in Africa	Annual revenues in Africa
Manufacturing	~ 12	~ $60 billion
Services	~ 5	~ $15 billion
Trade	~ 3	~ $15 billion
Construction and real estate	~ 50	~ $40 billion
Others*	~ 1	~ $50 billion

*Others refers to agriculture, utilities, oil and gas, and mining sector
Source Adapted from McKinsy & Co. (2017a)[19]

for nearly 50% of Africa's internationally contracted infrastructure construction market.[20]

Most countries in Africa have limited domestic financial resources to fill infrastructure gaps and energy shortages. Chinese financial institutions play a vital role in providing financial support for construction projects.[21] Since its announcement of the BRI, China has urged the banks under its control to provide financial support to the BRI construction projects in Africa. In general, there are three kinds of financial institutions that provide financial support for the infrastructure projects in Africa: Chinese national policy and development banks, including the CDB and China Exim Bank; Chinese central bank; and Chinese state-controlled commercial banks, such as the People's Bank of China and the ICBC. The Chinese government is a sole

[18] McKinsey & Co. (2017a).

[19] Ibid., 30.

[20] Ibid.

[21] Foster (2009).

shareholder or a controlling shareholder of these banks. These financial institutions and their functions in African investment are summarized and listed in Table 3.2.

3.1.2 China's Infrastructure Investment in Africa

As Table 3.1 shows, construction is an important area of investment. It is particularly reflected in infrastructure investment.[22] Inadequate infrastructure holds back Africa's economic growth and ability to provide sufficient water, electricity, and transportation services to a rapidly growing population, most notably in urban areas.[23] As infrastructure interconnectivity is the precondition for the flow of goods and people, one important aspect of the BRI is to enhance infrastructure construction so as to achieve interconnectivity and form networks.[24] In January 2015, China and the African Union agreed to put collective efforts into improving Africa's infrastructure, high-speed railways, aviation, and highways.[25] The Forum on China-Africa Cooperation (FOCAC) Summit is a platform for accelerating the cooperation between China and African states at multiple levels in the infrastructure sector, which has upgraded China-Africa relations to a "comprehensive strategic and cooperative partnership".[26] In December 2015, China declared that it would cooperate with Africa to promote the development of high-speed railways, expressways, and regional aviation networks.[27]

Chinese infrastructure commitments grew at an average rate of 16% per year from 2012 to 2015 and supported many of Africa's ambitious infrastructure developments, such as the Mombasa-Nairobi SGR railway in Kenya.[28] Chinese contractors today account for nearly half of Africa's international engineering, procurement, and construction workforce.[29] In international contracting, Chinese construction companies have a nearly 50% market share and control 42% of World Bank tenders in sub-Saharan Africa by value.[30] In 2016, China announced that it planned to help build a series of transportation grids (i.e., railroad, bridges, and roads) linking African countries.[31] In the same year, the gross annual revenues of Chinese companies' construction projects in Africa totaled $50 billion.[32]

---

[22] Chen (2018). See also, Foster (2009).

[23] Tang and Sun (2016).

[24] UNDP China (2017b).

[25] WWF (2016).

[26] Ministry of Commerce (2015). See also, Cui (2016).

[27] Ministry of Commerce (2015).

[28] McKinsey & Co. (2017b).

[29] Ibid., 30. See also, Kuo and Tang (2016).

[30] Gutman and Zhang (2015).

[31] China's Second African Policy Paper (2015).

[32] China Africa Research Initiative, "Data: Chinese Contracts in Africa", http://www.sais-cari.org/data-chinese-contracts-in-africa.

Table 3.2 Selective Chinese financial institutions participating in investment in Africa

Chinese National Policy Banks	China Development Bank	Up until June 2018, China Development Bank has financed over 50 billion USD to African countries, including about 36.8 billion loans, to mainly support the development of agriculture, manufacturing, infrastructure, civic areas, etc.[33] The cases include the US$50 million loans to the Equity Bank of Kenya, which supported Mataara Tea Factory Expansion Project, Kapkoros Tea Factory Project, Jetlink Logistics Project, the EURO€60 million loans to the West African Development Bank to support SMEs in the regions covered by Union Economique et Monétaire Ouest-Africaine,[34] and the US$100 million loans to United Bank for Africa (UBA) to support SMEs in the nineteen countries covered by UBA.[35] Up until the end of June 2024, China Development Bank has financed over 65 billion USD to African countries. This support primarily focused on the development of infrastructure, energy resources, trade cooperation zones, agriculture, green development, SMEs, telecommunications, etc. The cases include the 300 million USD special loan project for the development of African SMEs to an Egyptian bank, the 130 million USD loan to Kenya's Equity Bank to support various projects including tea cultivation and processing, biomass power generation, transportation and logistics, and the upgrading of rural power grids, and the 160 million EUR loans to the West African Development Bank to support SME development in the member countries[36]
	China Export–Import Bank	China Export–Import Bank has provided over US$67.2 billion loans to Sub-Saharan African countries and regions from 2001 to 2010, surpassing the US$54.7 billion loans provided by the World Bank during the same time.[37] Up until the end of August, 2018, the bank had a loan balance of RMB340 billion in African countries, which covered over 600 projects.[38] From 2007 to 2020, the China Export–Import Bank and the China Development Bank provided 23 billion USD in financing to Sub-Saharan Africa.[39] Up until September 2024, the China Export–Import Bank has a loan balance of 400 billion RMB in African countries, which covered over 700 projects[40]

(continued)

[33] CDB (2017).

[34] CDB (2016). See also, Ministry of Commerce of China (2015).

[35] Consulate General of the People's Republic of China in Lagos (2018).

[36] China Development Bank (2024).

[37] Xinhua News (2018).

[38] Jin (2017).

[39] Party School of the Central Committee of the CPC (2023).

[40] Zhao (2024).

Table 3.2 (continued)

Central Bank	The People's Bank of China	In 2014, the People's Bank of China and the African Development Bank (AfDB) set up the co-financing 30-year term "Africa Growing Together Fund" with a total amount of US$2 billion, all of which will be offered in loans to projects recommend by AfDB with the first ten years of the fund[41]
National Commercial Banks	Bank of China	As of the end of 2017, Bank of China has set up branches in 20 countries/regions along the OBOR, followed by about 500 major foreign projects with a total investment of more than US$100 billion.[42] Bank of China, as the first Chinese bank to have a presence in South Africa, opened its Johannesburg Branch in early October 2000, and after that other branches in Zambia, Kenya, Angola, Morocco, and Mauritius. Its present business radiates more than 30 countries and regions in Africa. Bank of China started the first RMB settlement business in Africa in 2010, and was prescribed by the People's Bank of China as the RMB clearing bank in Africa.[43] Over the past 27 years, the Bank of China Zambia Branch has provided over $3 billion in credit support, covering a wide range of large infrastructure projects, including mining, smelting, water supply, highways, and economic development zones. Additionally, the bank has invested a total of 12 billion kwacha (approximately 45.7 million USD) in Zambian government bonds. The Bank of China Luanda Branch has cumulatively provided 194 million USD to the Angolan National Oil Company[44]
	Industrial and Commercial Bank of China	From 2007 to 2017, the Industrial and Commercial Bank of China has financed US$20 billion in Africa and had a loan balance of US$6 billion which covered 106 projects.[45] Up until September 2024, the Industrial and Commercial Bank of China has provided over 28 billion USD in loans to more than 130 projects across Africa[46]
	China Construction Bank	From 2004 to 2014, China Construction Bank had financed over US$3 billion to support various industry and infrastructure projects in Africa[47]
	Agricultural Bank of China	In 2015, the Agricultural Bank of China and the Congolese government together established the Sino-Congolese Bank for Africa with a total capital of US$100 million, and 50% shares of it is held by the Agricultural Bank of China[48]

Author's Compilation

[41] African Development Bank Group (2014).

[42] People's Bank of China (2018).

[43] Lu (2017). See also, China-Africa Trade Research Center (2016).

[44] Bank of China (2024).

[45] People's Daily Online (2018).

[46] Industrial and Commercial Bank of China (2024).

[47] China Construction Bank (2015).

[48] Wan and Li (2018).

Table 3.3 Selective large Chinese-invested infrastructure projects in Africa

Country	Project	Value ($bn)
Nigeria	Coastal Railway	12
Tanzania	Bagamoyo Port	7
South Africa	Modderfontein New City Project	7
Kenya	SGR	3.8
Cong DRC	Infrastructure for Mines Barter Deal	6
Chad	Cha-Sudan Railway	5.6
Mozambique	Mphanada Nkuwa Dam and Hydroelectric Station Project	3.1
Sudan	Port Sudan-Khartoum Railway	1.3

Source Adapted from Johnston (2016)[52]

China's economic expansion in Africa is carried forward by thousands of companies, including SOEs and non-SOEs. While non-SOEs dominate investment in commerce and manufacturing, the majority of Chinese companies engaging in infrastructure construction in Africa are SOEs.[49] Six of the 10 largest infrastructure contractors operating in Africa are Chinese SOEs. These are China Communications Construction Company, China Railway Group, Sinohydro Group, China State Construction Engineering Corporation, China Railway Construction Corporation, and Citic Construction Company.[50] In recent years, the east Africa region in particular has been one of the most prominent beneficiaries of this development, with projects constructed by Chinese SOEs including Lamu Port in Kenya, the Southern Sudan-Ethiopia Transport (LAPSSET) corridor, and the SGR in Kenya. The transport sector has the potential to "connect African countries by reducing the costs of moving people and goods, and integrating markets".[51] The major infrastructure projects that have been or scheduled to be undertaken by Chinese SOEs in Africa are listed in Table 3.3.

In addition, the rise of infrastructure construction in Africa should also be contextualized within the influx of Chinese loans to African countries. China is now the largest bilateral infrastructure financier in Africa.[53] In 2015, Chinese commitments to infrastructure in Africa amounted to $21 billion, which is more than the combined total of the African Development Bank (AfDB), the European Commission, the IFC, and the World Bank.[54] Unlike Western donors, such as the European Union and the United States, which provide aid primarily in the form of aid loans, China has begun to shift from a focus on pure lump aid to new systems where recipient countries receive focused infrastructure building assistance through concessional loans and

[49] Ibid.

[50] Interview with former general counsel of China Civil Engineering Construction Corporation.

[51] Tukic and Kim (2015a).

[52] Johnston (2016).

[53] McKinsey & Co. (2017c).

[54] The Infrastructure Consortium for Africa (2015).

preferential export credits.[55] For the concessional loans, the Chinese government has designated the Chinese Exim Bank to provide the medium and long-term low-interest loans to developing countries.[56] These loans operate as "government-to-government official development assistance and are provided for projects that generate economic or social benefits", such as infrastructure projects.[57] The Chinese government also encourages financial institutions to offer lower interest rates to promote export and investment through preferential export credits.[58] Together with concessional loans, the two preferential facilities are "an arrangement made by the Chinese Government to support other developing countries with concessional funding".[59] China's concessional loans and preferential export credits are helpful to transfer China's manufacturing surplus to Africa and use its machinery, equipment, and export projects to enhance its international competitiveness. This offers China a unique opportunity to promote Chinese services, technologies, and management models overseas. Especially for railway construction projects, a recipient country is usually required to adopt Chinese Railway Technical Standards and/or equipment throughout the construction process under China's concessional loans.[60]

China's Ministry of Commerce is in charge of the Department of Foreign Aid, which "oversees projects financed through zero-interest loans and grants and signs off on China Exim Bank's concessional loans".[61] The vast majority of loans for overseas companies and large infrastructure projects from China to African countries come from China's official export credit agencies and policy banks, such as China Exim Bank, and state-owned banks, such as the ICBC.[62] Beginning in 2007, the China-Africa Development Fund has been instrumental in supporting the trade and cooperation between China and Africa. The fund has become the first equity investment arm China established to focus solely on investment in Africa and has managed to provide capital for major projects in Africa.[63] The NDB and Chinese infrastructure initiatives, such as the China-led Africa Growing Together Fund, "are

---

55 Manero (2017) and Zhang (2016). See more, according to OECD Glossary of Statistics, a concessional loan is "granted on terms substantially more generous than market loans either through below-market interest rates, by grace periods or a combination of both". Export credits are "government financial support, direct financing, guarantees, insurance or interest rate support provided to foreign buyers to assist in the financing of the purchase of goods from national exporters." For more information on Chinese government's concessional loans and export credits, see China-Africa Research Initiative, "Chinese Loans to Africa (2000–2014)" http://www.sais-cari.org/data-chinese-loans-and-aid-to-africa/.

56 Davies et al. (2008).

57 Brautigam and Hwang (2016a).

58 Ibid., 29.

59 China Exim Bank, "Preferential Facilities". http://english.eximbank.gov.cn/tm/en-TCN/index_640.html.

60 Interview with deputy director of Institute of International Development Cooperation at the Chinese Academy of International Trade and Economic Corporation, MOFCOM.

61 Brautigam and Hwang (2016b). See also, Moss and Rose (2006).

62 Hwang et al. (2016). See also, Global Markets-EY Knowledge (2015).

63 Schickerling (2012).

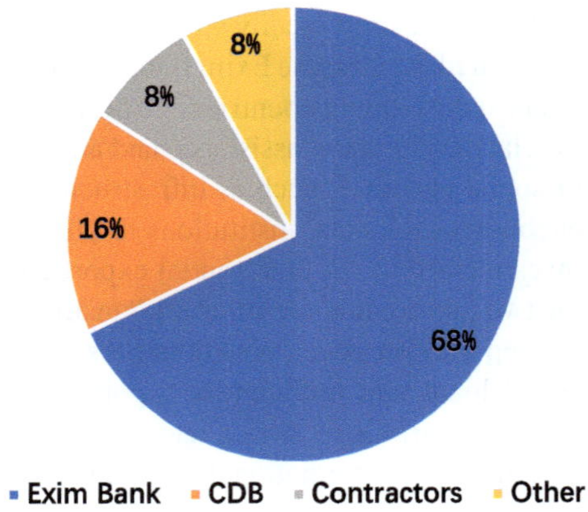

Fig. 3.3 Chinese Financiers' Contribution to African Loans (2000–2014). *Source* Adapted from Hwang al. (2016)[65]

expected to play a significant role ranging from financing to technology transfer".[64] Figure 3.3 shows that China Exim Bank has been the top provider of loans to Africa between 2000 and 2014.

3.2 The Impact of China's Investment in Africa

Given the rise of Chinese foreign investment in Africa, it is important to evaluate its impact on Africa. According to the surveys conducted by Pew Research Center, opinions of China and its expanding investment in Africa have generally been positive.[66] However, substantial variations in opinions exist across the continent, as shown in Table 3.4. The diverse economic development stages among African states partly explain different opinions on China as a foreign investor. In general, local people held favorable opinions on the economic benefits such as skill transfers and job creation by China's infrastructure projects.[67] The environmental concerns raised by China's infrastructure construction and natural resource extraction projects receive unfavorable opinions.[68] Critics of Chinese companies' investment activities claim that the primary motivation of Chinese investment in Africa is to extract resources. They also claim that Chinese companies export pollution from their industrial activities to non-democratic African countries with weak rule of law and weak legal institutions or high levels of corruption.[69] Given the controversial opinions surrounding China's investment in Africa, this section analyzes the potential economic, community, and environmental impact of China's investment in Africa.

64 Tukic and Kim (2015b). See also, African Development Group (2014).

65 Hwang et al. (2016).

66 Pew Research Center (2017).

67 Lekorwe et al. (2016).

68 Ibid.

69 Chen et al. (2015). See also, Taylor (2007). See also, Peh and Eyal (2010).

Table 3.4 Percent responding favorable of China's investment in Africa (2017)

Country	2017 (%)
Nigeria	72
Senegal	64
Tanzania	63
Tunisia	63
Kenya	54
Ghana	49
South Africa	45

Source Pew Research Center (2017)[70]

3.2.1 *Economic Impact*

At the macroeconomic level, host country governments and local communities in Africa generally acknowledge the contribution of Chinese investments to the economic development of their nations.[71] The economic, trade, and investment cooperation between China and Africa is still in its initial stage and has great potential. These emerging economies and developing countries urgently need opportunities for equal participation in the global economy and governance system.[72] China's ample capital and investment to host countries could boost their economic development and trade.[73] A World Bank report shows that development aid from China contributes to improving road construction projects, modernizing power distribution, rural electrification, technical training, and providing medical care and drugs.[74] However, as many of large infrastructure projects are supported through debt-based finance, questions are raised over its sustainability and the rising debt levels of African economies.[75] There are some criticisms that China's loans to African countries just sink them into financial traps.[76] Loans could also harm countries like Kenya in the long run because of their lack of transparency.[77] In addition, through concessional loans and debt from the Chinese government to African governments, Chinese companies and banks could also monopolize the complete industry and export chain.[78]

[70] Pew Research Center (2017).

[71] Wang et al. (2014).

[72] Van Dijk (2009).

[73] Martyn (2011a).

[74] Sanghi and Johnson (2016).

[75] Chen (2018). See also, Lee (2017).

[76] Beattie and Callan (2006). See also, Bavier (2018).

[77] Sanghi and Johnson (2016).

[78] Sun (2017).

As discussed above, infrastructure development is a critical issue for developing countries, especially in sub-Saharan Africa where lacking or outdated infrastructure has become a bottleneck for economic development.[79] Sub-Saharan Africa is currently in desperate need of paved road density, electricity generation capacity, and household access to water, and sanitation.[80] The lack of transnational infrastructure in Africa also restricts their import and export businesses, as "the inability of economies to integrate themselves with neighboring countries to promote wider markets continues to be a serious obstacle to trade".[81] Infrastructure development is therefore expected to be one of China's greatest contributions to host countries' economic infrastructure.[82] China's official policy toward Africa has advocated greater regional economic interconnection and promoted Chinese overseas companies "to participate in transnational and trans-regional infrastructure construction in Africa and provide preferential loans to support infrastructure building in Africa".[83] Some scholars observe that China's direct investment in the construction of roads, bridges, railways, and hydropower has increased local communities' access to transportation and electricity.[84] Farrell finds that for World Bank infrastructure projects, there is no significant difference in the quality of work performed by Chinese and non-Chinese contractors.[85] Burke shows that China's contribution to infrastructure in Africa comes with several benefits, such as easy access to capital and fast completion of construction with less redundant administrative approval process. The quality of infrastructure construction by Chinese companies is not compromised because of quick completion.[86] In addition, China's financing and construction of transport corridors could play a potential role in promoting regional integration.[87] For instance, the Kenyan SGR project will be expanded into a regional rail corridor connecting Kenya with Uganda, Burundi, and South Sudan. The implementation of transport networks and trade corridors is a key dimension of effective regional integration aimed at facilitating trade and investment within the region.

3.2.2 Community Impact

The community impact brought by Chinese companies' operation in Africa is controversial. There have been allegations against Chinese companies for their failure to localize their operations, for example, by importing workers from China instead of

[79] Martyn (2011a).

[80] Foster (2009). See also, Foster et al. (2008).

[81] Martyn (2011b).

[82] Corkin et al. (2008).

[83] Ministry of Foreign Affairs (2015).

[84] Arewa (2016). See also, Foster (2009), Schiere and Rugamba (2011) and Schiere (2011).

[85] Farrell (2016).

[86] Burke (2007).

[87] Esterhuyse et al. (2014).

hiring locally.[88] According to a study, Chinese laborers and engineers were imported to build infrastructure projects in African countries, which is unhelpful to the unemployment problem in Africa.[89] Many Chinese companies employ local staff only to engage in very basic physical work without providing them with systematic technical training.[90] According to Tang, even though Chinese companies hire local labor during construction, they only appoint Chinese managers.[91] In addition, working conditions in Chinese companies are problematic, often involving health and safety hazards and long working hours.[92] The labor protection measures of Chinese companies urgently require strengthening.[93] In addition, cultural and language barriers in communication often result in tensions and conflicts between local employees and Chinese workers or managers. It also leads to the inability of local staff to master more complex labor techniques and use more sophisticated production equipment.[94] Arsene's fieldwork in Kampala and Uganda, reveals that tensions between Chinese employers and African workers often arise because employees do not initially understand what their employers expect of them and because Chinese managers do not have adequate English-language skills to communicate.[95]

Conversely, some other researchers reveal the potential benefits when Chinese companies did employ local manpower. According to recent studies, Chinese investments have contributed to income generation and poverty reduction by creating a considerable number of employment opportunities for the host countries.[96] According to the UNDP 2017 Report on the Sustainable Development of Chinese Enterprises Overseas Supporting, at the end of 2015, "the total number of employees in overseas Chinese companies was 2,837,000, which included 1,225,000 non-Chinese employees, with an increase of 392,000 compared to the end of 2014".[97] This also indicates that Chinese overseas companies have started realizing the importance of localized operations in host countries. According to recent studies, during project subcontracting and procurement, Chinese overseas companies give priority to local personnel and suppliers in order to help local communities increase employment, enhance their functions, and support the development of local, small overseas companies and subcontractors in Africa.[98] The Business Perception Index survey conducted by Sino-African Centre of Excellence Foundation (SACE) shows that "Chinese companies hire Kenyans for 78 percent of full-time and 95 percent of part-time jobs. Ninety-three percent Chinese companies operating in Kenya reported

---

[88] Baah and Jauch (2009).

[89] Ibid.

[90] Zafar (2007).

[91] Tang (2010).

[92] Human Rights Watch (2011).

[93] Adolph et al. (2017).

[94] Arsene (2014).

[95] Ibid.

[96] Calabrese (2017). See also, Sautman and Yan (2015).

[97] UNDP China (2017c).

[98] Brautigam (2018). See also, Calabrese (2017). Sautman and Yan (2015).

hiring Kenyan workers".[99] The survey concluded that the employment of Kenyans by Chinese companies had grown over time. Chinese overseas companies have started to improve training and advancement opportunities for local workers as well. A recent study shows that comparisons of Chinese companies and their counterparts in OECD countries conclude that there are no substantial differences in working conditions between Chinese companies and those from other countries.[100]

3.2.3 Environmental Impact

Chinese foreign investment in Africa has been concentrated in environmentally-sensitive areas and carbon-intensive industries. First, Chinese foreign investment tends to flow to ecologically fragile African areas where there is a higher risk of environmental degradation. Second, a large proportion of Chinese foreign investment is located in carbon-intensive industries, such as infrastructure construction, oil and gas extraction, mining, hydropower, timber, and manufacturing.[101] These two features of Chinese investment cause significant environmental impact in Africa.

Existing literature generally presents a negative picture of the environmental performance of Chinese companies in Africa, particularly in the areas of mining, infrastructure, forestry, fishing, timber, and agricultural projects.[102] As many Chinese companies are developing projects in countries with weak governance structures, there are also concerns that China is exporting its pollution and environmental problems to Africa through this foreign investment strategy.[103] Moreover, as China adopts lower environmental standards for its aid and investment projects than multilateral institutions or Western companies, investment recipient countries may lower their environmental and social requirements for Chinese companies.[104] Furthermore, many Chinese companies operating in Africa are some of the most significant producers of global carbon emissions.[105] Africa is believed to be the most vulnerable and least able to adapt to global climate change.[106] As the world's largest producer and consumer of coal, and as an important actor in addressing global climate change, China faces international scrutiny to improve its environmental performance overseas.[107]

---

[99] Sino Africa Center of Excellence Foundation (2014).

[100] Farrell (2016).

[101] Ge et al. (2010). See also, González-Vicente (2011) and Greenovation Hub (2014).

[102] Mol (2011). See also, Bosshard (2008), Al-Aameri (2012), Butler (2005), Michelle (2007), Scott (2012), International Rivers (2012) and Alden (2009).

[103] Cissé et al. (2014). See also, Alden and Davies (2006).

[104] Shinn (2016). See also, Munson and Zheng (2011).

[105] Pike (2017).

[106] Besada and Sewankambo (2009). See also, Fields (2005).

[107] Interview with official from National Development and Reform Commission. See more, Walker (2016). "At present, more than 40% of China's coal-fired projects are planned (and signed) and under

Specifically, Chinese companies are frequently criticized for the negative environmental impact on African ecosystems when building dams and highways and conducting natural resource extraction in Africa.[108] There have been numerous cases of controversial negative environmental impact brought by Chinese companies in African countries. Table 3.5 shows a chronological list of well-known incidents. A high-profile case, for example, is Sinopec's suspension of oil prospecting in Loango National Park in Gabon due to pressures from NGOs.[109] More recently, in 2012, Chad withdrew five extraction permits and suspended all operations of the China National Petroleum Corporation for violations of environmental regulations.[110]

3.3 What Are the Incentives for China to Engage in CSR in Africa?

As discussed in Sect. 2.2, the Chinese government has political, economic, and social incentives to promote CSR internationally. The incentives may be enriched by African's context. As the discussion above illustrates, Chinese investment and industrial activities in Africa have triggered controversies over their social, economic and environment impact. Accordingly, the Chinese government and its affiliated entities—including SOEs and state-owned banks—may be motivated to promote CSR in Africa. This section analyzes the possible rationales for Chinese companies and financial institutions to promote sustainable investment in Africa.

3.3.1 Reducing Conflicts and Litigation Risks

Environmental and ecological conditions in Africa are complicated and volatile. Some areas have fragile and sensitive eco-environments that could cause severe natural disasters such as sandstorms, droughts, and erosion. Eastern Africa in particular has been suffering from prolonged droughts, hailstorms, extreme flooding, and other climate events in recent years.[111] These climate events are compounded by local environmental degradation caused by foreign investment, such as habitat loss, pollution, and deforestation.[112] Chinese infrastructure construction projects in Africa,

construction, such as the construction of a new pipeline across Myanmar and the construction of a number of coal-fired power plants in Indonesia, Pakistan, Turkey, and African and Latin American counties. From 2001 to 2016, the Chinese government invested in more than 50 coal-fired power plant projects overseas." See also, Pike (2017).

[108] Bosshard (2008). See also, Butler (2005). Michelle (2007).

[109] Deutsch (2010). See also, Mol (2011).

[110] Howit (2013).

[111] Lukamba (2010).

[112] OECD (2002).

Table 3.5 Selective environmental incidents caused by Chinese companies in Africa

Year	Country	Project in controversies	Chinese companies involved	Incident details
2003	Sudan	Merowe Dam Project on the Nile River	Sino Hydro; China International Water and Electric Corporation	Although Sudanese authorities had conducted and approved an ESIA, a few international NGOs and institutions insisted that the ESIA was sub-standard[113]
2005	Gabon	Oil Prospecting Project in Loango National Park	Sinopec	Conservation groups had pointed out that the ESIA had not been approved by the environment ministry[114]
2007	Zambia	Chiman Manufacturing's Manganese Mine in Kabwe	Chiman Manufacturing	Zambian government closed Chiman Manufacturing's manganese mine in Kabwe due to local concerns over air pollution and failures to implement pollution control measures[115]
2010	Gabon	Iron Ore Development Project	China National Machinery and Equipment Import and Export Corporation	A Gabonese environmental NGO successfully campaigned against a massive China Exim Bank-supported iron ore development project that threatened a national park[116]
2012	Zambia	Collum Coal Mine Industries in Sinazongwe	Collum Coal Mine	Zambian authorities shut down Chinese-owned Collum Coal Mine Industries in Sinazongwe for establishing sub-standard working conditions and failing to implement environmental and safety regulations[117]
2012	Chad	Oil Exploration Site in the South Western Town of Koudalwa	China National Petroleum Corporation	Chad withdrew five extraction permits and suspended all operations of the China National Petroleum Corporation for violations of environmental regulations[118]

Author's Compilation

which mainly focus on the construction of railways, container ports, and power plants, could further exacerbate these existing vulnerabilities and introduce additional risks. As important actors in international environmental governance and addressing global

113 Zhan (2014).

114 Bosshard (2008).

115 Bosshard (2008).

116 Zha (2014).

117 Okeowo (2013).

118 Van-Vliet and Magrin (2012).

climate change, Chinese companies are facing international scrutiny to improve their environmental performance overseas. International environmental NGOs have begun to apply legal pressure on companies in order to influence their environmental behaviors and urge them to operate in a more sustainable way.[119] To avoid conflicts regarding the negative environmental and social impact, Chinese infrastructure companies have incentives to develop infrastructure in African counties in an environmentally-friendly and socially responsible way.

The improvement of Chinese overseas companies' environmental and social behavior can also help to avoid regulatory violations in host countries. The traditional impression of Africa's environmental governance is that many African countries attach a low priority to environmental and social protection, and have bad records for countering corruption. In practice, African countries' approaches to environmental protection vary.[120] Some countries have "impressive legislation in place while others are lagging behind".[121] For example, countries such as Ethiopia, Mali, Mozambique, Zambia have relatively well-developed environmental legislation and implemented strategies and laws to support sustainable development.[122] Kenya also has a relatively developed environmental protection mechanism (see Chapter 4 for more details) due to the country's heavy reliance on nature tourism and international environmental organizations' monitoring. Due to the negative environmental impact brought by foreign investors, protection of the environment has become a particularly high priority for African governments.[123]

To promote sustainable development, many African countries have committed to transform their consumption and production processes and practices by embedding sustainable development into their legal system in order to protect the natural resources and environment for the current and future generations.[124] This shift toward a green economy has been reaffirmed by many different African initiatives, and there is now a growing awareness of the importance of transitioning to a green economy.[125] In addition, in response to the Intended Nationally Determined Contributions under the United Nations Framework Convention on Climate Change, many African countries have required foreign investors to reduce their industrial carbon emissions.[126] The regulatory authorities of host countries in Africa may continue to intensify their monitoring, assessment, and management of environmental and social considerations. Stricter environmental regulations and policies therefore pose a threat to the

[119] Frank and Pattberg (2013). See also, Kanie and Haas (2004).

[120] Shinn (2015).

[121] Ibid.

[122] Ibid.

[123] UN Economic Commission for Africa (2014).

[124] UNEP (2016). See also, UN Economic Commission for Africa (2016a).

[125] UN Economic Commission for Africa (2016a).

[126] Ibid., 69. See also, World Bank (2015).

survival of Chinese high-polluting infrastructure projects overseas,[127] and this will in turn affect the financial institutions that have provided loans to these companies.

In addition, Chinese companies may also face pushback for their lack of attention to protecting the interests and welfare of local communities in host countries. The historically unequal distribution of resources, revenues, and compensation as well as communication gaps and misunderstandings between the government, companies, and local communities have exacerbated the political, cultural, and economic marginalization of local communities and triggered conflicts.[128] Chinese overseas companies often face complex social risks and challenges in host countries, such as a lack of social acceptance or inclusiveness, inadequate regard for labor and working conditions, land acquisition and compensation, localized operations and management.[129] However, Chinese companies generally tend to invest more energy in building relations with the government instead of paying attention to economic benefits for landowners in Africa.[130] These actions would further destabilize relationships and cause new internal divisions over access to wealth, creating a vicious cycle that ignites, prolongs, and exacerbates conflicts between interested parties.

As the negative impact of climate change caused by multinational companies' and operation activities is gradually becoming a global issue, the litigation risks of multinational companies are increasingly rise. Given that multinational companies which account for the majority of total global emissions are more sensitive to the costs of legal liability, reputational damage, and ongoing public scrutiny, avoiding potential climate litigation against multinational companies is also an important consideration of promoting sustainable investment overseas. Given the increasingly strict domestic regulation from host countries and potential social conflicts during the investments in host countries, Chinese overseas companies are exposed to the risk of liability and litigation.[131] As multinational companies have encountered civil and criminal litigations worldwide for their irresponsible behavior,[132] it is just a matter of time before Chinese companies will encounter lawsuits, if they do not handle social and environmental issues properly. As mentioned earlier, the negative environmental and social impact brought by Chinese companies have drawn much attention form regulatory authorities in some African countries. Potential legal suits regarding land

---

[127] UNDP China (2017b). See also, UN Environment Financial Initiative (UNEP FI). https://www.unpri.org/.

[128] McKenna (2016).

[129] Interview with director of Institute of International Development Cooperation at the Chinese Academy of International Trade and Economic Corporation, MOFCOM. See also, Gu (2015).

[130] Interview with project manager of WWF-Africa.

[131] Han (2013).

[132] For example, in the case of *Texaco Oil Company and Chevron vs Lago Agrio Plaintiffs* illustrates the disputes over environmental pollution and civil health, and investors were prosecuted by victims' organizations in the Federal Court of New York and in Ecuador's domestic courts. As one of the world biggest environmental litigation between foreign investors and local communities in host countries, this case could be seen as a warning to foreign business investors and executives, and urges them to pay attention to investment projects that would pose great threat to the environment. See more, Moreta and Liu (2018).

acquisition and relocation, labor protection, and environmental protection may push Chinese companies to pay attention to integrating environmental and social protection elements into their daily operations.

3.3.2 *Reducing Economic Losses*

Chinese overseas companies and financial institutions conforming to a higher global environmental standard can also reduce economic losses and achieve lower lending risks during their operations in Africa. Current research has shown that it is in the companies' interest to minimize activity that may have negative impact on the environment.[133] Investors have recognized that if there are social and environmental risks or concerns, companies that successfully and effectively manage these risks through effective self-regulation will generate higher returns on investment capital.[134] As discussed in Sect. 3.3.1, as African countries are strengthening their social and environmental regulations, Chinese companies in violation of the regulations may face an increasing risk of civil claims and criminal fines. Moreover, negative publicity from even just one project could threaten Chinese companies' business future access to resources and markets in Africa.[135]

In recent years, socially responsible investing (SRI) has made inroads into Africa, particularly in the three major economies including Nigeria, Kenya, and South Africa.[136] The assets under SRI management in the three economies grew to $678 billion USD.[137] SRI investors only invest in companies that effectively govern their impact on climate change, human rights, social interests, and the environment.[138] With the development of SRI, companies that have better environmental conservation practices in their operations may attract more capital from private and multilateral financial institutions.[139] Chinese companies can use the environment as a strategic competitive advantage, by adopting higher environmental standards to help companies gain financial access and greater acceptance and access to markets in African host countries, and improve their public images relative to their competitors in Africa.

[133] Graham and Woods (2006).

[134] Analysis of a sample of 89 manufacturing and extracting companies drawn from the Standard & Poors 500 Index found that those companies choosing to follow their own strict global environmental standard had an individual value approximately $10.4 billion higher than those companies that met only the less stringent US legal requirements. See, Dowell et al. (2000). See more, Blacconiere and Patten (1994).

[135] AmeWiig (2011).

[136] Global Sustainable Investment Alliance (2016).

[137] Ibid., 17.

[138] African Development Bank Group, "Climate Change Action Plan (2011–2015). https://www.afdb.org/fileadmin/uploads/afdb/Documents/Policy-Documents/Climate%20Change%20Action%20Plan%20%28CCAP%29%202011-2015.pdf. See also, Guo (2008).

[139] Frank and Pattberg (2013). See also, Blacconiere and Patten (1994).

In addition, promoting Chinese companies' CSR in Africa could also help Chinese financial institutions reduce lending risks, such as valuation risk and credit risk.[140] Chinese financial institutions have come to realize that environmental and social risks are potential causes of volatile markets and financial instability.[141] Chinese financial institutions' investment in high pollution-risk projects would therefore increase their lending risks and affect their financial returns. As China's infrastructure projects in Africa are handled mainly by SOEs with financial support from China's state-owned banks, a financial loss for an infrastructure project overseas equals a financial loss for the Chinese government.[142] The case Lamu Coal Power Plant in Kenya, clearly shows the financial risks of Chinese financial institutions in Africa. As Kenya's first and East Africa's first coal-fired power plant project, Lamu Plant has been suspended by Kenya's National Environmental Court on June 26, 2019.[143] The coal plant cost $2bn, of which $1.2bn was financed by the Industrial and Commercial Bank of China (ICBC). Thus, to maximize the returns on their investments and to reduce the potential damage to state assets, Chinese companies and state-owned financial institutions have an incentive to ensure that environmental and social risks are adequately addressed and enhance their environmental behavior during foreign investment activities in Africa.

3.3.3 *Protecting Political Image*

Chinese infrastructure and development projects undertaken by China's SOEs with financial supports from state-controlled financial institutions are often seen as a form of soft power designed to win local support for China's economic policies and diplomatic positions internationally. As most of the Chinese companies engaging in infrastructure construction in Africa are SOEs, their behavior may be ultimately traceable to the Chinese government. In particular, Chinese companies' expansion in Africa under the sponsorship of the Chinese government has attracted the accusation that China is becoming a new colonial power in Africa.[144] Especially, China's investment on the continent mainly involves in natural resources exploitation that can result in serious environmental consequences. The way Chinese companies manage local employees has also raised the social exploitation concerns. As discussed previously, the managerial echelon of Chinese companies operating in Africa is dominated by virtually all Chinese and local African employees are hired only to work at the lower levels.

[140] Ma (2017).

[141] For an analysis of environmental risk in the financial sector, see UNEP Inquiry (2016).

[142] Interview with official from National Development and Reform Commission.

[143] A Ochieng, 'Tribunal Cancels Lamu Coal Power Project Licence' (Daily Nation, June 27 2019). The project was opposed by local residents and civil society groups regarding its adverse potential effects on the local environment, cultural heritage, health and biodiversity.

[144] Walsh (2006). See also, Esposito et al. (2014), French (2010) and Kelly (2017).

Moreover, the ostensibly generous financial aids provided by the Chinese government and financial institutions have been criticized for creating a deep financial trap that makes African countries subordinate to China's control.[145] In the face of "neo-colonialism" allegations in Africa, the Chinese government and Chinese companies may have strategic incentives to alleviate the concerns through CSR practices and thus improve China's political image in the international community.

3.3.4 Responding to the International Sustainable Investment Regime Reform

Traditional IIAs have long focused on protecting the interests of international investors while restricting the host country's regulatory measures. In recent years, with the international investment regime's concern over climate change issues, climate governance and international investment regime reform have been mutually reinforcing.[146] As multinational companies become increasingly powerful in investment activities, they often challenge the regulatory measures of the host country in international investment arbitration, and the incongruity between the interests of investors and the public interests of the host country becomes increasingly obvious. In recent years, host states have come to realize the importance of environmental public interests and have begun to pay attention to preserving regulatory space to carefully oversee the activities of foreign investors. Moreover, in the context of the evolving concept of green investment, the international community has also added new requirements for the international investment policy framework, calling for the balance between the rights of the host state and foreign investors to be given close attention in IIAs in order to promote the sustainable development of the host state.[147] Incorporated into the new generation of IIAs are investor obligation clauses related to climate governance, environmental protection, human rights protection, representing a gradual evolution of IIAs in terms of their function and value orientation and marking a shift from a focus solely on protecting the private rights and interests of foreign investors to balancing and reconciling the interests of both host states and investors. UNCTAD is now actively reforming and redrafting IIAs to incorporate more investor obligations related to sustainable development.[148]

In the context of international sustainable investment reform in response to climate change, climate regulation clauses have undergone development, and the value tendency has evolved from emphasizing the protection of investment interests to balancing the regulatory rights of the host country's environmental public interests, and the content of clauses has also evolved from abstract environmental clauses

[145] Beattie and Callan (2006). See also, Bavier (2018), Pandey (2018) and Mclntyre (2018).

[146] Liu (2024a).

[147] Xiao (2015).

[148] UNCTAD (2015).

to specific climate regulation clauses.[149] Among them, climate change regulatory clauses are expected to become an essential tool for balancing the host country's public interest and investor protection. It is expected that the climate regulatory provisions can further increase the chances of host countries to defend and win lawsuits, encourage host countries to fulfill relevant international emission reduction obligations, and ensure the balance between the public interests of host countries and the protection of investors' interests.[150] Moreover, there is an increasingly tendency of establishing climate-change-related investor obligations in IIAs that balance the regulatory rights of host states and the protection of investor interests.[151] In order to effectively address climate change, host countries have gradually begun to encourage climate-friendly investments by restricting or banning high-carbon non-climate-friendly investments by revoking licenses for fossil fuel exploration or extraction activities, and phasing out fossil fuel energy sources and eliminating fossil fuel subsidies.[152] Some countries have begun to exclude carbon-intensive industries from the treaty's protection.[153] As investors and host countries increasingly apply environmental rules to international investment arbitration, climate change claims will continue to flourish in investment arbitration, and conflicts between international investment rules and climate change governance rules will continue to increase.

3.4 What is the Relevancy of China's "State-Centric" Approach to the African Context?

As discussed above, Chinese companies and financial institutions may have incentives to engage in CSR in Africa for a host of reasons. However, CSR engagement does not mean it has to be through the state-led approach. Many Western multinational companies operating in Africa, for example, have a wide range of CSR activities in Africa by following the conventional market-based approach. Thus, it raises an important question: Is there any particular significance of the state-centric approach in the African context to make Chinese companies and financial institutions engage in CSR?

As discussed in Chapter 2, the effectiveness of the market-based CSR approach entails active NGOs as well as a range of educated and responsive information users including consumers and investors. It relies on market pressure to force companies to engage in CSR. The market pressure may come locally and internationally. In many African countries, the local market pressure has not become a sophisticated force to make companies integrate CSR into their daily business management. Existing empirical research has shown that the market-based CSR approach has made African

---

149 Liu (2024b).

150 Paine and Sheargold (2023).

151 Liu and Ai (2025).

152 Paine and Sheargold (2023).

153 Council of European Union (2022).

companies engage in CSR only in a very superficial manner such as by treating it as public relations and philanthropy.[154] In this regard, the international market force is particularly important. The international market force may come from multinational companies' home-country market. Consumers and investors in the multinational companies' home country market take actions in response to irresponsible behavior of the multinational companies. A well-known example is that the anti-apartheid shareholder activism in the 1980s in the U.S. to pressure U.S. companies to divest from South Africa.[155] Led by institutional investors from religious and public institutions, apartheid-minded investors used shareholder resolutions to pressure U.S. companies to curtail their investment in South Africa.

The home-country market pressure has been more observable in the West than in China. To date, China's public has not demonstrated much particular concerns and corresponding reactions to irresponsible overseas behavior of Chinese companies and financial institutions. Chinese civil society and market remain focused on domestic CSR issues. In this regard, the compliance pressure from the state-led approach may be a substitute for the home-country market pressure in the Western context. The state as a home-country regulator and a major international investor may exert great power over Chinese companies operating in Africa. China's state-centric approach may be a complement to the local albeit immature market pressure in Africa as well as a substitute for the home-country market pressure.

Meanwhile, China's state-centric approach may aggravate the "neo-colonialism" suspicion in Africa. As discussed above, the pervasiveness of state control over Chinese overseas SOEs that dominate infrastructure and extractive sector projects in Africa has already raised the fear that Chinese investments are to realize China's neo-imperialist ambitions. The state-centric approach emphasizes "top-down" control instead of "bottom-up" community engagement. Under the state-centric approach, local priorities would not been adequately reflected in Chinese companies' CSR policies and practices.[156]

Moreover, the Chinese government and its affiliates are usually known for insufficient transparency. It raises concerns on how China's state-centric approach may be effective to protect disadvantaged local people in Africa where there is a relatively high level of corruption as well.[157] The lack of transparency of China's state-centric approach could further cultivate corruption and deepen the concern that Chinese foreign investment always goes to African countries with weak rule of law and high level of corruption.

154 Visser (2008). See also, Hilson (2013). Mumo et al. (2005). Ite (2004).

155 Broyles (1998).

156 Roe (2013).

157 Warf (2017). See also, UN Economic Commission for Africa (2016b), Davies (2009) and Bersselaar (2011).

3.5 Conclusion

This chapter examines the contexts, motivations, and reasons for Chinese companies and financial institutions to promote sustainable investment in Africa. The Chinese government and its affiliates may want to engage in CSR in Africa to avoid potential legal liabilities and economic losses, to respond to the latest international sustainable investment regime reform, to improve the international reputation and political image, as well as to respond to the international sustainable investment regime reform.

This chapter also analyzes the promises and concerns of the state-centric approach in the particular context of Africa. China's state-centric approach may potentially complement the market-based approach to better advance Chinese companies' CSR in African countries. However, the top-down nature of the state-centric approach may lack sufficient considerations of true needs of African local communities. It could aggravate the suspicion of Chinese "neo-colonialism" in Africa. The transparency problems of the Chinese government and its affiliates raise doubts how the state-centric approach may effectively protect local communities in Africa where it has its own serious corruption problems as well. The next chapter will provide a case study to more concretely contextualize the promises and concerns of the state-centric approach raised in this chapter.

References

Adolph C et al (2017) The Shanghai effect: do exports to China affect labor practices in Africa? World Dev 89:1–18

African Development Bank Group (2014) AfDB announces US$2 Billion fund with China. https://www.afdb.org/en/news-and-events/afdb-announces-us-2-billion-fund-with-china-13165/

African Development Group (2014) AfDB announces US $2 billion fund with China. https://www.afdb.org/en/news-and-events/afdb-announces-us-2-billion-fund-with-china-13165/. The resources from the Africa Growing Together Fund are expected to be provided over a 10-year period and will be used alongside the AfDB's own resources to finance eligible sovereign and non-sovereign guaranteed development projects in Africa

Al-Aameri N et al (2012) Environmental impact of China's outward foreign direct investment. https://oaktrust.library.tamu.edu/bitstream/handle/1969.1/152080/Final%20Bush%20School%20Report_2012.pdf?sequence=1

Alden C (2009) China and Africa's natural resources: the challenges and implications for development and governance. http://www.voltairenet.org/IMG/pdf/China_and_Africa_s_Natural_Resources.pdf

Alden C, Davies M (2006) A profile of the operations of Chinese multinationals in Africa. S Afr J Int Aff 13(1):83–96

AmeWiig I (2011) Better the devil you know? Chinese foreign direct investment in Africa. J Afr Bus 12(1):31–50

Arewa O (2016) Constructing Africa: Chinese investment, infrastructure deficits, and development. Cornell Int Law J 49:101–139

Arsene C (2014) Chinese employers and their Ugandan workers: tensions, frictions and cooperation in an African City. J Curr Chin Aff 43(1):139–176

Baah A, Jauch H (eds) (2009) Chinese investment in Africa: a labour perspective. Africa Labour Research Network. https://www.fnv.nl/site/over-de-fnv/internationaal/mondiaal-fnv/documenten/english/publications/Chinese_investments_in_Africa_final_report1.pdf

Bank of China (2024) Bank of China: the financial bridge for China-Africa economic and trade cooperation. https://www.bankofchina.com/aboutboc/bi1/202409/t20240904_25147682.html

Bavier J (2018) China overloading poor nations with debt though infrastructure projects. Reuters. https://news.abs-cbn.com/focus/07/16/18/china-overloading-poor-nations-with-debt-though-infra-projects

Beattie A, Callan E (2006) China loans create 'New Wave of Africa Debt'. Financial Times. https://www.ft.com/content/640a5986-863a-11db-86d5-0000779e2340

Bersselaar D (2011) No longer at ease: corruption as an institution in West Africa. Int J Public Adm 34(11):741–752

Besada H, Sewankambo N (2009) Climate change in Africa: adaptation, mitigation and governance challenges. The Center for International Governance Innovation Special Report. https://www.unicef.org/esaro/Climate_Change_in_Africa.pdf

Blacconiere W, Patten D (1994) Environmental disclosures, regulatory costs, and changes in firm value. J Account Econ 18(3):357–377

Blue Book of Outbound Investment and Risks (2017) Annual report on China's outbound direct investment and host country risk. Social Science Academic Press China

Bosshard P (2008) China's environmental footprint in Africa. China in Africa Policy Briefing. https://www.internationalrivers.org/sites/default/files/attached-files/saiia_policy_briefing_508.pdf

Brautigam D (2018) U.S. politicians get China in Africa all wrong. The Washington Post. https://www.washingtonpost.com/news/theworldpost/wp/2018/04/12/china-africa/?noredirect=on&utm_term=.1c64caa6983b

Brautigam D, Hwang J (2016a) Eastern promises: new data on Chinese loans in Africa, 2000 to 2014. China Africa Research Initiative Working Paper No. 4, 24. https://static1.squarespace.com/static/5652847de4b033f56d2bdc29/t/58ac91ede6f2e1f64a20d11a/1487704559189/eastern+promises+v4.pdf

Brautigam D, Hwang J (2016b) Eastern promises: new data on Chinese loans in Africa, 2000–2014. China-Africa Research Initiative Working Paper No. 4, 23. https://static1.squarespace.com/static/5652847de4b033f56d2bdc29/t/58ac91ede6f2e1f64a20d11a/1487704559189/eastern+promises+v4.pdf

Broyles P (1998) The impact of shareholder activism on corporate involvement in South Africa during the reagan era. Int Rev Mod Sociol 28(1):1–19

Burke C (2007) China's entry into construction industries in Africa: Tanzania and Zambia as Case Studies. China Report. http://journals.sagepub.com; https://doi.org/10.1177/000944550704300304

Butler T (2005) Growing pains and growing alliances: China, timber and Africa. Afr Renaissance 2(4):42–46

Calabrese L (2017) Chinese investment and knowledge transfer in Africa. Growth Research Programme. https://dl.orangedox.com/Brief-China-Africa-investment-1

CDB (2016) Special loan product for small and medium-sized African businesses. http://www.cdb.com.cn/cpfw/gjyw/zxfw_440/201602/t20160222_2675.html

CDB (2017) CDB has Financed over US$5 Billion for Africa. http://www.cdb.com.cn/xwzx/khdt/201709/t20170927_4616.html

Chen H (2016) China's 'One Belt, One Road' initiative and its implications for Sino-African investment relations. Transnatl Corp Rev 8(3):178–182

Chen Y (2018) Silk road to the Sahel: African ambitions in China's belt and road initiative. Johns Hopkins SAIS-CARI Policy Brief No.23. https://static1.squarespace.com/static/5652847de4b033f56d2bdc29/t/5b67f63b562fa7f5d579f835/1533539945322/Yunnan+Belt+and+Road+-+Final+Version.pdf

Chen W et al (2015) Why is China investing in Africa? Evidence from the firm level. Brookings Institution. https://www.brookings.edu/wp-content/uploads/2016/06/Why-is-China-investing-in-Africa.pdf
Cheng C (2018) Blood cell finance and the belt and road initiative: new model for China-Africa development cooperation. Renmin University Press, Beijing
Chhibber A (2017) China's one belt one road strategy: the new financial institutions and India's options. Institute for International Economic Policy Working Paper Series. https://www2.gwu.edu/~iiep/assets/docs/papers/2017WP/ChhibberIIEPWP2017-7.pdf
China-Africa Trade Research Center (2016) The practitioner of China-Africa finance: a collection of bank of China branches in Africa. http://toutiao.manqian.cn/wz_58005fb9e4b0f812e551ac13.html
China Construction Bank (2015) China Construction Bank and South Africa industrial development company signed a strategic corporation agreement to support the industrialization of Africa. http://ccb.com/cn/ccbtoday/newsv3/20151204_1449191625.html
China Development Bank (2024) Deepening financial cooperation and building a high-level China-Africa community with a shared future. https://www.cdb.com.cn/xwzx/khdt/202409/t20240903_11886.html
China's Second African Policy Paper (2015). http://www.china.org.cn/world/2015-12/05/content_37241677_5.htm. The Chinese Government intends to step up China-Africa cooperation in transportation, communication, water conservancy, electricity and other infrastructure's; vigorously to encourage Chinese companies to participate in the building of infrastructure in African countries
Cissé D et al (2014) State-directed multi-national enterprises and transnational governance: Chinese investments in Africa, corporate responsibility and sustainability norms. http://scholar.sun.ac.za/handle/10019.1/95493
Consulate General of the People's Republic of China in Lagos (2018) United Bank for Africa Obtained US$100 Million Special Loans from CDB. http://www.mofcom.gov.cn/article/i/jyjl/k/201803/20180302716926.shtml
Corkin L et al (2008) China's role in the development of Africa's infrastructure. SAIS Working Papers in African Studies. https://www.sais-jhu.edu/sites/default/files/China's-Role-in-the-Development-of-Africa's-Infrastructure.pdf
Council of European Union (2022) Agreement in principle on the modernization of the energy charter treaty
Cui X (2016) China's 'Belt and Road': Where Is Africa?. The Diplomat. https://thediplomat.com/2016/06/chinas-belt-and-road-where-is-africa/
Davies J (2009) Parliamentarians and corruption in Africa: the challenges of leadership and the practice of politics. African Parliamentarians Network Against Corruption. https://agora-parl.org/resources/library/parliamentarians-and-corruption-africa-challenge-leadership-and-practice-politics
Davies M et al (2008) How China delivers development assistance to Africa. Center for Chinese Studies. http://www0.sun.ac.za/ccs/wp-content/uploads/2009/04/dfid_fa_final.pdf
Deutsch J (2010) Partnering with SINOPEC in Loango National Park, Gabon. Wildlife Conservation Society & the African Biodiversity Collaborative Group. http://www.frameweb.org/adl/en-US/5345/file/756/Deutsch%20ABCG%20-20WCS%20Sinopec%20in%20Loango%20NP%20Gabon.pdf
Dowell G et al (2000) Do corporate global environmental standards create or destroy market value? Manag Sci 46(8):1059–1074
Eom J et al (2016) Looking back and moving forward: an analysis of China-Africa economic trends and the outcomes of the 2015 forum on China Africa cooperation. China-Africa Research Initiative. http://static1.squarespace.com/static/5652847de4b033f56d2bdc29/t/56aa3a95a12f44bc3732d26e/1453996965486/CARI_PolicyBrief_9_Jan2016
Esposito M et al. (2014) Recolonizing Africa: a modern Chinese story?. CNBC. https://www.cnbc.com/2014/12/30/recolonizing-africa-a-modern-chinese-story.html

Esterhuyse W et al (2014) African regional economic communities engagement with China. China-Africa Relations Policy Briefing. http://urban-africa-china.angonet.org/content/african-regional-economic-communities-engagement-china
Farrell J (2016) How do Chinese contractors perform in Africa? Evidence from World Bank Projects. Johns Hopkins SAIS-CARI Working Paper 3. https://static1.squarespace.com/static/5652847de4b033f56d2bdc29/t/573c970bf8baf3591b05253f/1463588620386/Working+Paper_Jamie+Farrell.pdf
Fields S (2005) Continental divide: why Africa's climate change burden is greater. Environ Health Perspect 113(8):534–537
Foster V (2009) Building bridges: China's growing role as infrastructure financier for Sub-Saharan Africa. World Bank. https://openknowledge.worldbank.org/handle/10986/2614
Foster V et al (2008) China's emerging role in Africa: part of the changing landscape of infrastructure finance. World Bank. https://documents.worldbank.org/en/publication/documents-reports/documentdetail/888291468029095977/chinas-emerging-role-in-africa-part-ofthe-changing-landscape-of-infrastructure-finance
Frank B, Pattberg P (2013) Global environmental governance: taking stock, moving forward. Annu Rev Environ Resour 33:277–294
French H (2010) The Next Empire. The Atlantic. http://www.theatlantic.com/magazine/archive/2010/05/the-next-empire/308018
Gallagher N, Shan W (2009) Chinese investment treaties: policies and practice. Oxford University Press, Oxford
Ge C et al (2010) Environmental policies on China's investment overseas. China Environmental Science Press, Beijing
Global Markets-EY Knowledge (2015) Riding the silk road: China sees outbound investment boom: outlook for China's outward foreign direct investment. http://www.ey.com/Publication/vwLUAssets/ey-china-outbound-investment-report-en/$FILE/ey-china-outbound-investment-report-en.pdf
Global Sustainable Investment Alliance (2016) 2016 Global Sustainable Investment Review. http://www.gsi-alliance.org/wp-content/uploads/2017/03/GSIR_Review2016.F.pdf
González-Vicente R (2011) China's engagement in South America and Africa's extractive sectors: new perspectives for resource curse theories. Pac Rev 24(1):65–87
Graham D, Woods N (2006) Making corporate self-regulation effective in developing countries. World Dev 34(5):868–883
Greenovation Hub (2014) China's mining industry at home and overseas: development, impact and regulation. http://www.ghub.org/cfc_en/wp-content/uploads/sites/2/2014/11/China-Mining-at-Home-and-Overseas_Main-report2_EN.pdf
Gu J (2015) China's new silk road to development cooperation: opportunities and challenges. United Nations University Centre for Policy Research. https://collections.unu.edu/eserv/UNU:3324/unu_cpr_china_dev.pdf
Guo P (2008) Socially responsible investment emerges in China. (China Dialogue). https://www.ChinaDialogue.net/article/2020-Socially-responsible-investment-emerges-in-China
Gutman J, Zhang C (2015) Who wins world bank-financed government contracts?. Brookings Institution. https://www.brookings.edu/blog/africa-in-focus/2015/06/24/who-wins-world-bank-financed-government-contracts-four-things-we-learned-from-the-data-1-lingering-question/
Han X (2013) Study on Chinese companies on environmental protection during overseas investment. Law Press China, Beijing, pp 121–127
Hilson G (2013) Corporate social responsibility in the extractive industries: experiences from developing countries. Resour Policy 37(2):131–137
Howit N (2013) Chad suspends CNPC's oil operations after oil spill. China Dialogue. https://www.ChinaDialogue.net/blog/6315-Chad-suspends-CNPC-s-oil-opera-tions-after-oil-spill/en
Human Rights Watch (2011) Labor abuses in Zambia's Chinese state-owned copper mines. Human Rights Watch. https://www.hrw.org/sites/default/files/reports/zambia1111ForWebUpload.pdf

Hwang J et al (2016) How Chinese money is transforming Africa: it's not what you think. China Africa Research Initiative, Policy Brief No. 11. http://www.africa-platform.org/resources/how-chinese-money-transforming-africa-its-not-what-you-think

Industrial and Commercial Bank of China (2024) The Industrial and Commercial Bank of China and Standard Bank Group jointly hosted a China-Africa Economic and Trade Investment Forum. https://www.icbc.com.cn/page/1022090829038731264.html

International Rivers (2012) The new great walls: a guide to China's overseas Dam Industry. http://www.internationalrivers.org/files/attached-files/intlrivers_newgreatwalls_2012_2.pdf

Ite U (2004) Multinationals and corporate social responsibility in developing countries: a case study of Nigeria. Corp Soc Responsib Environ Manag 11:1–11

Jian J (2017) Africa in the maritime silk road: challenges and prospects. In: Mayer M (ed) Rethinking the silk road: China's belt and road initiative and emerging eurasian relations. Springer, New York

Jin X (2017) The Financial Engine Assist China-Africa Comprehensive Corporation. People's Daily. http://paper.people.com.cn/rmrb/html/2017-12/07/nw.D110000renmrb_20171207_3-14.htm

Johnston L (2016) Africa, and China's one belt, one road initiative: why now and what next. International Centre for Trade and Sustainable Development. https://www.ictsd.org/bridges-news/bridges-africa/news/africa-and-china%E2%80%99s-one-belt-one-road-initiative-why-now-and-what

Kanie N, Haas P (eds) (2004) Emerging forces in environmental governance. United Nations University Press, New York

Kazeemm Y (2017) China doubled its investment spend in Africa in 2016 as UK and US Fell. Quartz Africa. https://www.google.com.hk/amp/s/qz.com/africa/978419/china-influence-has-an-investor-in-africa-grew-in-2016/amp/

Kelly R (2017) How China's soft power is building a new-colonial system in Africa. Ketagalan Media. http://www.ketagalanmedia.com/2017/10/09/how-chinas-soft-power-is-building-a-neo-colonial-system-in-africa/

Kuo M, Tang A (2016) China's Africa strategy: going global with infrastructure investment. The Diplomat. https://thediplomat.com/2016/01/chinas-africa-strategy-going-global-with-infrastructure-investment/

Lee CK (2017) The specter of global China: politics, labor and foreign investment in Africa. University of Chicago Press, Chicago

Lekorwe M et al (2016) China's growing presence in Africa wins largely positive popular reviews. Afrobarometer Dispatch No. 122. http://afrobarometer.org/sites/default/files/publications/Dispatches/ab_r6_dispatchno122_perceptions_of_china_in_africa1.pdf

Liu B (2024a) Investment arrangements for climate governance: tracing, evolution and new approaches. Study Law Bus 4:56–57

Liu B (2024b) Investment arrangements for climate governance: tracing, evolution and new approaches. Study Law Bus 4:55–60

Liu B, Ai S (2025) Establishing binding climate-change-related investor obligation clauses in international investment agreements: obstacles and pathways. Rev Eur Comp Int Environ Law 4(1):136–154

Lu A (2017) The RMB business of the Bank of China Johannesburg branch covers 29 African countries. CHINAFRICA. http://www.chinafrica.cn/chinese/mrxw/201705/t20170526_800097103.html

Lukamba MT (2010) Natural disasters in African countries: what can we learn about them? J Transdiscip Res South Afr 6(2):478–485

Ma J (2017) Establishing China's green financial system. China Financial Publication House, Beijing

Manero E (2017) Chinas investment in Africa: the new colonialism?. Harvard Political Review. http://harvardpolitics.com/world/chinas-investment-in-africa-the-new-colonialism/

Martyn D (2011a) How China is influencing Africa's development. In: Men J, Barton B (eds) China and the European Union in Africa: partners or competitors? College of Europe, Belgium, pp 187–205

Martyn D (2011b) How China is influencing Africa's development. In: Men J, Barton B (eds) China and the European Union in Africa: partners or competitors? College of Europe, Belgium, p 195

McKenna K (2016) Corporate social responsibility and natural resource conflict. Routledge, Oxon

McKinsey & Co. (2017a) Dance of the Lions and Dragons: How are Africa and China Engaging, and How will the Partnership Evolve? 10. https://www.mckinsey.com/global-themes/middle-east-and-africa/the-closest-look-yet-at-chinese-economic-engagement-in-africa

McKinsey & Co. (2017b) Dance of the lions and dragons: how are Africa and China engaging, and how will the partnership evolve? 24. https://www.mckinsey.com/global-themes/middle-east-and-africa/the-closest-look-yet-at-chinese-economic-engagement-in-africa

McKinsey & Co. (2017b) Dance of the Lions and Dragons: how are Africa and China engaging, and how will the partnership evolve?. https://www.mckinp27sey.com/global-themes/middle-east-and-africa/the-closest-look-yet-at-chinese-economic-engagement-in-africa

McIntyre J (2018) "'Game of loans: how china uses 'Debt-trap Diplomacy' to extend its military reach". Examiner. https://www.washingtonexaminer.com/policy/defense-national-security/how-china-uses-debt-trap-diplomacy-to-extend-its-military-reach

Michelle C-F (2007) Environmental impact: more of the same. In: Manji F, Marks S (eds) African perspectives on China in Africa. Pambazuka Press, pp 139–152

Ministry of Commerce (2015) The interpretations of the Johannesburg summit of the FOCAC and the sixth ministerial conference on the 10 major China-Africa cooperation plans in economic and trade domains. http://english.mofcom.gov.cn/article/policyrelease/Cocoon/201512/20151201219036.shtml

Ministry of Commerce (2016) 2016 China Foreign Direct Investment Statistical Bulletin. http://fec.mofcom.gov.cn/article/tjsj/tjgb/201709/20170902653690.shtml

Ministry of Commerce of China (2015) Introduction of the CDB special loans product for small and medium-sized African businesses. http://www.mofcom.gov.cn/aarticle/i/jshz/rlzykf/201204/20120408048826.html

Ministry of Foreign Affairs (2015) The forum on China-Africa cooperation Johannesburg action plan (2016–2018). http://www.fmprc.gov.cn/mfa_eng/zxxx_662805/t1323159.shtml

Mol A (2011) China's ascent and Africa's environment. Glob Environ Chang 21(3):785–794

Moreta M, Liu B (2018) The challenge of bringing to justice transnational corporations for environmental damages: case of study texaco oil company and Chevron vs Lago Agrio Plaintiffs. In: Voigt C et al (eds) Courts and the environment. Edward Elgar, Cheltenham

Moss T, Rose S (2006) China Exim Bank and Africa: new lendings, new challenges. Centre for Global Development. https://www.cgdev.org/files/11116_file_China_and_Africa.pdf

Mumo K et al (2005) How can corporate social responsibility deliver in Africa? Insights from Kenya and Zambia. International Institute for Environment and Development. http://pubs.iied.org/pdfs/16006IIED.pdf

Munson P, Zheng R (2011) Feeding the dragon: managing Chinese resource acquisition in Africa. Seattle J Environ Law 2:373–376

National Development and Reform Commission, Ministry of Foreign Affairs, and Ministry of Commerce (2015) Vision and actions on jointly building silk road economic belt and 21st-century maritime silk road. http://en.ndrc.gov.cn/newsrelease/201503/t20150330_669367.html

NDRC, Ministry of Foreign Affairs and Ministry of Commerce of China (2015) Vision and action on joint building silk road economic belt and 21st-century maritime silk road. https://reconasia-production.s3.amazonaws.com/media/filer_public/e0/22/e0228017-7463-46fc-9094-0465a6f1ca23/vision_and_actions_on_jointly_building_silk_road_economic_belt_and_21st-century_maritime_silk_road.pdf

OECD (2002) Environmental impact of Foreign direct investment in the mining sector in Sub-Saharan Africa. https://www.oecd.org/env/1819582.pdf

Okeowo A (2013) China, Zambia, and a Clash in a Coal Mine. The New Yorker. https://www.newyorker.com/business/currency/china-zambia-and-a-clash-in-a-coal-mine
Omoruyi E (2018) Xi's visit Bolsters China-Africa relations. Belt and Road Portal. https://eng.yidaiyilu.gov.cn/home/rolling/60999.htm
Paine J, Sheargold E (2023) A climate change carve-out for investment treaties. J Int Econ Law 26(2):285–304
Pandey E (2018) China's debt-trap diplomacy is spreading across Africa. Axios. https://www.axios.com/china-debt-africa-djibouti-kenya-angola-belt-and-road-initiative-c65b82fa-48a6-4140-bb01-bc19580a16c9.html
Party School of the Central Committee of the CPC (2023) How developing countries can move towards modernization—summary of the fourth high-level think tank forum on National Governance for Developing Countries. https://www.ccps.gov.cn/xyyw/202311/t20231112_159850.shtml
Peh K, Eyal J (2010) Unveiling China's impact on African environment. Energy Policy 38(8):4729–4730
People's Bank of China (2018) People's Bank of China reponses to the OBOR initiative and build global first-class bank. http://www.boc.cn/aboutboc/bi1/201803/t20180312_11698999.html
People's Daily Online (2018) Together with South Africa's largest bank, industrial and commercial Bank of China assists Africa development. http://world.people.com.cn/n1/2018/0724/c1002-30165973.html
Pew Research Center (2017) Opinion of China, do you have a favorable or unfavorable view of China?. http://www.pewglobal.org/database/indicator/24/
Pike L (2017) Is the belt and road compatible with Paris?. China Dialogue. https://www.chinadialogue.org.cn/article/show/single/en/10284-Is-the-Belt-and-Road-compatible-with-Paris
Roe E (2013) Is CSR the missing ingredient in the China-Africa relationship?. Devex. https://www.devex.com/news/is-csr-the-missing-ingredient-in-the-china-africa-relationship-81747
Sanghi A, Johnson D (2016) Deal or no deal: strictly business for China in Kenya?. World Bank Policy Research Working Paper 7614. http://documents.worldbank.org/curated/en/801581468195561492/pdf/WPS7614.pdf
Sautman B, Yan H (2015) Localizing Chinese enterprises in Africa: from myths to policies. Institute for Emerging Market Studies, Thought Leadership Brief No. 5. http://iems.ust.hk/assets/publications/thought-leadership-briefs/tlb05/hkust_iems_thought_leadership_brief_tlb05.pdf
Schickerling E (2012) Foreign development aid in China's foreign policy Africa: exploring the China-Africa development fund. University of Lovemore Chikova
Schiere R (2011) China and Africa: an emerging partnership for development? An overview of issues. African Development Bank Group Working Paper Series. https://www.afdb.org/fileadmin/uploads/afdb/Documents/Publications/WPS%20No%20125%20China%20and%20Africa%20%20An%20Emerging%20Partnership%20.pdf
Schiere R, Rugamba A (2011) Chinese infrastructure investments and African integration. African Development Bank Group Working Paper Series. https://www.afdb.org/fileadmin/uploads/afdb/Documents/Publications/WPS%20No%20127%20Chinese%20Infrastructure%20Investments%20.pdf
Scott D (2012) Do Chinese extraction (Mining, Oil & Gas) activities in Africa overlap with areas of conservation value?. (Conservation International). http://www.academia.edu/1002354/Do_Chinese_Extraction_Mining_Oil_and_Gas_Activities_in_Africa_overlap_with_Areas_of_Conservation_Value
Shinn D (2015) The environmental impact of China's investment in Africa. Cornell Int Law J 49:44
Shinn D (2016) The environmental impact of China's investment in Africa. Cornell Int Law J 25:25–65
Sino Africa Center of Excellence Foundation (2014) Business Perception Index Kenya 2014, 18. http://www.focac.org/eng/lhyj_1/zxxx/P020150803357007793815.pdf

Sun Y (2017) China and East Africa railways: beyond full industry chain export. Brookings Institution. https://www.brookings.edu/blog/africa-in-focus/2017/07/06/china-and-the-east-africa-railways-beyond-full-industry-chain-export/

Tang X (2010) Bulldozer or locomotive? The impact of Chinese enterprises on the local employment market in Angola. J Asian Afr Stud 45(3):350–368

Tang X, Sun Y (2016) Social Responsibility or development responsibility-what is the environmental impact of Chinese investments in Africa: what are its drivers, and what are the possibilities for action. Cornell Int Law J 49(1):66–99

Taylor I (2007) China's environmental footprint in Africa. China Dialogue. https://www.ChinaDialogue.net/article/741-China-s-environmental-footprint-in-Africa

The Infrastructure Consortium for Africa (2015) Infrastructure financing trends in Africa. https://www.icafrica.org/fileadmin/documents/Annual_Reports/ICA_2015_annual_report.pdf

Tian J (2016) One belt and one road: connecting China and the world. McKinsy &Co. https://www.mckinsey.com/industries/capital-projects-and-infrastructure/our-insights/one-belt-and-one-road-connecting-china-and-the-world

Tukic N, Kim Y (2015a) Paving the road ahead–China-Africa co-operation in the infrastructure sector. http://scholar.sun.ac.za/handle/10019.1/98935

Tukic N, Kim Y (2015b) Paving the road ahead-China-Africa co-operation in the infrastructure sector. Center for Chinese Studies, Policy Briefing. http://scholar.sun.ac.za/handle/10019.1/98935

UN Economic Commission for Africa (2014) Common African Position on the Post-2015 Development Agenda. https://sustainabledevelopment.un.org/index.php?page=view&type=400&nr=1329&menu=35

UN Economic Commission for Africa (2016a) Green Africa's Industrialization, pp 54–58. http://repository.uneca.org/bitstream/handle/10855/23017/b11560861.pdf?sequence=1

UN Economic Commission for Africa (2016b) Measuring corruption in Africa: the International Dimension Matters. https://www.uneca.org/sites/default/files/PublicationFiles/agr4_eng_fin_web_11april.pdf

UN Conference on Trade and Development (2016) Foreign direct investment to Africa fell by a moderate three per cent in 2016. http://unctad.org/en/pages/PressRelease.aspx?OriginalVersionID=408

UNCTAD (2015) Investment policy framework for sustainable development. https://unctad.org/system/files/official-document/diaepcb2015d5_en.pdf. 77–78

UNDP China (2017a) 2017 Report on the Sustainable Development of Chinese Enterprises Overseas Supporting—The Belt and Road Regions to Achieve the 2030 Agenda for Sustainable Development, 12. http://www.cn.undp.org/content/china/en/home/library/south-south-cooperation/2017-report-on-the-sustainable-development-of-chinese-enterprise.html. Note that while the report was published under an affiliation with the UNDP China, the research team was led by the Ministry of Commerce of the People's Republic of China and Commission of the State Council of the People's Republic of China

UNDP China (2017b) 2017 Report on the sustainable development of Chinese enterprises overseas supporting—the belt and road regions to achieve the 2030 agenda for sustainable development. http://www.cn.undp.org/content/china/en/home/library/south-south-cooperation/2017-report-on-the-sustainable-development-of-chinese-enterprise.html

UNDP China (2017c) 2017 Report on the Sustainable Development of Chinese Enterprises Overseas Supporting—The Belt and Road Regions to Achieve the 2030 Agenda for Sustainable Development, 31. http://www.cn.undp.org/content/china/en/home/library/south-south-cooperation/2017-report-on-the-sustainable-development-of-chinese-enterprise.html

UNEP (2016) UNEP's compendium of innovative laws: promoting green economy & sustainable development, pp 157–162. http://wedocs.unep.org/handle/20.500.11822/9947

UNEP Inquiry (2016) Environmental risk analysis of financial institutions. unepinquiry.org/wpcontent/uploads/2016/09/2_Environment_Risk_Anlysis_by_Financial_Institutions.pdf

Van Dijk M (2009) Introduction: objectives of and instruments for China's new presence in Africa". In: Van Dijk M (ed) The new presence of China in Africa. Amsterdam University Press, Amsterdam
Van-Vliet G, Magrin G (2012) The environmental challenges facing a Chinese oil company in Chad. Agence Française de Développement. https://portals.iucn.org/library/sites/library/files/documents/SPE-Int-674.3-001.pdf
Visser W (2008) Corporate social responsibility in developing countries. In: Andrew C et al (eds) The Oxford handbook of corporate social responsibility. Oxford University Press, Oxford, pp 473–499
Walker B (2016) China Stokes Global Coal Growth. China Dialogue. https://www.chinadialogue.org.cn/article/show/single/en/9264-China-stokes-global-coal-growth
Walsh C (2006) Is China the new colonial power in Africa. The Guardian. https://www.theguardian.com/business/2006/oct/29/china.theobserver
Wan Y, Li Z (2018) Sino-Congolese Bank for Africa Building Inaugurated in Congo. People's Daily. http://en.people.cn/n3/2018/0413/c90000-9448984.html
Wang B et al (2014) Overseas impact of China's outward direct investment: China's outward direct investment. Asian Econ Policy Rev 9(2):227–249
Warf B (2017) Geographies of African corruption. PSU Res Rev 1(1):20–38
World Bank (2015) Africa Climate Business Plan: Accelerating Climate-resilient and Low-carbon Development. Working Paper. http://documents.worldbank.org/curated/en/401711468185370301/pdf/101130-REPLACEMENT-FILE-SAME-BOX-PUBLIC-K8545.pdf
WWF (2016) China's Belt and Road Initiative and Its Implications for Africa. http://assets.wwfke.panda.org/downloads/china_s_belt_and_road_initiative_and_its_implications_for_africa.pdf
Xiao J (2015) How can a prospective China–EU BIT contribute to sustainable investment: in light of the UNCTAD investment policy framework for sustainable development. J World Energy Law Bus 8:521–523
Xinhua News (2018) The Export-Import Bank of China Financed US$67.2 Billion, Surpassing the World Bank. http://www.mofcom.gov.cn/aarticle/i/jyjl/k/201201/20120107913576.html
Yu L et al (eds) (2016) National strategy: policy and investment of "Belt and Road" initiative. Zhejiang University
Zafar A (2007) The growing relationship between China and Sub-Saharan Africa: macroeconomic, trade, investment and aid links. World Bank Res Observer 22(1):103–130
Zha D (2014) Case study of social and environmental risk of Chinese Foreign Investment. Peking University Press
Zhan D (2014) Case study of social and environmental risk of chinese foreign investment. Peking University Press, Beijing
Zhang J (2016) Chinese Foreign Assistance Explained. Brookings Institution. https://www.brookings.edu/blog/order-from-chaos/2016/07/19/chinese-foreign-assistance-explained/
Zhao M (2024) What has the China export-import bank brought to Africa. Financial News. https://www.financialnews.com.cn/2024-09/03/content_407548.html

Chapter 4
China's Sustainable Investment in Africa: The SGR Project in Kenya as a Case Study

While Chapter 3 has provided a general assessment of the potential impact of China's BRI across Africa, it remains important to remember that Africa is not a homogenous bloc and African countries are quite different in their historical, political, legal, social, and environmental backgrounds. Even within a country, there may have regional differences. Furthermore, each project may have features not shared by others. In other words, country-specific and project-specific attributes should be taken into account.

Accordingly, this chapter empirically analyzes the role of the state-centric CSR approach in the SGR project in Kenya. First, it situates Kenya's importance within the overall landscape of Chinese infrastructure projects in Africa. Second, it briefly discusses Kenya's political, economic, social, and environmental environments, which provides contextual information for better understanding the SGR project. Third, it focuses on the details of the SGR project. The analysis is based on information collected from my six-month long fieldwork in Kenya through face-to-face and semi-structured interviews between September 2016 and February 2017. A total of 39 interviewees participated. Specifically, interviews were conducted with Chinese and local specialists, government officials from Kenya and China, managers from the CRBC Kenya branch, two locally-elected county government officials of affected counties, staff members of environmental NGOs and media outlets in Kenya and China, officers of UN Environment in Kenya, (project) managers and officers at branch operations of Chinese companies, and project managers of China Exim Bank. To better represent the local communities' voices and reflect their opinions on the SGR, the elected government officials of Mombasa and Kajiado Counties were interviewed on the assumption that they represent the interests of their people. In addition, liaison officers of the two counties who were born and raised in the area, and thus have experience and familiarity with local NGOs, governments, and the community were interviewed. Lastly, representatives from six NGOs in Kenya and China were interviewed to better reflect diverse opinions on the impact of the SGR.

B. Liu, *China's Green Investment in Africa: A State-Centric Corporate Social Responsibility Perspective*, Modern China and International Economic Law,
https://doi.org/10.1007/978-981-95-2157-9_4

4.1 The Importance of Kenya in China's BRI

I selected Kenya as a case study because of its increasing importance in Africa and its increasing level of cooperation with China under the BRI. Within the context of the BRI, China is using Chinese companies and financial institutions to strengthen its relationship with Kenya and using that relationship as a stepping-stone to increase its presence in eastern Africa. China's infrastructure construction in Kenya aims to facilitate its trade and investment in East and Central Africa. This section provides an overview of China's investment, especially in infrastructure construction, in Kenya.

4.1.1 China's General Investment in Kenya

As one of Africa's four largest economies, Kenya is China's key partner in Africa. China views Kenya as a "gateway to East African region and is a focal point in terms of China's trade and economic strategy in Africa" under the BRI.[1] China-Kenya cooperation has been at the forefront of China-Africa cooperation.[2] Since Kenya and China established their formal relation in 1963, the relation between the two countries has continued to develop. In recent years, Kenya and China have steadily increased mutual political trust, increasing cultural and economic exchanges in infrastructure, energy, technology, youth employment, and entrepreneurship.[3] According to a World Bank study, Chinese companies "have taken interest in more than natural resources in Kenya", and the size, operations, and financing of Chinese companies are quite diverse.[4]

In recent years, China's economic presence in Kenya has risen rapidly. China is a leading source of Kenya's FDI. Figure 4.1 shows the investment flows from China between 2003 and 2012. China's FDI has grown rapidly. A big jump of Chinese FDI in Kenya took place between 2009 and 2010, increasing by 261%.[5] Figure 4.2 shows that China's FDI represents a large share of Kenya's total FDI. Moreover, in 2015, the number of ongoing engineering projects contracted by Chinese companies has "grown to 172, reaching total revenue of $9.5 billion, an increase of 173%. There are 48 newly contracted projects, with revenue of $2.25 billion, reaching an increase of 127%".[6] In May 2017, during the BRI International Cooperation Summit, President

[1] Andiva (2015). See also, Falk (2013).

[2] Kenya China Economic and Trade Association (2017b).

[3] Interview with an official of Chinese embassy in Kenya.

[4] Sanghi and Johnson (2016a). See also, Buxbaum (2016).

[5] Sanghi and Johnson (2016b).

[6] China Daily (2016).

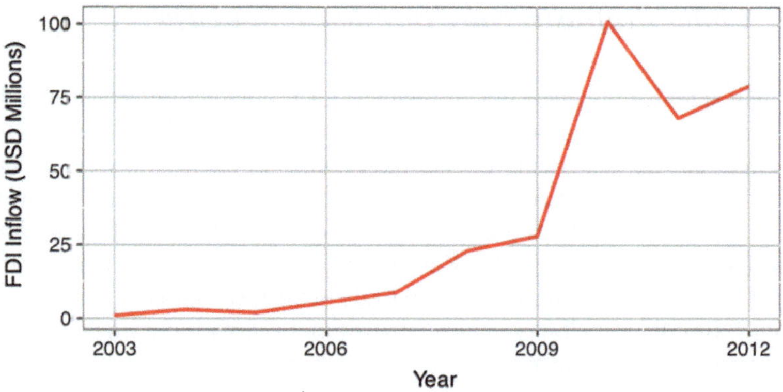

Fig. 4.1 Kenya's FDI inflow from China (2003–2012). *Source* Sanghi and Johnson (2016b)[8]

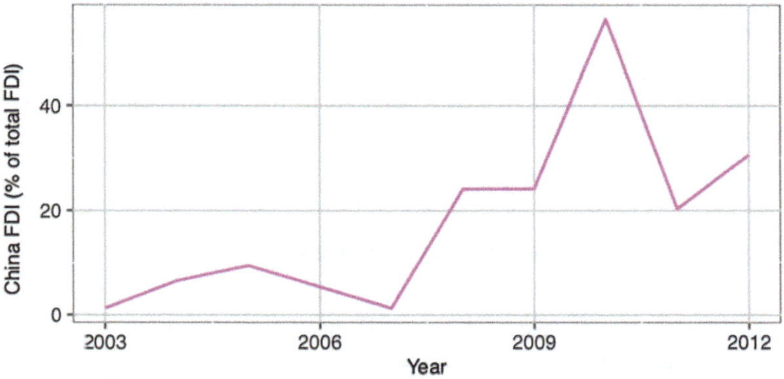

Fig. 4.2 China's FDI share of Kenya's Total FDI (2003–2012). *Source* Sanghi and Johnson (2016b)[9]

Xi and President Kenyatta decided to further enhance the China-Kenya relationship, leading to the prime period of bilateral relations between the two countries.[7]

[7] Ministry of Foreign Affairs of the Republic of Kenya, "5th Diplomatic Brief/ 2016–2017". http://www.mfa.go.ke/wp-content/uploads/2017/06/Diplomatic-briefing-Speech-by-Amb.-Monica-Juma-on-June-14-2017.pdf.

[8] Sanghi and Johnson (2016b).

[9] Ibid.

4.1.2 *China's Infrastructure Investment in Kenya*

China has significantly increased investment in infrastructure projects in Kenya, mainly in projects related to energy generation, power distribution, rural electrification, and railway construction.[10] During Premier Li Keqiang's visit to Africa in 2010, Li proposed the construction of high-speed railways as well as highways and regional aviation networks and other infrastructure. Furthermore, China's financial institutions are actively involved in Kenya's infrastructure construction by providing loans.[11] China's aid to Kenya is almost entirely in the form of loans, mainly provided by China Exim Bank.[12] Chinese financial institutions provide the single largest bilateral infrastructure financial assistance source in Kenya.[13] The projects with financial assistance from China mainly include the SGR, the Olkaria IV drilling project, the Nairobi-Thika project, and the Two Rivers Shopping Mall project. The Chinese government gave a total of KES 20.6 billion in loans for development in the fiscal year ending in 2015. Table 4.1 shows the funding and contractor details of Chinese infrastructure projects as well as recent ongoing infrastructure projects funded by China in Kenya. By funding Kenyan infrastructure projects through bilateral lending, China help contribute to Kenya's realization of its Vision 2030 and help accelerate economic growth in the country.[14]

4.2 Kenya's Institutional Environments

As Sect. 4.1 shows, Chinese SOEs and financial institutions have been actively involved in infrastructure construction projects in Kenya. To better understand the CSR implications of the infrastructure projects, this section will provide a general introduction of Kenya's institutional environment. A better understating of the political, economic, social, and environmental conditions in Kenya helps understand the tensions and investment risks associated with the SGR project.

---

[10] Interview with counselor of the Economic and Commercial Councilor's Office of the Chinese government. to Kenya.

[11] Brautigam and Gallagher (2014). See also, Foster (2009).

[12] Sanghi and Johnson (2016c).

[13] Interview with the director of Chinese Academy of International Trade and Economic Corporation, MOFCOM.

[14] Interview with project manager of China-Africa Excellency Foundation.

Table 4.1 Funding and contractor details of selective Chinese infrastructure projects in Kenya

Year	Project	Contractor	Project cost	Funding
2015	Emali-Oloitoktok	Synohydro Corporation Ltd (SOE)	4.2 billion	BADEA/ OPEC Fund/ Gok
2015	Southern Bypass Roads Project	CRBC (SOE)	16.9 billion	China Exim Bank/GoK
2014	Mombasa-Nairobi Standard Gauge Railway	CRBC (SOE)	3.8 billion	China Exim Bank/GoK
2014	Olkaria IV Geothermal Field Production Wells Drilling Project	Great Wall Drilling Company of China (SOE)	7.5 billion	China Exim Bank/GoK
2014	Kenya Power Distribution System Modernization and Strengthening	China CAMC Engineering Co. Ltd (SOE)	1.4 billion	China Exim Bank/GoK
2014	Kenyatta University Teaching, Research and Referral Hospital	China Jiangxi Company (SOE)	9.85 billion	China Exim Bank/GoK
2012	Marsabit-Turbi	Jiangxi Zhongmei Engineering Co. Ltd (SOE)	13 billion	AfDB/GoK
2011	Athi River-Namanga	China Overseas Engineering Group Co. Ltd (SOE)	6.2 billion	AfDB/GoK
2008	Nairobi-Thika	China Wu Yi Co. Ltd (SOE)	8.1 billion	AfDB/GoK

Author's Compilation

4.2.1 Kenya's Political and Social Conditions

Kenya has a population of approximately 50.9 million people by January 2017.[15] The five largest native ethnic groups are "the Kikuyu (22%), the Luhya (14%), the Kalenjin (12%), the Luo (13%), and the Kamba (11%)".[16] Kenya is a presidential representative democratic republic and the President is both the head of state and head of government. The politics in Kenya has long been influenced by ethnicity and historical tribal conflicts.[17] From 1920 to 1963, Kenya was under the rule of the British colonial government, which adopted a "Divide and Rule" approach to governance.[18] This entailed the compartmentalization and separation of the different ethnic communities and locked each group in its own reserve to weaken intermingling

[15] World Population Review (2018).

[16] CIA World Factbook (2018).

[17] Mungai et al. (2010).

[18] Morrock (1973).

among many communities in Kenya.[19] Since independence in 1963, Kenya's politics has been dominated by two political parties, namely the Kenya Africa National Union that is a Kikuyu and Luo alliance party, and the Kenya African Democratic Union, which consists of other small tribes.[20] This two-party situation has colored the current system of tribal politics in the country.[21] Currently, the "tribe" factor is the most important element in politics.[22]

Because of these historical and political reasons, there have been tensions within and between local communities, ethnic groups, and socioeconomic groups; these tensions have been exacerbated by foreign investment. In particular, land issues have been politically sensitive in Kenya for decades. Kenya's land ownership is complex, involving political, cultural, and religious factors. The ethnic identity of the Kenyan people shows a strong association between people and the land. The local communities, especially the ethnic groups, reserve ownership of the land and resources in their area.[23] The land is also where ethnic groups' identities come from.[24] In many cases of construction or natural resource extraction, land compensation and resource/revenue distribution have been a long-standing source of grievance. Acquisitions of community and private lands trigger conflicts over involuntary resettlement. These conflicts between state ownership rights and rights governed by customary law illuminate the subtle power relationships between states, local authorities, and landowners that reinforce the inequitable distribution of resources, revenues, and compensation to displaced communities.[25] The complex and vague land ownership system in Kenya is an investment challenge not only for Chinese companies but also for companies from other countries. Without careful consideration of Kenya's social and cultural conditions throughout construction, land disputes can easily become an obstacle to the development of Chinese infrastructure projects in Kenya.

4.2.2 Kenya's Economic Development

Kenya has played an important role in the eastern and central African economy due to its relatively well-established economic base and outstanding geographic location.[26] In recent years, with the east African regional integration, Kenya attracted foreign investors.[27] According to the 2018 Economic Survey Report launched by the Kenya National Bureau of Statistics (KNBS), Kenya's economy expanded by 4.9

[19] Lynch (2013).

[20] Ibid.

[21] Ibid.

[22] Spear (1993).

[23] Ibid.

[24] Interview with head manager of China Daily, Africa Station.

[25] Mungai et al. (2010).

[26] Kenya National Bureau of Statistics (2018).

[27] Sanghi and Johnson (2016c).

percent in 2017 and 5.9 percent in 2016.[28] The main sectors driving the economy were agriculture and forestry, wholesale and retail trade, transport and communication, manufacturing and financial intermediation.[29] In 2007, the Kenyan government formulated Vision 2030 to focus on three key political, economic, and social areas to promote Kenyan industrialization. Vision 2030 outlines the need to provide and expand Kenya's infrastructure so that the country can be extensively connected by an excellent network of roads, railways, ports, airports, and telecommunications.[30] According to Deloitte's research, in 2015, Kenya's infrastructure projects ranked first in east Africa, with projects focusing on roads, ports, energy, and water.[31]

Kenya's location implies the significance of transport infrastructure development. Investment in Kenya's transport infrastructure linking it to neighboring countries is expected to facilitate regional integration and investment, trade, and economic advancement. However, there is a physical infrastructure deficit in Kenya. African's infrastructure was constructed with a "colonial external extractive paradigm that focused on extracting resources for the benefit of the home country", and did not sufficiently focus on "internal infrastructure development and networked connectivity".[32] In the post-colonial era, a lack of capacity and underinvestment by post-colonial African states led to the deterioration of existing infrastructure and the insufficient construction of new infrastructure. This lack of networked infrastructure has contributed to economic isolation in sub-Saharan Africa.[33] Infrastructure networks are also an essential element of regional integration on the continent.[34] Connecting these areas is clearly the key infrastructure task at hand for the Kenyan government to realize the goals of Vision 2030 and promote Kenya as a stable geographical gateway to Africa.

Meanwhile, some economic and social problems hold back Kenya's long-term development. Unemployment and poverty affect a large number of Kenyan people.[35] About 45% of Kenyans are below the poverty line.[36] The 2015 unemployment rate in Kenya was roughly 11%, and the total rate of youth (ages 14–25) unemployment was about 22%.[37] The livelihoods of indigenous peoples still depend on natural rangelands through traditional pastoralism, and these groups face challenges such as land pressure and an undeveloped livestock market.[38] At the same time, corruption in Kenya is one of the biggest obstacles for foreign investors' operations. Kenya

---

[28] Kenya National Bureau of Statistics (2018).

[29] Ibid.

[30] Kenya "Vision 2030". http://www.vision2030.go.ke/.

[31] Deloitte (2016).

[32] Arewa (2016). See also, Gwilliam (2011).

[33] Ndulu et al. (2007).

[34] Rosnes and Shkaratan (2011).

[35] World Bank (2017).

[36] The Guardian (2013).

[37] UNDP (2016).

[38] Interview with government official of Kajiado County.

ranks 145 out of 175 in Transparency International's corruption-perception index.[39] Chinese companies identify corruption as the most significant obstacle to conducting business in Kenya. According to a survey by SACE, 53% of respondents said corruption was a "very significant obstacle" and 15% mentioned corruption as a "significant obstacle".[40]

4.2.3 Kenya's Regulatory Environment for Environmental and Social Protection

Kenya is rich in natural resources and biodiversity with a wide range of natural ecosystems, including arid and semi-arid areas, savannahs, and forests. The country has over 35,000 known species of flora and fauna, for which remarkable conservation efforts have been made. Kenya is also home to 53 national and international protected areas, including five biosphere reserves, four Ramsar sites, and three world heritage sites.[41] Kenya is also rich in wind, solar, and geothermal energy. The Great Rift also boasts the largest storage of geothermal energy in east Africa. The economic importance of its natural environment, especially to tourism, leads to the Kenyan government and local communities attaching great importance to environmental protection.

Given the significance of natural resources and environment to Kenyans, the regulatory authorities of Kenya have intensified the monitoring, assessment and management of environmental and social considerations.[42] Kenya's legal framework is quite well developed and addresses many of the most important challenges facing environmental management. As the UN Environment headquarters and many international environmental organizations are based in Kenya, the external supervision from international organizations pushes the Kenyan government to attach importance to environmental protection.[43] Green growth in Kenya has its roots in the country's constitution, which prioritizes a clean and healthy environment and seeks to increase and maintain forest cover for at least 10% of its land area. The need for environmental protection is also highlighted in Vision 2030 to achieve a clean, secure, and sustainable environment by 2030.[44]

The Kenyan government has put a wide range of policy, institutional, and legislative arrangements in place to regulate investment projects and associated activities to minimize negative impact on the environment and the socioeconomic well-being of people. The National Environmental Management Authority (NEMA) along with other lead agencies like the Kenya Wildlife Service (KWS), Kenya Parks Service, and the Water Regulation Management Authority are regulatory authorities responsible

---

39 Transparency International (2018).

40 Sino Africa Center of Excellence Foundation (2014).

41 ETC East Africa Ltd (2006).

42 Mwenda and Kibutu (2012).

43 Interview with officer of UN Environment.

44 Kenya "Vision 2030". http://www.vision2030.go.ke/.

for environmental protection in Kenya. Importantly, the 2010 Constitution of Kenya gives the environment a prominent place in its structure.[45] Kenya has a comprehensive legal framework on land expropriation to protect the interests of landowners.[46] Specifically, in 2011, the Kenyan Parliament passed the Environment and Land Court Act to ensure the court retains original and appellate jurisdiction over disputes relating to environmental planning and protection, trade, climate issues, land use planning, and mining minerals.[47] Legislation, such as The National Land Commission Act,[48] the Prevention, Protection, and Assistance to Internally Displaced Persons and Affected Communities Act,[49] has also been enacted to protect the social rights of local people and communities who may be affected by overseas investment.

Kenya's environmental and social protection regulatory framework is perceived as a significant reason for Chinese companies to pay attention to social and environmental performance. Although there are many factors that weaken the implementation of Kenyan laws and policies, such as low enforcement capacity among government institutions, weak rule of law and corruption, the interviewed project managers of Chinese SOEs in Kenya reported that local environmental regulations are quite strict.[50] They perceived compliance with Kenya national laws as an essential way to reduce operational risks, and protect themselves from environmental and

45 "The 2010 Constitution of Kenya".http://www.kenyalaw.org/lex/actview.xql?actid=Const2010. Article 42 of the fundamental rights and freedoms granted to Kenyan citizens states that "the Kenyan governments must ensure a clean and healthy environment that benefits both current and future generations". Article 69 outlines specific environmental duties of the Kenyan government, including sustainable exploitation and conservation of the environment and requires that the country maintain a tree cover of at least 10% of the land area of Kenya. Article 70 gives citizens the right to petition a court for redress if they feel their environmental rights have been infringed.

46 Part VIII of "The Land Act of Kenya" stipulates the compensation method for the compulsory acquisition of land, especially for large scale investments and development activities that may present challenges of involuntary resettlement, and displacement for affected communities. "The Prevention, Protection and Assistance to Internally Displaced Persons and Affected Communities Act" is Kenya's legal safeguard to govern displacement caused by development projects, especially the projects constructed by foreign investors. See more details, The Land Act of Kenya, Part VIII. http://kenyalaw.org/kl/fileadmin/pdfdownloads/AmendmentActs/2016/LandLaws_Amendment_Act_28of2016.pdf. "The Prevention, Protection and Assistance to Internally Displaced Persons and Affected Communities Act", 2012. http://www.refworld.org/docid/511219962.html; For more information, Kibugi et al. (2016).

47 "The Environment and Land Court Act", 2011, § 18. http://extwprlegs1.fao.org/docs/pdf/ken112134.pdf.

48 "The National Land Commission Act", 2012, § 3. https://www.ecolex.org/details/legislation/national-land-commission-act-2012-no-5-of-2012-lex-faoc112132/.

49 "The Prevention, Protection and Assistance to Internally Displaced Persons and Affected Communities Act", 2012. http://www.refworld.org/docid/511219962.html; For more information, Kibugi et al. (2016).

50 Interview with project managers of Great Wall Drilling Company of China National Petroleum Corporation, Power China (Kenya), China Gezhouba Group Company Limited (Kenya), SinoHydro Corporation Limited (Kenya) and CRBC.

labor disputes, or punitive measures by local government authorities.[51] Local environmental NGOs in Kenya and international organizations have also begun to urge Chinese companies to operate sustainably.[52] As discussed in Chapter 3, environmental and social litigation risks can potentially hurt Chinese companies' economic performance and reputation. Kenya's existing regulatory environment presents some legal risks that cause Chinese companies to adopt responsible investment strategies.[53]

4.3 The History and Impact of the SGR Project

As part of China's BRI, China aims to use Kenya's SGR project to gain access to trade and investment in eastern Africa. It is a railway construction project undertaken by CRBC. Like other Chinese infrastructure projects in Africa, the SGR has sparked controversy for its community and environmental impact. This section introduces the background and impact of the SGR project.

4.3.1 History of the SGR

Kenya's existing narrow gauge railway network was in a poor state and unable to meet Kenya's increasing transportation needs. This situation not only puts huge pressure on Kenya's railway system, but also increases freight costs, which has a negative impact on the development of regional trade. Therefore, Kenya, Uganda, Rwanda, Burundi, South Sudan, Tanzania, and Ethiopia have agreed to construct more than 10 new railways in the region in the next 12 years to promote regional economic growth.[54] Since its commencement, the SGR project has received great attention from the Kenyan government and people. It is Kenya's first railway in nearly a century and a flagship project of Vision 2030 (Fig. 4.3). It is the first segment of the railway network in east Africa and a model project of "high-speed railway network, highway network, regional aviation network, and industrialization" in Africa.[55]

The contractor for the SGR is CRBC, a subsidiary of the China Communications Construction Company (CCCC), which is ultimately controlled by the Chinese central government. The CCCC is a leading transportation construction company with more than 60 wholly-owned and controlled subsidiaries. CRBC is one of China's

[51] Ibid.

[52] Interview with project manager of WWF-Africa; interview with program officer of China House; interview with official of UN Environment.

[53] Interview with director of WWF-China.

[54] Wissenbach and Wang (2016).

[55] More information on Kenya "Vision 2030". http://www.vision2030.go.ke/.

Fig. 4.3 Proposed SGR network. *Source* Reprinted from A Tale of Two Railways (2015)[56]

first large companies with a presence in international contracting markets.[57] CRBC's office in Kenya has been established for over 30 years. It is committed to the construction of large-scale infrastructure in Kenya, including roads, bridges, ports, and railways. In May 2014, during his visit to Kenya, Premier Li Keqiang witnessed the signing of a USD $3.8 billion contract for the SGR between CRBC and the Government of Kenya.[58] Due to increased demand for quality and affordable transport, telecommunications, energy, transport, water and sewage, and social services, Kenya enacted the Public Private Partnerships (PPPs) Act in 2013, which paved the way for capital and infrastructure projects to gravitate toward PPPs.[59] Eighty-five percent of the project's funding came from China Exim Bank, while Kenya provided 15% in co-financing. Construction of the Mombasa-Nairobi SGR project started in October

[56] A Tale of Two Railways (2015).

[57] CRBC specializes in "the contracting of domestic and international projects for roads, bridges, ports, railways, airports, tunnels, water conservancy, municipal works and dredging, and also engages in investment, industry, trade, leasing and service for over 50 years. It has set up branches in more than 50 countries and regions in Asia, Africa, Europe and America". For more information on CRBC. http://www.crbc.com/site/crbcEN/index.html.

[58] More information on CCCC. http://en.ccccltd.cn/.

[59] "Public Private Partnerships Act", No. 15 of 2013, National Council for Law Reporting with the Authority of the Attorney-General. http://www.kpda.or.ke/documents/Policies/Public%20Private%20Partnerships%20Act%20No.15,%202013.pdf.

2014 and finished on May 31, 2017.[60] From June 2017 until the end of June 2018, the SGR transported more than 1.3 million travelers and more than 60,000 containers.[61]

4.3.2 Concerns Over the SGR Project

The development of the SGR is expected to bring many benefits to Kenya. It is expected to reduce the cost of transportation, making Kenya an attractive and competitive investment destination in the region. Hence, it is expected to accelerate industrialization through the availability of easier and cheaper transport and help turn Kenya's Vision 2030 into reality. It is anticipated that it would also create employment opportunities as well as demand and markets for local construction materials during the construction and operation phases.[62] The project affects eight counties—Mombasa, Kilifi, Kwale, Taveta, Makueni, Machakos, Kajiado, and Nairobi—the most.[63]

However, the project may also bring some negative impact. In general, objections to the SGR Project were based on the following concerns. The first concern was the negative environmental impact. The SGR goes through the middle of Nairobi National Park for six kilometers, dividing the 12,000-hectare park in two. Conservationists protested the project, arguing that it would disrupt the park's ecosystem, negatively impact wildlife migration, and increase cases of human-wildlife conflict.[64] Environmentalists expressed concerns that the project would negatively affect the wildlife migration and conservation.[65] The park plays a priceless role in preserving Nairobi's biodiversity and cultural heritage. Therefore, there were concerns over whether the contractor carried out a proper ESIA prior to the project's commencement.[66] The second concern was the negative social impact brought by the project. There were some land ownership disputes between private owners and local Maasai communities along the SGR route.[67] The project required the acquisition of public, community, and private lands, which would result in involuntary resettlements and

[60] Wissenbach and Wang (2016).

[61] Embassy of the People's Republic of China in the Republic of Kenya (2018).

[62] Interview official of the Chinese embassy in Kenya and director of Institute of International Development Cooperation at the Chinese Academy of International Trade and Economic Cooperation.

[63] Interview with counselor of the Economic and Commercial Councilor's Office of the Chinese government in Kenya.

[64] Interview with staff of Kenya Wildlife Service and program officer of China House. See more, Mwendwa (2017).

[65] Interview with staff of Kenya Coalition for Wildlife Conservation and Management during one demonstration before Chinese Embassy to Kenya in October, 2016.

[66] Interview with staff of Kenya Coalition for Wildlife Conservation and Management and project manager of WWF-Africa.

[67] Interview with liaison officer of Mombasa County.

Table 4.2 The interested and affected parties of the project

Types of parties involved or affected	Details of subjects involved or affected
Government Institutions Officials	Kenya Pipeline Company, KWS, Kenya Ports Authority, Kenya Railway Corporation, Kenya Highways Authority, Kenya Urban Roads Authority, Kenya Rural Roads Authority, Kenya Electricity Generating Company, Kenya Electricity Transmission Company, Kenya Forest Service, Water Resource Management Authority, Ministry of Mining, Relevant ministries in the County governments of Nairobi, Kajiado, Mombasa such as Environment, Transport, National Transport Safety Authority, National Land Commission, Kenya Association of Transporters, Kenya Association of Manufacturers, Kenya Association of Tour Operators, Kenya Chamber of Commerce, Local Political and Community Leaders
Business Operators	Hotel owners, shop owners, service stations, freight terminal owners, truck owners among others
Communities with an Interest in Land Affected by the Project	Affected communities in areas such as Kima, Simba, Kiboko, Maungu, etc.; Rural private and communal land in areas such as Kivati, Nagwata, Wangala, etc
Conservation NGOs	Nature Kenya, WWF, Centre for Training and Integrated Research for ASAL Development etc

Author's Compilation

land acquisitions of affected communities' private and communal lands.[68] Table 4.2 outlines the interested and affected parties of the project. These are those that were likely be affected by or had an interest in the proposed railway corridor.

On September 19, 2016, the National Environment Tribunal issued a stop-work order following a petition by activist Okiya Omtatah and the Kenya Coalition for Wildlife Conservation and Management, who filed a petition against the National Environmental Management Authority (NEMA), the KWS, CRBC, the Kenya Railways Corporation, the attorney general, and the Ministries of Environment and Transport. The National Environment Tribunal stopped the construction of a section of the SGR set to pass through Nairobi National Park until the assessment of the project's environmental and social impact was completed.[69] NEMA was accused of "failing to conduct a feasibility study for the project" and allowing the project to go on before an ESIA was done. As such, the tribunal demanded that "all activities relating to the appeal in question must be stopped until the appeal is heard and determined by the tribunal".[70] This, alongside criticisms from local conservation NGOs and the media,

[68] Interview with project coordinator of Centre for Training and Integrated Research for ASAL Development; interview with official from UN Environment.

[69] National Environment Tribunal, "Net/192/2016(2) Re: Stop Order for Construction of Phase 2A of the Standard Gauge Railway (SGR) Nairobi-Naivasha Section".

[70] KenyaForum (2016).

shows that the environmental and social impact of the project raised heated debates in Kenya.

4.4 Key Actors in Addressing the Environmental and Social Concerns in the SGR Project

Stakeholder engagement is a critical process that helps companies understand key environmental and social impact and identify sustainability risks and opportunities.[71] Besides CSR stakeholder theory, the sociological network analysis approach emphasizes that the interactions between social actors (e.g., individuals, organizations, or nations) shape their behavior. Social actors are interdependent and linked by social ties.[72] Institutional theory in economic sociology suggests that an organization's behavior is influenced by the economic, legal, and political environment in which it operates.[73] Together, stakeholder theory, network analysis, and institutional theory provide an analytical framework to understand how a company may change its CSR practices because of institutional pressure and other factors.

Different stakeholder groups should be examined to get a comprehensive picture of the problem. In this section, this book empirically examines the key actors in addressing the environmental and social concerns in the SGR project. This book mainly focuses on the role of the Chinese government, China Exim Bank and CRBC during the construction of the SGR, as they are the implementers of the state-centric approach. This book also extends to the stakeholders in Kenya including the Kenyan government, local NGOs, and media to understand how they interact with the Chinese actors. The stakeholder approach helps to show how the state-centric approach was implemented in advancing CRBC's CSR in the SGR project.

4.4.1 The Kenyan Government

The host country government can be regarded as the most critical player that can significantly affect overseas companies' environmental and social behavior through rule setting and regulatory powers.[74] The environmental and social policies in host countries as well as the political will and capacity of the institutions that enforce and implement the policies are usually considered as the determining factors of foreign investments' environmental and social impact.[75] As shown in Appendix 6,

[71] Hu et al. (2014).

[72] Lin (2015). See more, Granovetter (1985).

[73] Ibid.

[74] Petrović-Ranđelović (2011).

[75] Hu and Wang (2015). Interview with research fellow of International Cooperation Centre of National Development and Reform Commission.

the Kenyan government had a legal obligation to take the listed national environmental policies and the affected communities' plans into consideration to assess the environmental and social impact of the SGR project. It also required CRBC to comply with Kenyan domestic regulations to ensure the sustainable operation of the SGR project. In addition, as the construction of the SGR took place before Kenya's national elections, the politicization of the project determined the Kenyan government's vital role in the process and its subsequent commitment to the sustainable operation of the project. The successful completion of the SGR project would add campaign capital for the incumbent election. Under electoral uncertainty, to better deal with contestation from the opposition party, the incumbent Kenyan politicians committed to the project and lobbied CRBC to ensure the project's sustainability.[76]

As mentioned above, land ownership has been a long-standing political grievance in Kenya, and the SGR project exacerbated the conflict and "brought issues around land ownership and compensation to the forefront of political debate".[77] Much of the land that the railway passes through had to be expropriated from private owners. Especially in Mombasa County, the land compensation disputes had posed significant obstacles to construction. The government official of Mombasa County claimed that the historical context should be considered during the valuation regarding resettlement and compensation.[78] One long-standing source of political land grievances stems from land ownership disputes between indigenous community members who live on the land without title deeds and migrants from other parts of Kenya who were issued title deeds by the government without considering the incumbent residents' traditional forms of land ownership.[79] Given the long-standing conflicts over land ownership in Kenya, land compensation had become one of the biggest challenges for CRBC, even though it was not its responsibility in the SGR project.

Most of the land along the project is considered private land and community land, which, according to the 2010 Constitution of Kenya, is held in trust by the respective Country Governments. To guarantee fair land compensation and expropriation, public participation is a significant aspect to ensure positive social impact on local communities.[80] In the SGR project, the National Land Commission (NLC) was accountable for managing the valuation of as well as the compensation claims deriving from the acquisition and leasing of these lands. Land surveyors and appraisers had been assigned by NLC to sites to conduct land compensation evaluation and help facilitate the process that determined when CRBC could begin construction.[81] An estimated 10% share of the KES 380 billion from the Kenyan government was allocated toward resettlement and compensation.[82] Before the construction of the SGR, the Kenyan Railway Corporation appointed Limcom Africonsults to conduct the ESIA. According to the

[76] Interview with government official of Mombasa County.

[77] Wissenbach and Wang (2016). See also, Nyassy (2015).

[78] Interview with government official of Mombasa County.

[79] Ibid.

[80] Interview with project manager of WWF-Africa.

[81] Ibid.

[82] Interview with government official of Mombasa County.

local government officials, views from local residents, leaders, institutions, and development partners were collected through interviews, technical consultative forums, and public consultation meetings.[83] According to the liaison officer, about 2,000 residents and business owners along SGR railway line were consulted during these public meetings.[84] Local residents, chiefs of affected villages, administrative leaders, and relevant line ministries from the county governments along the proposed route were invited to attend.[85] These extensive consultation efforts laid a helpful foundation for the construction of the SGR. During an official visit to the Mombasa County in December 2016, the Managing Director of Kenya Railway complained that dealing with land acquisition issues was very difficult. At the time of his public speech, approximately KES 90 billion had already been spent toward issues of land acquisition, double the initial budget allocation for land issues.[86]

During the construction of the SGR, land compensation disputes arose. Due to the complexity of Kenya's land ownership and historical grievances among tribes, the NLC's land valuation process generated many disputes. For example, for some farmers or indigenous groups who wanted to claim compensation without the legal documents to prove land ownership would likely lose compensation in the name of public interest. In addition, tensions and grievances among tribes were barriers to construction. The villages outside the SGR route envied the affected communities who were able to obtain land compensation and other benefits from CRBC's CSR programs, such as schools and jobs for the local community.[87] When the Kenyan government faced difficulties in fully compensating affected landowners in time, CRBC had to be involved to help the Kenyan government resolve the land compensation issue due to the political pressure from the Chinese and Kenyan government.[88] According to the liaison officer of Mombasa County, since CRBC did not want media attention on land compensation to cause unnecessary troubles, it usually assigned liaison officers to communicate with affected landowners and pay the land compensation fees to ensure that the project could be finished before the deadline.[89]

4.4.2 The Chinese Government

Home country governments can provide financial and technical assistance to help host countries govern foreign investments and maximize economic, environmental, and social benefits.[90] CRBC could not address the potential environmental and social

[83] Ibid.

[84] Interviews with liaison officer of Mombasa County.

[85] Ibid.

[86] Ibid.

[87] Ibid.

[88] Interview with project manager of the SGR project.

[89] Interview with liaison officer of Mombasa County.

[90] Hu et al. (2015).

impact of the project without the guidance and support of the governments and leaders of the two countries. During President Kenyatta's visit to China in 2013, President Xi and President Kenyatta jointly witnessed the signing of the financing memorandum of understanding of the SGR project. In May 2014, Premier Li and President Kenyatta, together with leaders of other east African countries, attended the signing ceremony of the financing agreement for the SGR. Premier Li urged the CCCC to meticulously construct the SGR, provide the Kenyan counterparts with necessary and qualified equipment, and offer operation and management training to local employees. President Kenyatta and other Kenyan leaders all attached immense importance to the SGR. They conducted inspection visits to various sections of the SGR each quarter and held on-site meetings with the Chinese embassy, CRBC, Kenyan cabinet secretaries, governors, and heads of relevant Kenyan departments to guarantee the rapid implementation of the project.[91]

As discussed before, to better deal with the opposition's contestations and win the 2017 Kenyan election, incumbent Kenyan politicians demanded CRBC to carry out the project in a sustainable manner.[92] The political significance of the SGR for both Kenya and China and the political pressure from both governments played an important role in pushing CRBC to ensure the quality and sustainability of the project. As a Chinese SOE, the successful completion of the SGR sustainably would not only represent the CRBC's CSR efforts but also demonstrate China's railway construction capabilities and professionalism.[93] Given the project's political salience, the united and concerted efforts of the Chinese and Kenyan governments created favorable conditions for the construction of the SGR.

The Chinese embassy in Kenya played an important oversight role in the CRBC's CSR performance in the SGR. According to an officer from the Chinese embassy in Kenya, the Chinese government issued a strict directive to the embassy to ensure that the SGR was constructed sustainably, out of recognition that the international community paid a significant amount of attention to the project. The central government instructed the Chinese embassy in Kenya to educate and train staff of CRBC and other SOEs to comply with local environmental laws and social regulations as well as international regulations and guidelines during construction.[94] Such direct engagement with the Chinese embassy and the Economic and Commercial Counselor's Office (ECCO) provided Chinese companies with informal governance oversight.[95]

The Chinese embassy in Kenya and the ECCO made concerted efforts to establish effective communication channels with CRBC through regular visits and meetings. They required CRBC to report the progress of the project and other related issues to them. The Chinese embassy in Kenya also organized relevant trainings once every two months to help CRBC managers and other SOEs learn local laws and regulations,

[91] Interview with project manager of WWF-Africa and WWF-China.

[92] Interview with government official of Mombasa County.

[93] Interview with official of Chinese embassy in Kenya.

[94] Ibid.

[95] Ibid.

familiarize themselves with the local business environment, strengthen their awareness of legal compliance, and help address financial arrangements during overseas operations, including customs clearance, taxation, and investment risks. The embassy also invited professionals for on-site consultations.[96] Chinese SOEs' familiarity and compliance with policies, guidelines, and initiatives related to promoting sustainable foreign investment were also encouraged by the Chinese embassy and the ECCO.

I attended and observed three of these training sessions at the Chinese embassy in Kenya during my fieldwork. All of the three training sessions were organized for Chinese SOEs engaging in hydropower, railway, highways, and real estate construction in Kenya. Project managers of branch officers of a total of 21 Chinese SOEs attended the three compulsory training sessions. Both the Chinese ambassador and counselor of the ECCO also attended all the three training sessions. The trainings usually proceeded in this way: Firstly, the invited companies gave 20-min presentations to report their construction progress over the past two months. In addition to reporting the construction progress, the companies also had the chance to express their concerns and reflect difficulties encountered during the constructions period. For example, they could seek advice on how to build effective communication with local people from the embassy. After the presentations, the embassy and the ECCO responded to questions before appointed legal and economic experts conducted training workshops on Kenyan policies and regulations regarding taxes, labor, and environmental protection. By sharing good practices and drawing lessons from presentations, the embassy and the ECCO encouraged Chinese SOEs in Kenya to learn from each other's practices and draw lessons from negative cases. Managers of some invited Chinese companies claimed that through the compulsory trainings and group study sessions, they became more familiar with Kenya's local laws and regulations and developed more of a sense of responsibility to complete the construction projects, given the social and environmental impact on the local community and people.[97]

The Chinese embassy also encouraged CRBC to hire liaison officers to build connections with local communities and pay attention to the local employment and labor warfare. According to the interview with an official from the Chinese embassy in Kenya, project managers of Chinese SOEs who violated Kenyan regulations and caused negative environmental and social impact would be warned by the Chinese embassy and incidents would be reported back to CCCC. In serious cases that caused huge financial losses or reputational damage for Chinese SOEs, the political careers of project managers or even senior managers of CCCC could be affected.[98] Such political punishment could have a lifelong effect on these officials and they could even face further disciplinary actions (such as demotion, delayed promotions, or removal from current position) or even criminal prosecution.[99] Given that the managers of

[96] Ibid.

[97] Interviews with project managers of China Wu Yi Co., Ltd. (Kenya Branch), China Road and Bridge Corporation (Kenya), and Power China (Kenya).

[98] Interview with official from Chinese embassy in Kenya.

[99] Interview with project manager of WWF-China.

CRBC and China Exim Bank would not want to jeopardize their political career for their negligence of the laws, CRBC and China Exim Bank were reasonably motivated to ensure that the SGR project conformed to the established guidelines. According to an official from the Ministry of Environmental Protection in China, other regulatory systems of the Chinese government were also used to hold CRBC accountable. These include procedures for approval by Chinese ministries, certificates, and guarantees from financial institutions, and due diligence inspections by project managers of China Exim Bank.[100]

In addition to the efforts and political guidance of the Chinese embassy in Kenya and the ECCO, Chinese business associations led by the ECCO also influenced CRBC's environmental and social behavior in Kenya. One such association is the Kenya China Economic and Trade Association (KCETA), a social organization comprising Chinese companies operating in Kenya. The association was founded in 2001, and its membership grew to 73 by the end of May 2017. According to statistics, its members are involved in project contracting, trade, real estate, logistics, technology services, and manufacturing.[101] The mission of the KCETA is to help Chinese companies in Kenya resolve difficulties during operation and encourage members to arrange CSR programs to build closer ties with the community in order to protect their rights and promote business development. Specific efforts include advocating and organizing public welfare activities, helping members familiarize themselves with the local market, and building close community ties.[102] The association also encourages its members to vigorously promote the localization of employees, conduct technical training and assistance activities, establish training centers in universities to help local people improve their work capacity, and organize donations to charity organizations such as the Red Cross and the Rhino Conservation Organization.[103] The association also has the capacity to organize large-scale public welfare activities in Kenya.[104]

The KCETA also released its 2017 Chinese Overseas Companies in Kenya Social Responsibility Report in both English and Chinese to report on the overall environmental and social behavior of Chinese companies in Kenya.[105] The report was written with technical support from the ECCO. It is the first CSR report regarding Chinese companies in Kenya, showing the Chinese government's increasing attention toward CSR performance of Chinese companies in Kenya. The KCETA and the ECCO in Kenya offered an opportunity for the private sector to comment on legislative and regulatory proposals and give feedback on the CSR report. Therefore, companies were able to provide constructive criticisms that help new CSR measures be practicable and reflective of business realities.[106] The report includes the CSR practices

---

[100] Interview with deputy director of Ministry of Environmental Protection of China.

[101] Interview with the vice secretary of the KCETA.

[102] Ibid.

[103] Ibid.

[104] Kenya China Economic and Trade Association (2017b).

[105] Interview with vice secretary of the KCETA.

[106] Ibid.

of several SOEs operating in Kenya, including CRBC's CSR practices in the SGR project, to encourage other Chinese companies in Kenya to learn from them.[107]

4.4.3 China Exim Bank

Eighty-five percent of the funding for the SGR came from the China Exim Bank. Therefore, China Exim Bank could play an influential role in minimizing the environmental and social risks of the project. The consistent application of green financing standards would address host countries' concerns, protect China's image as a responsible country, increase the effectiveness of China's soft power, and enhance its role an increasingly active global power.[108] In the Mombasa-Nairobi SGR, China Exim Bank was responsible for conducting ESIAs, project reviews, public consultations with communities affected by the project, and ex-post ESIAs in its lending policy.

China Exim Bank is a government bank under the direct leadership of the state council. The operation of China Exim Bank is overseen by the Ministries of Finance and Commerce, the People's Bank of China, and the CBRC. The bank has a dual purpose of financing the operations of Chinese companies abroad and promoting Chinese exports. China Exim Bank achieves these objectives by providing export credits to Chinese companies, loans to overseas construction and investment projects, and concessional loans to foreign governments.[109] China's BRI has now brought China Exim Bank's commercial and policy lending to the international stage. The bank extends 90% of its export credits to state-owned overseas companies and large projects. In China Exim Bank's 2007 Guidelines on Environmental and Social Impact Assessment of Loan Projects, the bank stipulates an ex-ante ESIA requirement and further states that those projects that are harmful to the environment or do not gain approval from environmental administration will not be funded.[110] China Exim Bank is required to conduct ex-post ESIAs of overseas investment projects. Based on the findings of this ESIA, China Exim Bank should revise the measures taken before and during the project implementation for similar projects.[111] China Exim Bank also needs to conduct public consultations and project reviews in the duration of the loan; accordingly, it should take immediate remedial or preventive measures to deal with environmental and social risks.[112]

According to the interview with a general manager of China Exim Bank, the following performance standards were considered when extending loans for the SGR project: assessment and management of environmental and social risks and impact; labor and working conditions; resource efficiency and pollution prevention;

---

[107] Kenya China Economic and Trade Association (2017a).

[108] Gallagher et al. (2016).

[109] More information on Chinese Exim Bank. http://english.eximbank.gov.cn/.

[110] China Exim Bank (2007).

[111] Ibid., Article 18.

[112] Ibid., Article 12 (4) and Article 19.

community health, safety, and security; preparation of land acquisition and involuntary resettlement action plans; biodiversity conservation; assessments of impacted protected areas and mitigation measures; and the protection of indigenous peoples and cultural heritage.[113] During the construction of the SGR, CRBC and Kenyan government were responsible for reporting to China Exim Bank regarding the social and environmental impact of the project. Upon completion of the project, the Kenyan government handed in the environmental acceptance documents.[114] Based on the documents, China Exim Bank conducted post-evaluation on the environmental and social impact and monitored the post-loan management of the SGR.[115]

Interview evidence suggests that China Exim Bank had some enforcement of its internal social and environmental rules, which played an important role in encouraging CRBC's legal compliance behavior. According to a project manager of the SGR project, there were three staff members in China Exim Bank in charge of the assessment, management, and monitoring of the SGR project. All three personnel had at least five years of project approval and supervision experience in the Approval and Management Department of China Exim Bank. The project manager in charge of the SGR project visited the project sites in 2014 and in 2017 to conduct due diligence and post-evaluation reports regarding the project's impact on the local community and people. During construction, CRBC's project manager was obligated to report on the construction's progress and emergencies to China Exim Bank through email and telephone conferences.[116] For example, when the Kenya's National Environmental Tribunal issued a stop-work order for the construction of a section of the SGR in 2016, China Exim Bank immediately learned the situation and urged CRBC to adopt adaptive measures to reduce potential negative fallout regarding the project.[117]

However, China Exim Bank's assessment report on the environmental and social impact of the SGR is not open to the public. As China Exim Bank has no legal obligation to disclose project evaluation information and there is no third-party monitoring nor grievance mechanism to allow affected community and people to file complaints during construction, the overall credibility of the sustainable lending process is in doubt. In addition, the project manager reflected that there was generally not enough staff involved in China Exim Bank's lending processes.[118] According to the manager, the three persons in charge of the SGR project were also responsible for reviewing and approving other infrastructure projects at the same time. The manager explained that with more projects awaiting approval under the BRI, the workload of the thirty full-time staff members in the Approval and Management Department of China Exim Bank has become very heavy.[119] Without adequate technical personnel involved in

[113] Interview with project manager of China Exim Bank.

[114] Interview with staff of Kenyan Wildlife Service.

[115] Interview with project manager of China Exim Bank.

[116] Interview with project manager of the SGR project.

[117] Interview with project manager of China Exim Bank.

[118] Ibid.

[119] Ibid.

the lending process, the credibility of China Exim Bank as a monitoring body could be compromised.

4.4.4 *The CRBC's CSR Efforts*

4.4.4.1 Internal Management System

The SGR project faced many challenges, such as tight deadlines before the Kenyan election; strict environmental requirements; and relationships with the government, owners, consultants, and local NGOs and communities that the project affected.[120] To ensure the sustainable environmental and social operations of the project, CRBC established a three-level (head office, branch offices, and site offices) responsibility management system.[121] According to a project manager of the SGR project, the design of the organizational system aimed to ensure social and environmental commitment to the local government and community.[122] The head office was responsible for safety, and the quality department was responsible for the overall management of energy conservation and environmental performance. The branch offices were responsible for assisting the head office in the supervision and guidance of environmental protection management work within their jurisdiction. The site offices oversaw environmental and social protection at various sections by tracking and analyzing the environmental situation, formulating specific environmental policies and measures, and implementing related schemes of environmental protection.[123] Under the project, there were ten departments, one administrative office, four branch offices, eleven site offices, two track-laying bases, and one hundred and eighty construction teams. The head office's instructions cascaded through the branch and site offices to the construction sites.[124]

Throughout the project, CRBC's quality management included regular or irregular inspections and special inspections of material procurement, testing, and quality control at each section. Special sites were built to monitor the mixing stations, and each section submitted pictures of roadbed transition sections to the head office each day. The head office inspected the construction quality of each section twice a month; notified sites of problems and required rectification within a limited period (usually within one month), punished sections with serious quality, environmental, and social problems.[125] Punishments included oral warnings in regular meetings organized by project managers, written warnings posted in corporate internal newsletters, and

[120] Interview with counselor of the Economic and Commercial Councilor's Office of the Chinese government in Kenya.

[121] Interview with project manager of the SGR project.

[122] Ibid.

[123] Ibid.

[124] Ibid.

[125] Interview with government officials of Mombasa and Kajiado.

reduced payments for the head manager and engineer responsible for the section construction work.[126] According to the project manager of the SGR project, direct administrative monitoring from the head office motivated each section to ensure the sustainable construction of the project.[127]

CRBC also tried to address community concerns by hiring liaison officers to build close connections with the local community. Hiring local liaison officers, as in the CRBC offices in Mombasa and Kajiado County, could be an effective way to improve communication between Chinese companies and local communities. Liaison officers who have roots in the local community served as the bridge between the company and the community and conveyed residents' needs to the company. According to the SGR CSR report released by CRBC, CRBC believed the three-level management system with the appointment of liaison officers was effective to promote the sustainable construction of the SGR project.[128]

4.4.4.2 Environmental Protection Efforts

In terms of the environmental protection performance, CRBC sought to comply with the environmental laws and regulations of Kenya. The head office of CRBC formulated and issued a series of environmental management rules including the Administrative Measures for Environmental Protection, the Administrative Measures for Soil and Water Conservation, and the Administrative Measures for Environmental Impact Assessment.[129] According to the liaison officers, CRBC carried out environmental inspections of all sections once a month to supervise the implementation of environmental protection measures. This enabled them to rectify any irrational behaviors in a timely manner, and standardized environmental management practices throughout the project.[130] CRBC also engaged with professional ESIA consulting companies and appointed a professional ESIA engineer to each site office from commencement to completion to provide a professional guarantee of standard environment management.[131] China-based Third Railway Survey and Design Institute Group Corporation (TSDI), Kenya-based APEC Consortium, and Edon Consultants International Limited were chosen as the professional ESIA consultants.[132] The consulting consortium monitored the operation of the project, aiming to ensure the project was in compliance with local laws and regulations.

---

[126] Interview with project manager of the SGR project.

[127] Ibid.

[128] Interview with public relations officer of CRBC. See also, "China Road and Bridge Corporation Social Responsibility Report 2015 on Mombasa-Nairobi SGR Report". The report is China's first overseas project CSR report.

[129] Interview with project officer of the SGR project.

[130] Interview with liaison officers of Mombasa County.

[131] Interview with general engineer of the SGR project.

[132] Interview with project manager of the SGR project.

Before the commencement of the SGR project, CRBC was required to undertake an ESIA study guided by the 2003 Environmental Management and Coordination Act. The assessment of the SGR included the planning and design, construction, operation, and decommissioning phases.[133] The aspects of the SGR project identified for monitoring included vegetation, water quality, air quality, solid waste generation, occupational health and safety risks, wildlife/livestock/human accidents, soil erosion, resettlement, and livelihood and environmental risks.[134] CRBC also put effort into various environmental protection activities. For water pollution control and solid waste pollution control, for example, CRBC set up cleaning devices and vehicles at designated points; simple sewage treatment facilities in the camps for the centralized collection and disposal of domestic sewage; and sedimentation tanks on work sites generating high-turbidity waste water or other measures to treat the wastewater. The government official in Mombasa County reflected that, with regard to the solid waste pollution control, CRBC properly and promptly processed and removed the waste unsuitable for recycle.[135] CRBC also set up temporary stack points in camps and entrusted local sanitation departments to dispose of municipal waste in a centralized way.[136]

To reduce negative impact to wildlife, CRBC analyzed more than ten possible routes and chose a route that could bypass Nairobi Wildlife Park and meet the requirements of the KWS.[137] According the KWS, allowing 11 km of track to pass through Nairobi National Park is a pragmatic alternative with the economic and development needs of the Kenyan people in mind.[138] In consideration of the migratory patterns and paths of wildlife in the wildlife reserves along the railway as well as the habitats of elephants, giraffes, and other animals, CRBC installed a number of wildlife channels and facilities to help animals cross the rail safely. These included fences on both sides of the railway to prevent roaming animals from colliding with the train, extending the approach of the crossing bridge, and increasing its height to facilitate the passing of animals, and setting up lower-profile culverts to meet the drinking needs of small animals.[139] CRBC also set up electronic systems to detect and deter animals. Stationary signal-warning systems are used to scare wildlife away from fenced areas and bridges.[140] According to the Kenyan Wildlife Services, these methods effectively reduced the adverse impact of the SGR on wildlife migration and human-wildlife conflicts.[141]

[133] "China Road and Bridge Corporation Social Responsibility Report 2015 on Mombasa-Nairobi SGR Report".

[134] Interview the project manager of the SGR project.

[135] Interview with government official of Mombasa County.

[136] Interview with government official of Mombasa County.

[137] Interview with Chairman of The Kenyan Wildlife Service and officer of Chinese embassy in Kenya.

[138] Interview with staff of The Kenyan Wildlife Service.

[139] Interview with Chinese engineer of the SGR project.

[140] Ibid.

[141] Interview with staff of The Kenyan Wildlife Service.

4.4.4.3 Social Interests Protection

As the SGR encompasses a land area that extends over 472 km, it is imperative for CRBC to adopt effective measures to minimize negative social impact to local communities that occupy or use the land it covers. According to the project manager of the SGR project, before the construction of the project, field visits had been carried out by CRBC to inspect the site characteristics and the environmental status of the surrounding areas.[142]

As the railway passes through many tribal lands, communication with local communities and respect for local customs and traditions during the construction of the project, including the rights and interests of tribal people, were important to ensure the smooth development of the SGR project. CRBC communicated with the local people affected by the project through group consultation, public announcements, notices, and explanatory letters. It also set up billboards around the site to smooth communication and resolve dissatisfactions.[143] Nonetheless, according to the liaison officer, CRCB encountered some difficulties in communicating with a particular group, the Maasai tribe. The Maasai tribe living along the SGR route has historically been a marginalized community. The tribe had long-standing conflicts and struggles with other ethnic groups over resources.[144] During the construction, the affected Maasai tribe was unhappy that CRBC also provided jobs to other ethnic groups and communities. They believed that, since the railway was being built on Maasai land, only the Maasai tribe was entitled to the job opportunities.[145] In addition, disputes over wages, employment benefits, land compensation, environmental impact, and supply contracts all caused disagreement within and between the local communities and CRBC.[146] The pre-existing tensions between ethnic and socioeconomic groups were exacerbated by the SGR project.[147] In order to get construction underway as soon as possible due to political pressure from the Chinese and Kenyan governments, CRBC became involved the land compensation issue, as "the company didn't want the thing to be out of control".[148] When communication efforts did not work as expected, CRBC had to help the Kenyan government to resolve land compensation issues.[149]

In the SGR, liaison officers were "assigned to every section by the SGR and CRBC as part of CRBC's CSR strategy".[150] The liaison officers were responsible for connecting and communicating with external stakeholders to ensure effective communication with local people and communities in order to address their

142 Interview with project manager of the SGR project.

143 Interview with liaison officers of Mombasa County.

144 Interview with UN Environment officer.

145 Interview with liaison officer in Mombasa County.

146 Interview with program manager of China House and head of China Daily, African Station.

147 Wissenbach and Wang (2016).

148 Interview with government official of Mombasa County.

149 Interview with project manager of the SGR project.

150 Wissenbach and Wang (2016).

concerns.[151] The liaison officers collected complaints from the local community and send them to CRBC. The liaison officers also had the responsibility of advising CRBC managers on the ways to deal with the ethnic diversity of the local communities to ensure diverse and equitable representation.[152] In Mombasa and Kajiado County, I met with two liaison officers after being introduced by the county government. One officer had experience with local NGOs and was familiar with the local community. The other officer served Mombasa County as a civil servant for many years and became a counselor in the local government before taking the position as a liaison officer. Born and raised in the Counties, both believed that they were trusted by the local community. Hiring recognized liaison officers seemed to be an effective strategy for gaining greater acceptance from the local community and reducing friction over land, employment, and communication issues between CRBC and local residents and workers. The two liaison officers collected appeals and complaints from the local community to discuss them with CRBC. In response to some of the feedback, CRBC helped renovate schools, water infrastructure, health centers, churches, and disease protection trainings.[153] Furthermore, following the directions and arrangements set by the head office of CRBC, section offices investigated the expectations and demands of the local communities with the support of the county governments.[154] In addition, according to the manager, CRBC held quarterly meetings with top officials of the Government of Kenya. To maintain communication with concerned landowners and work toward solving problems regarding land acquisition and demolition, CRBC established regular communication channels with the National Land Commission, the Kenya Railways, the KWS, and other agencies.[155]

In addition to efforts to work with external organizations and institutions in the host country, employee localization was a critical concern in the SGR project. As of the end of 2015, 21,858 employees, including 2000 Chinese management and technical personnel, and 19,858 local employees (4690 technical workers, 907 management personnel and 14,261 ordinary workers) were officially registered in the project.[156] By the end of June 2018, the SGR project had provided jobs for almost 50,000 people, trained over 5,000 technical workers and operation managers, and supported over 100 Kenyan students in earning bachelor degrees in railway construction in China.[157] CRBC also cooperated with leading domestic universities and the Railway

---

[151] Ibid.

[152] Interview with liaison officers of Mombasa and Kajiado.

[153] Interview with public relations Officer of the SGR project. "Since the project commenced, CRBC have organized more than 100 social activates, from which over 10,000 Kenyan people have benefited. Activities include built water reservoir along the railway line to ensure water safety of local residents; built primary campus and donated stationery and sports goods, organized AIDs campaigns including prevention training, prophylactic distribution; made emergency plans for major epidemics, conducted training on epidemic prevention and treatment, etc."

[154] Interview with project manager of the SGR project.

[155] Ibid. Interview with liaison officer of Mombasa County.

[156] China Road and Bridge Corporation Social Responsibility Report 2015 on Mombasa-Nairobi SGR Report.

[157] CRI Africa (2018).

Training Institute (RTI) to train railway operation personnel in preparation for railway operation. CRBC reached an agreement with a leading Chinese railway training institute to send outstanding employees to China for training.[158]

In addition, local government officials were concerned about whether the SGR would truly benefit local industries, provide business opportunities for local contractors, and help promote local employment.[159] During the construction of the SGR project, county government officials learned the local subcontractor information through regular meetings with SGR project managers and local liaison officers.[160] According to a local government officer, the Chinese government promised labor localization to create a "win–win" outcome throughout the construction process.[161] Under the Chinese government's instructions, CRBC cooperated with more than 200 local subcontractors.[162] It communicated with local subcontractors, conducted efficient and timely coordination and investigations, and dealt with key issues that could affect the quality, safety, and progress of the project.[163] These activities enabled better communication with local communities and turn economic investments into mutually beneficial outcomes.[164] CRBC adopted social and environmental criteria for subcontractors. Based on its experience in railway construction and management in Kenya, CRBC formulated internal quality management measures, quality assurance plans, and administrative measures to investigate whether subcontractors complied with its social and environmental standards. According to the CRBC's Administrative Measures for Investigation of Environmental-related Activities, CRBC could stop contracting with subcontractors who violate the internal regulations and Kenyan laws, and section managers responsible for monitoring the construction would be warned and fined in accordance with the severity of the subcontractors' violation.[165] These internal rules provided a general framework for CRBC to deal with subcontractor activities. However, these internal measures were not open to the public. The actual implementation depended on the discretion of the SGR project manager.

---

[158] Interview with public relations officer of the SGR project. See more, China Road and Bridge Corporation Social Responsibility Report 2015 on Mombasa-Nairobi SGR Report. From July to December 2015, CRBC sent 13 outstanding local employees in four groups to the seminar on Railway Project Management and Construction for Developing Countries sponsored by the Ministry of Commerce of PRC and organized by Southwest Jiaotong University. Through class lectures and on-site teaching, trainees got a clearer picture of the leading technologies and advanced development of Chinese railways, especially the high-speed railways, comprehensively assimilated the knowledge and skills of railway project management and enhanced their ability to solve Kenya's problems concerned. After the training, each of the designated local employees finished all courses and obtained a training certification issued by Southwest Jiaotong University.

[159] Interview with government officials of Mombasa and Kajiado County.

[160] Interview with government official of Mombasa County.

[161] Ibid.

[162] Interview with project manager of the SGR project.

[163] Interview with government official of Mombasa County.

[164] Ibid.

[165] Interview with project manager of the SGR project.

According to the liaison officer in Mombasa, there was strict screening of subcontractors in the bidding process and the chances of subcontractor violation against either CRBC's internal rules or Kenyan laws should be pretty low.[166]

4.4.5 NGOs and Media in Kenya

While the Chinese government may exert tight control over the domestic civil society, its administrative influence over overseas civil society is very limited. This is reflected in the SGR project. In the empirical research, I interviewed six NGOs both in Kenya and China, including the WWF-Africa, WWF-China, Kenya Coalition for Wildlife Conservation and Management, Centre for Training and Integrated Research for ASAL Development, China House, and the China-Africa Excellency Foundation. Five of the above NGOs are based in Kenya. All these NGOs have at least one researcher or staff member who conducts research on the SGR project. Apart from the China-Africa Excellency Foundation, which only conducts research on the macroeconomic impact of the SGR on local people and community, all the other interviewed NGOs pay special attention to the environmental and social impact brought on by the SGR. According to the interviews, not only Kenyan NGOs but also Chinese NGOs in Kenya (China House) did not meaningfully engage in dialogues with the Chinese government, the China Exim Bank, or CRBC throughout the construction process.

Since its commencement, the SGR project received great attention from local and international media. However, the CRBC's attitude toward local NGOs and media was "keeping a distance from them". The project manager of the SGR project admitted that that "we seldomly get in touch with local NGOs and media as some of them interpret some issues without deep understanding the reasons lying behind". A responsible media, to the project manager's understanding, should "assume the responsibility to report more positive stories to better facilitate the construction of the SGR project".[167] The public relations officer of the SGR project believed that the Kenyan media always focused on eye-catching stories to attract their audience and sometimes they failed to carry the social responsibility of independent social media.[168] The language barrier between CRBC, local NGOs, and the media made it more difficult to achieve effective communication. Even though many staff members at the management level of CRBC found no problem in daily communication with local people, it was still difficult for CRBC to deal with the questions of local NGOs and the media in the public debate.[169] Due to the above reasons, according to the program officer of China House, CRBC tended to contact local media only when it had positive stories to spread out.[170] For example, CRBC "invited local media

[166] Interview with liaison officer and government official of Mombasa County.

[167] Interview with project manager of the SGR project.

[168] Interview with public relations officer of the SGR project.

[169] Ibid.

[170] Interview with program officer of China House.

to participate in project exhibitions and CSR report release events, but they seldom participated".[171]

Due to the lack of communication with local NGOs and media—even though the liaison officers were hired to help communicate with the local community—CRBC believed that its voice was not heard by local communities. One concrete example is the misunderstanding regarding the land compensation issue.[172] Although the responsibility of land compensation for the local community did not belong to CRBC, "local villagers believed that the CRBC was conspiring with the government to destroy their land and property by building railways".[173] The CRBC often believed that it was wrongly accused by such complaints.[174] Whenever it received such complaints from local NGOs and media, the CRBC always preferred to communicate with local governors to express any unspoken concerns and raise suspicions about the true intentions of local NGOs and media.[175] Without an effective dialogue with the CRBC, some NGO staff members became relatively critical, believing that "if the Chinese contractor doesn't fully communicate with them, it means they want to hide something".[176] The communication breakdown further exacerbated the misunderstanding between CRBC and local NGOs and media.[177]

4.5 Evaluation

4.5.1 The State-Centric Approach in Advancing CRBC's CSR

The SGR case shows the role of the state-centric approach in regulating CRBC's environmental and social behavior in the SGR project. The CRBC's CSR advancement, which benefits from the direct governing and monitoring power from the Chinese government and China Exim Bank, is an example of implementation of the state-centric CSR approach overseas. Figure 4.4 summarizes how the state-centric approach plays out in advancing CRBC's CSR.

As discussed in previous chapters, considering that the Chinese SOEs are linked to the state through institutionalized channels and political practices, their performance and behavior are closely intertwined with the political interests of the Chinese government and the commercial interests of Chinese national and policy banks. Due to the SGR's political importance to both the Chinese and Kenyan governments,

[171] Ibid.

[172] Interview with project manager of WWF-Africa.

[173] Ibid.

[174] Interview with liaison officer in Mombasa County.

[175] Interview with program officer of China House.

[176] Interview with staff of Kenya Coalition for Wildlife Conservation and Management.

[177] Interview with program officer of China House.

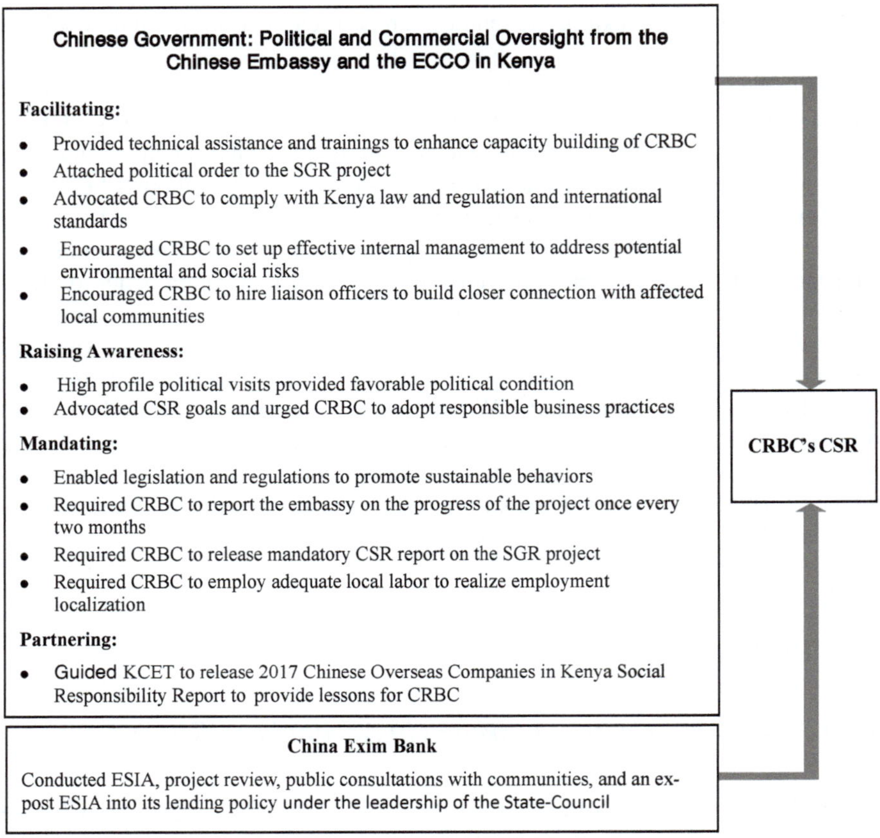

Fig. 4.4 State-centric approach in advancing CRBC's CSR in the SGR. Author's Diagram

the Chinese government attached significant importance to the sustainable construction of the SGR project. In the SGR project, the Chinese embassy and the ECCO in Kenya facilitated CRBC's practice by providing technical assistance and facilitating trainings for project managers, encouraging CRBC to set up effective internal management, and hiring liaison officers to build closer connections with affected local communities to better address potential environmental and social challenges and risks. In addition, the Chinese embassy and the ECCO in Kenya also raised the CRBC's CSR awareness in the SGR project through high profile political visits to provide favorable political conditions in advocating CSR goals. Combined with their evolving efforts to integrate environmental and social protection into foreign investment regulations and green finance, the Chinese government helped increase the CRBC's tendency to construct the railway in a sustainable manner. Furthermore, the Chinese embassy and the ECCO in Kenya also propelled the CRBC's CSR practices in the SGR project by requiring the CRBC to report to the embassy on the progress of the project regularly, to release mandatory CSR report on the SGR project, and to employ adequate local labor to realize employment localization. Lastly, the ECCO also partnered with the KCTA to release the 2017 Chinese Overseas Companies in Kenya Social Responsibility Report to further advocate for CSR in the CRBC and other Chinese SOEs in Kenya.

In addition, as the main financial provider for the SGR, China Exim Bank monitored and reviewed the project throughout the construction process. As a stated-owned policy bank under the direct leadership of the state council, China Exim Bank was encouraged to comply with the CSR standards established by the Chinese government. Beyond the basic requirement to comply with Kenyan domestic law regarding environmental and social protection, China Exim Bank mainly under the political pressure to maintain the Chinese government's image overseas required CRBC to meet requisite social and environmental standards. The governance and monitoring from the Chinese government and China Exim Bank pressed CRBC to acknowledge and practice sustainable construction concepts.

In general, the Chinese government contributed to the improvement of CRBC's CSR performance in the SGR project in a number of ways. First, the Chinese "Going Out" policy framework provides a regulatory framework for CRBC's operations in Kenya. As demonstrated in Chapter 2, the policy framework, which includes policies and regulations on China's sustainable investment overseas, helps promote Chinese companies' CSR development and financial institutions' practice of green finance. Second, the Chinese government established a strong and inter-locking institutional network to regulate and support CRBC's operation in Kenya. Together with the financial loans and support from the state-owned China Exim Bank, the political and financial supervision from the Chinese government further facilitated, endorsed, and mandated CRBC's responsible behavior in the SGR project. Third, significant political willingness by the Chinese government to complete the SGR successfully also enhanced the effectiveness of the state-centric approach in advancing CRBC's CSR activities. Such diplomacy, reflected in extensive high-level political visits to Kenya with loans and technical assistance promises from the Chinese government, promoted a favorable environment for the construction of the SGR project.

4.5.2 Limitations of the State-Centric Approach in the SGR Project

The case study has methodological limitations and substantive implication limitations. As to the methodological limitations, it should be noted that the SGR case presents the environmental and social behavior of a single Chinese SOE engaging in infrastructure construction in Kenya rather than a comprehensive examination of Chinese companies' behavior as a whole. As a result, there is an important caution on the generalization of the lessons learned from the SGR case. African countries are quite heterogeneous in their institutional qualities. It is uncertain whether the findings here in Kenya are equally applicable to other Chinese infrastructure projects in other African countries. Moreover, the company in the case study is a SOE. There are various types of Chinese companies operating in Kenya - from SOEs to fully private companies. The state-centric approach of CSR may not be equally effective to influence privately-owned Chinese companies' CSR, given the diverse political and business cultures of different types of Chinese companies.

In addition, the interview sampling is imperfect. Although it covers a wide spectrum of population and occupations, as can be seen from the interview list, a small number of interviewees in different fields cannot fully represent the full population of Chinese overseas companies and affected stakeholders. Besides the sample issues, information credibility is hard to verify, particularly for information from the Chinese government and the agents under its control. The Chinese government and its affiliated institutions including Chinese SOEs and state-controlled banks may have incentives to present a positive image to the outside world, especially in the face of surrounding criticisms.

Leaving the methodological limitations aside, the SGR case confirms some theoretical limitations of the state-centric approach as discussed in Chapter 2. In the SGR project, CRBC preferred to deal with the local governments and stay away from local NGOs and media in Kenya. This tendency was mainly rooted in its limited experience with civil society engagement back in its home country, i.e., China. As a result, local NGOs and media held more suspicion of CRBC and did not engage in any meaningful dialogues with CRBC in the construction process. As discussed in Chapter 2, an important weakness of the state-centric approach is the lack of input from civil society, which is an important additional source of monitoring over corporate behavior and shaping corporate image. This weakness is evident in the SGR case. China's state-centric approach developed in isolation from local NGOs and media does not help its CSR strategies responsive to local needs. Local NGOs and media are an important driving force of CSR. They can be partners with Chinese companies in designing, implementing, and monitoring CSR programs. As NGOs are independent intermediaries, they can act as a bridge between companies, communities, and the government to help them discuss viable solutions when conflicts arise. Moreover, China's state-centric approach without substantive engagement with local NGOs and media does not help China gain good international reputation that it desires. As seen in the SGR case, CRBC often complained about unfair treatment by local NGOs and thus avoided its contact with them. Insufficient communication breeds distrust and misunderstanding. Meaningful and interactive engagement rather than defensive avoidance is a better way to gain trust and reputations with the international community. To correct the weakness of the state-centric approach, it is important to encourage the Chinese government and its affiliated institutions to get more involved with civil societies.

Furthermore, as mentioned in Chapter 2, the effectiveness of the state-centric approach depends on the political commitment of the government. The SGR project had a high political value for both the Chinese government and the Kenyan government. This political value created a favorable environment to press CRBC to engage in CSR practices. This political value is an important feature of the state-centric approach as the traditional market-based CSR approach mainly sees business value.

The SGR case suggests that the state-centric approach may be weaker when projects are not politically important.

Finally, as discussed in Chapter 2, the Chinese government and its affiliated institutes have published numerous rules on promoting CSR. However, due to the vague and broad nature of the guidelines, the implementation of CSR initiatives and information disclosure of CSR policies and green finance are mainly rule-deep. There is not enough disclosure at the implementation level. This is also evident in the SGR case. China Exim Bank did not disclose its assessment report on the environmental and social impact of the SGR project. Neither the Chinese government made enough disclosure about the implementation of CSR measures in the SGR project. Poor transparency is a salient weakness of China's state-centric approach. It undermines the credibility of the state-centric approach in advancing Chinese companies' CSR overseas.

4.6 Conclusion

China's infrastructure investment in Kenya has increased dramatically in recent years. Given the particular economic, environmental, and social conditions in Kenya, the chapter specifically uses the SGR project in Kenya as a case study to illuminate the strengths and limitations of the state-centric approach. The empirical case study demonstrates the usefulness of the state-centric approach through mandating, facilitating, endorsing, and partnering to improve CRBC's CSR behavior. Meanwhile, this case study shows important limitations of the state-centric approach, including the lack of engagement with local NGOs and media, the dependence on political stakes at issue, and the poor transparency at the implementation level.

References

A Tale of Two Railways (2015). https://www.theeagora.com/a-tale-of-two-railways/

Andiva YM (2015) The impact of Chinese led infrastructure development on Sino-African relations: the case of Kenya. http://erepository.uonbi.ac.ke:8080/xmlui/handle/11295/102651

Arewa O (2016) Constructing Africa: Chinese investment, infrastructure deficits, and development. Cornell Int Law J 49:114

Brautigam D, Gallagher K (2014) Bartering globalization: China's commodity- backed finance in Africa and Latin America. Global Pol 5(3):346–352

Buxbaum P (2016) What in the world is China doing in Kenya?. http://www.globaltrademag.com/global-trade-daily/commentary/what-in-the-world-is-china-ng-in-kenya

China Daily (2016) China, Kenya launch direct cash exchange. http://www.chinadaily.com.cn/world/2016-07/14/content_26080669.htm

China Exim Bank (2007) Guidelines for environmental and social impact assessments of the China export and import bank's loan projects. (中国进出口银行贷款项目环境与社会评价指导意见). https://www.globalwitness.org/sites/default/files/library/Chinese%20guidelines%20EN.pdf

CIA World Factbook (2018) Kenya Demographics Profile 2018. https://www.cia.gov/library/publications/the-world-factbook/geos/ke.html.

CRI Africa (2018) Chinese ambassador to Kennya accepted CGTN INTERVIEW on anniversary of SGR operation. https://www.sohu.com/a/233508865_99934374

Deloitte (2016) Kenya, Africa's grounding growth. https://www2.deloitte.com/content/dam/Deloitte/za/Documents/africa/DeloitteAfrica_Kenya_Country_Report_Africa_Nov2016.pdf

Embassy of the People's Republic of China in the Republic of Kenya (2018) Interview with the Ambassador of Chinese Embassy in Kenya. http://www.fmprc.gov.cn/ce/ceke/chn/xw/t1564247.htm

ETC East Africa Ltd (2006) Country Environmental Profile of Kenya. https://europa.eu/capacity4dev/public-environment-climate/document/country-environmental-profile-kenya

Falk T (2013) China identifies Kenya as its next continental industrial Hub why China is investing $5 billion in Kenya's infrastructure (ZDNet). https://www.zdnet.com/article/why-china-is-investing-5-billion-in-kenyas-infrastructure

Foster V (2009) Building bridges: China's growing role as infrastructure financier for sub-saharan Africa. (World Bank). https://openknowledge.worldbank.org/handle/10986/2614

Gallagher K et al (2016) The globalization of Chinese development finance. Boston University, Global Economic Governance Initiative

Granovetter M (1985) Economic action and social structure: the problem of embeddedness. Am J Sociol 19(3):481–510

Gwilliam K (2011) Africa's transportation infrastructure: mainstreaming maintenance and management. World Bank. http://documents.worldbank.org/curated/en/728801468191665263/pdf/608030PUB0Afri10Box358332B01PUBLIC1.pdf

Hu T, Wang Y (2015) Environmental and social risk management of chinese transnational corporations. Yale School of Forestry and Environmental Studies and WWF. http://www.wwfchina.org/content/press/publication/2015/Yale-WWF_final.pdf

Hu T et al (2014) Managing environmental impact: international experience and lessons in risk management for overseas investments. World Resources Institute. www.wri.org/managing-environmental-impact-international-experience-and-lessons-in-risk-management-for-overseas-investments

Hu T et al (eds) (2015) Analysis of key players in China's outward foreign direct investment based on the conceptual matrix-Part I: case study in Latin America. In: Hu T, Wang Y (eds) Environmental and social risk management of Chinese transnational corporations. Yale School of Forestry and Environmental Studies and WWF. http://www.wwfchina.org/content/press/publication/2015/Yale-WWF_final.pdf

Kenya China Economic and Trade Association (2017a) 2017 Chinese overseas companies in Kenya social responsibility report. 16, 28, 30, 48. http://ke2.mofcom.gov.cn/17en.pdf

Kenya China Economic and Trade Association (2017b) 2017 Chinese overseas companies in Kenya social responsibility report. http://ke2.mofcom.gov.cn/17en.pdf

Kenya National Bureau of Statistics (2018) 2018 Economic Survey Report. https://www.knbs.or.ke/economic-survey-2018-launched/

KenyaForum (2016) Tribunal halts construction of SGR through National Park. http://www.kenyaforum.net/2016/09/20/environmental-tribunal-halts-construction-of-sgr-through-national-park/

Kibugi R et al (2016) Large scale land acquisitions for investment in Kenya: is the participation, and benefits of affected local communities meaningful, and equitable?. http://profiles.uonbi.ac.ke/rmkibugi/publications/large-scale-land-acquisitions-investments-kenya-participation-and-benefits-aff

Lin L (2015) China's National champions: governance change through globalization? Univ Pennsylvania Asian Law Rev 11(1):82–126

Lynch G (2013) The politics of ethnicity. In: Cheeseman N et al (eds) Routledge handbook of African politics. Routledge, Oxon

Morrock R (1973) Heritage of strife: the effect of colonialist 'divide and rule' strategy upon the colonized peoples. Sci Soc 37(2):129–151

Mungai M et al (eds) (2010) (Re)membering Kenya: identity, culture and freedom. Twaweza Communications Ltd

Mwenda A, Kibutu T (2012) Implications of the new constitution on environmental management in Kenya. Law Environ Dev J 8(1):76–87

Mwendwa M (2017) SGR will destroy the Ecology of Nairobi National Park. http://www.talkafrica.co.ke/sgr-will-destroy-the-ecology-of-nairobi-national-park-experts-warn/

Ndulu B et al (2007) Challenges of African growth: opportunities, constrains and strategic directions. World Bank. http://siteresources.worldbank.org/AFRICAEXT/Resources/AFR_Growth_Advance_Edition.pdf

Nyassy D (2015) Hands off Railway Project, Company Tells County Officials. Daily Nation. http://mobile.nation.co.ke/counties/Mombasa-Standard-Gauge-Railway-CRBC/-/1950480/2761446/-/format/xhtml/-/8y1o2bz/-/index.html

Petrović-Ranđelović M (2011) Host country policy as a determinant of environmentally sustainable foreign direct investment inflows. Econ Org 8(2):235–246

Rosnes O, Shkaratan M (2011) Africa's power infrastructure: investment, integration, efficiency. World Bank Publications

Sanghi A, Johnson D (2016a) Deal or no deal: strictly business for China in Kenya?. World Bank Policy Research Working Paper 7614, 42. http://documents.worldbank.org/curated/en/801581468195561492/pdf/WPS7614.pdf

Sanghi A, Johnson D (2016b) Deal or No Deal: Strictly Business for China in Kenya?. World Bank Policy Research Working Paper 7614, 21. http://documents.worldbank.org/curated/en/801581468195561492/pdf/WPS7614.pdf

Sanghi A, Johnson D (2016c) Deal or no deal: strictly business for China in Kenya?. World Bank Policy Research Working Paper 7614. http://documents.worldbank.org/curated/en/801581468195561492/pdf/WPS7614.pdf

Sino Africa Center of Excellence Foundation (2014) Business Perception Index Kenya 2014, iii. https://www.focac.org/eng/lhyj_1/zxxx/P020150803357007793815.pdf

Spear T et al (eds) (1993) Being Maasai: ethnicity and identity in East Africa. Jame Currey Ltd., Oxford

The Guardian (2013) How has Kenya changed since independence. https://www.theguardian.com/global-development/datablog/2013/dec/12/kenya-how-changed-independence-data

Transparency International (2018) Corruption Perceptions Index 2017. https://www.transparency.org/news/feature/corruption_perceptions_index_2017?gclid=CjwKCAiA24PVBRBvEiwAyBxf-S2YUEBHgUxMZNbVo-dOsRxyhgnDMixrqJ7Y7WFbC5mbOiW-gQ2eCxoCLVEQAvD_BwE

UNDP (2016) The 2016 human development reports of UNDP. http://hdr.undp.org/sites/default/files/2016_human_development_report.pdf

Wissenbach U, Wang Y (2016) Local politics meets Chinese engineers: a study of the Chinese-built standard Gauge Railway Project in Kenya. (China Africa Research Initiative Policy Brief, No. 16). https://static1.squarespace.com/static/5652847de4b033f56d2bdc29/t/58136e42b3db2ba8eafb7cbb/1477668419649/kenya+v3.pdf

World Bank (2017) The World Bank in Kenya. http://www.worldbank.org/en/country/kenya/overview

World Population Review (2018) Kenya Population 2018. http://worldpopulationreview.com/countries/kenya-population/.

Chapter 5
China's Sustainable Investment in Africa Under the State-Centric CSR Approach: Green Finance as a Case Study

Environmental law does not generally regulate financial institutions, on the assumption that its environmental sequelae are most appropriately governed at the level of enterprises and other economic actors.[1] Green finance has to some extent sought to fill this gap by disciplining enterprises to improve their environmental performance. Green finance has become a critical issue in financial innovation. It requires financial institutions to integrate consideration of environmental and social protection into lending decisions, to ensure the transparency of environmental information and measures, and to facilitate oversight and accountability in the lending process.[2] On September 22, 2019, the Principle for Responsible Banking (PRB), signed by 130 Banks worldwide, was officially launched.[3] The principles and supported documents provide guidelines for banks on how to conduct sustainable lending and investment. In the context of promoting green BRI, Chinese enterprises and financial institutions are required to conduct responsible investment to ensure the sustainable development in BRI countries.

Financial institutions can not only drive the transition to a low-carbon and climate-resilient economy, but also benefit themselves by managing and addressing environmental and social risks. It has the potential to shape borrowing enterprises' behavior, which in turn may lead to more socially acceptable business practices.[4] Enterprises that have better environmental conservation practices for their operations may have

[1] Richardson (2019).

[2] Ma (2017) and Lindenberg (2014).

[3] The Principles, along with the Principles for Responsible Investment (PRI) and the Principles for Sustainable Insurance (PSI) become important benchmarks for the financial sector to implement the United Nations 2030 Sustainable Development Goals (SDGs) and the Paris climate agreement. For more information, see Principles for Responsible Banking (PRB). https://www.unepfi.org/wordpress/wp-content/uploads/2019/07/FINAL-PRB-Signature-Document-2-Interactive-22-07-19.pdf?.

[4] Clark and Dariusz (2007). The geography of finance: corporate governance in the global marketplace. Oxford University Press, Oxford.

B. Liu, *China's Green Investment in Africa: A State-Centric Corporate Social Responsibility Perspective*, Modern China and International Economic Law,
https://doi.org/10.1007/978-981-95-2157-9_5

better chances of acquiring capital from private and multilateral financial institutions.[5] The green finance development of financial institutions therefore can play a significant role in monitoring environmental risks and implementing sustainable finance policies. With dramatic increase of Chinese enterprises going abroad and the rise of socially responsible investment, there is a growing need to promote socially responsible investment under the BRI.

As most countries in Africa have limited domestic financial resources to fill infrastructure gaps and energy shortages, since its announcement of the BRI, China has urged the banks under its control to provide financial support to the BRI construction projects in Africa.[6] However, as many of large infrastructure projects are supported through debt-based finance, questions are raised over its sustainability and the rising debt levels of African economies.[7] There are some criticisms that China's loans to African countries just sink them into financial traps.[8] Moreover, as China adopts lower environmental standards for its aid and investment projects than multilateral institutions or Western enterprises, investment recipient countries may lower their environmental and social requirements for Chinese enterprises.[9] To ensure the sustainable and green investment of Chinese foreign investment and address the criticism from the international community, there is a need to improve the sustainable and green finance from Chinese financial institutions under the BRI.

This chapter explores the development of green finance by Chinese financial institutions under a state-centric approach. It begins by analyzing the motivations behind China-Africa green cooperation and examines the evolution and characteristics of their climate cooperation. Against this backdrop, the chapter then delves into China's green finance cooperation with Africa, using it as a case study to contextualize China's overseas green finance development in Africa. It investigates how China's green finance initiatives in Africa are predominantly shaped by the state-centric approach and outlines the policy supports that facilitate green finance both domestically and internationally. Finally, the chapter assesses the challenges and limitations associated with the current state-centric approach and its related policies.

[5] Hu et al. (2014).

[6] Foster (2009).

[7] Chen (2018).

[8] Beattie and Callan (2006).

[9] Shinn (2016). See also, Munson and Zheng (2011).

5.1 The Necessity of Green Finance Cooperation Between China and Africa

5.1.1 Africa and China's Development Needs

With the development of the concept of sustainable development, the demand for green transformation and green development in Africa is becoming increasingly intense. The Sixth Global Environment Outlook released by the UNPE shows that Africa has rich natural capital in soil, geology, biodiversity, water, landscape, and habitat diversity. If properly managed, it has the potential to lead the region to a future of improved ecosystem integrity and human health and well-being.[10] Particularly, Africa is one of the continents that is most severely affected by climate damage and is a key region in global climate governance. The UNDP estimates that Africa will warm faster than the global average in the twenty-first century, with the increase likely to reach 4–6 °C in tropical West Africa and the Sahel region.[11] Climate change has rendered Africa more susceptible to extreme weather events, water scarcity, rising sea levels, food insecurity, and fragile ecosystems, thereby threatening its security and development and undermining the well-being of its people.[12] The escalating climate crisis necessitates that Africa pursue a green transformation and implement measures for climate change mitigation and adaptation.

Against this background, Africa has an increasingly urgent and strong demand for green energy transition, and is looking forward to finding a green development path more suitable for Africa. Agenda 2063 of the African Union (AU) sets "environmentally and climate-sustainable economic and social development" as one of its key objectives.[13] More than 90 percent of African countries have formally ratified the Paris Agreement on climate change, and more than 70 percent of African countries have included the development of clean energy and clean agriculture in their NDC to address climate change.[14] Many African countries have submitted their NDCs under the Paris Agreement, and more than 40 African countries have set clear national energy transition targets.[15]

However, energy remains the primary bottleneck hindering Africa's green development, particularly due to the low levels of energy production and consumption across the continent. The energy structure of African countries is still heavily reliant on fossil fuels and traditional biomass energy, with serious issues such as the lack of electricity for approximately 50 percent of its population. African countries are

---

[10] UNEP (2016b).

[11] UNEP (2020).

[12] Zhao and Zhang (2021c).

[13] Agenda 2063 of the African Union. https://au.int/en/agenda2063/overview.

[14] Zhou (2023b).

[15] The State of Climate Finance in Africa: Climate Finance Needs of African Countries. https://www.climatepolicyinitiative.org/wp-content/uploads/2022/06/Climate-Finance-Needs-of-African-Countries.pdf.

actively seeking to promote a clean energy transformation and develop a new path for industrialization. Most African countries are currently in a critical period of economic development and social transformation, and the choice of renewable energy development path could significantly impact their overall development. Therefore, Africa is the continent with the most potential for renewable energy development, and there is a vast market for renewable energy technology. It is thus significant for China and Africa to build a green BRI, enhance energy accessibility in Africa, and advance South-South cooperation on energy governance.[16] New energy technology cooperation with Africa can not only open up overseas markets for renewable energy technology but also serve as an effective means to export national technical standards.[17]

From China's perspective, with the desire to play a leadership role in global climate governance and to present itself as a responsible country, China has endeavored to adopt China's endeavor to strengthen its soft power or leadership role in global environmental governance.[18] In the era of global green and low-carbon development, China-Africa green cooperation and global ecological civilization construction are generally consistent, interactive, and integrated.[19] In particular, it is of great significance for China to help Africa cope with climate threats and enhance climate resilience through climate aid.

First, China's climate aid to climate-vulnerable African countries is an important practice in realizing the vision of "a community with a shared future for mankind"(CSFM). African developing countries, as the biggest victims of climate change, generally lack the capacity to cope with its impacts. Constraints in climate finance, low-carbon technologies, and capacity have left them vulnerable to climate disasters, with significant repercussions for development and human rights.[20] China's climate aid significantly boosts these countries' ability to address climate change, exemplifying China's commitment to building CSFM. Moreover, climate aid is strategically important for China. From the perspective of political and economic interests, developed countries are increasingly prioritizing assistance and cooperation with developing countries to combat climate change. This trend accelerates global strategic deployment and develops potential climate technology markets.[21] Recent research indicates that the U.S. plans to enhance support for its allies and partner governments in the climate field, providing aid for adaptation and resilience to strengthen alliances and assert international climate security leadership.[22] China's climate aid strategy also aims to consolidate friendly cooperation with African countries. Green investment between China and Africa promotes technology transfer and innovation. This not only helps upgrade Africa's industrial level but also opens new

[16] Zhang and Sun (2023a).

[17] Wang and Zhang (2022c).

[18] Qin and Liu (2024).

[19] Wang and Zhang (2022a).

[20] Duyck et al. (2018).

[21] Liu and Feng (2011).

[22] Liu and Wang (2023).

markets for Chinese enterprises, thereby strengthening economic ties and diversifying bilateral trade and investment. Furthermore, climate aid is a crucial dimension of international cooperation. Addressing climate challenges through bilateral and regional climate aid can enhance China's image as a responsible country and increase climate cooperation with Western nations. Such cooperation not only deepens mutual trust and the willingness to cooperate between China and Africa but also provides a new model for the international community, demonstrating the potential of South-South cooperation in tackling global challenges.

Overall, China's green cooperation with Africa holds great practical significance. From a governance standpoint, green cooperation and investment can enhance the recipient countries' ability to cope with climate change and mitigate its adverse effects. Diplomatically, it helps shape China's image as a country committed to green development and responsible global citizenship. China's green cooperation with Africa will also influence the future landscape of international relations. By leveraging the opportunity of the new energy revolution to promote reform of the global governance system and build a community with a shared future for mankind with African countries, China can further advance the development of the BRI. Developmentally, China's green cooperation plays a positive role in expanding the international environmental protection market and promoting green development. China-Africa green cooperation is not only an integral part of global ecological progress but also a model for it. Therefore, the green investment cooperation between China and African countries not only contributes to environmental protection and economic development but also provides crucial support for the realization of global sustainable development goals, holding extensive social, economic, and environmental significance.

5.1.2 Global Pressure

Many factors contribute to China's participation in climate change governance. In general, China's seeking to lead in global climate governance is motivated by China's own national conditions and is a strategic response to international expectations, manifesting China's intention to be responsible for protecting global ecological security.[23] Climate change poses an increasingly severe threat to global ecology, and, to secure the common interests of mankind, China has deemed it prudent to take a more active role in international climate negotiations. Thus, economics, ecology and the ever-intensifying global trend of green and low-carbon development have jointly compelled China to assume a leadership role.[24] Surpassing the U.S. as the world's largest carbon emitter in 2006, China has found that its energy consumption has increased rapidly owing to its unprecedented industrialization and urbanization. With China's rapid economic growth, the international community's expectations for

[23] Teng and Wang (2021).

[24] Trombetta (2019).

China's participation in international climate negotiations increased, and continue to increase, accordingly.[25] Against this background, China has faced mounting international pressure to reduce GHG emissions. Coupling that pressure with a desire to play a leadership role in global climate governance and present itself as a responsible developing country, China has endeavored to strengthen its soft power in global climate governance.

Under the framework of the Paris Agreement, China and African countries are required to report their NDCs in light of their respective national conditions, and provide regular feedback to the international community on their emission reduction progress through national communications, biennial reports, and biennial update reports. The framework requires to update and strengthen emission reduction actions in accordance with relevant regulations in the five-yearly global stocktaking.[26] This means that the emission reduction targets and actions of China and African countries require China and African countries to establish long-term emission reduction targets and set up feasible emission reduction that are compatible with the targets.

In the context of global pressure to provide climate aid, international climate aid has emerged as a crucial means for the international community to jointly address climate change,[27] as it can support the funds and technologies needed by developing countries to cope with climate change.[28] According to the 1992 UNFCCC, developed countries should take the lead in limiting greenhouse gas emissions and providing relevant funds and technologies to developing countries. Developing countries, in turn, should also take measures to mitigate and adapt to climate change while receiving technical and financial support.[29] Addressing climate change has now become a mainstream focus of foreign aid.

Moreover, in recent years, there has been a trend of mainstreaming climate change in the plans of donors. "Climate mainstreaming" is the integration of climate factors into planning and decision-making processes, in particular the integration of climate change mitigation and adaptation considerations into policies and actions.[30] The advocate for "climate mainstreaming" in development aid dates back to the 1990s, with the Paris Agreement requiring global financial flows to be more aligned with climate change adaptation and mitigation efforts in 2016, a trend that has become more pronounced in foreign aid and broader development finance in recent years. The mainstreaming of climate change is mainly reflected in the following aspects.[31] First, integrating climate impacts and climate risks into aid policies and assessment processes. Some donors have formulated climate and international development strategy to regulate the ecological environment and climate impacts of aid projects

---

25 Engels (2018).

26 UNFCCC, "Decision 1/CP.21, Adoption of the Paris Agreement", UN Doc CCC/CP/2015/10/Add.1 (29 January 2016).

27 Toetzke et al. (2022).

28 Kono and Montinola (2019).

29 UNFCCC, Art. 4.

30 Sun (2021).

31 Ibid.

and call for a more rigorous accounting system for environmental and climate change impacts. Second, phasing out fundings for projects with negative climate impacts. Major donor countries have pledged to reduce or stop funding for high-emission areas such as coal power to show their support for climate change in 2021. The Ministers agreed to end direct government support for coal projects, including development aid, loans, investments and financial services by the end of 2021, and to phase out fundings for all fossil fuels.[32]All these developments have become global pressures for China and Africa to promote climate finance and take climate factor as an integrated part of climate aid.

5.2 Development and Characteristics of China-Africa Green Finance Cooperation

5.2.1 China's Efforts in Contributing to Global Climate Governance

China's role in climate governance is becoming more prominent. China has been active in international lawmaking concerning climate governance, including in negotiating the UNFCCC, the Kyoto Protocol, and the Paris Agreement.[33] In general, China is a defender of the goals and principles of the UNFCCC and the Paris Agreement, a mediator of the North–South climate-related political conflicts, a supporter of developing countries' efforts to deal with climate change and an initiator of the green development of the BRI. With respect to its position in international climate change negotiations, from being an active participant China has evolved into being an active contributor and, further, is becoming an active leader. During the 75th session of the UN General Assembly, China announced that it would increase its NDC and expend more effort to achieve peak carbon emissions by 2030 and carbon neutrality by 2060. This further demonstrates China's consistent commitment to addressing climate change.[34]

Additionally, its domestic climate actions have evolved along with its international commitments. China has set domestic targets and taken steps to achieve carbon neutrality as well as assumed leadership responsibility among the international community to fight climate change. China's shift from the pursuit of a high GDP growth rate to high-quality development has contributed to China's assumption

[32] Ibid.

[33] Gao (2018). See also, Li al. (2021).

[34] China Headed Towards Carbon Neutrality by 2060. news.un.org/en/story/2021/09/1100642; "Xi's Statements at UN Meetings Demonstrate China's Global Vision, Firm Commitment". english.cctv.com/2020/10/03/ARTIHvrMfX8O1nBZAx0LIBSa201003.shtml; "China Carbon Neutrality in 2060: A Possible Game-Changer for Climate". https://bit.ly/3se54HW.

of a leadership role in fighting climate change.[35] All these efforts are designed to help China fulfill its responsibility to address the climate crisis.

5.2.1.1 Participation in Climate Lawmaking, Green Investment and Green Aid

China is the world's largest GHG emitter, its climate policy framework is of considerable importance for the future of global climate governance. In recent years, China has been proactive in climate change policymaking and has improved its climate governance through progressive policymaking and institution building domestically and internationally. China's climate policy framework demonstrates a stable movement toward developing a sustainable industrial transformation and a low-carbon economy.

In 1997, when the Kyoto Protocol was adopted, China actively participated in devising the Clean Development Mechanism, one of the Kyoto Protocol's financial mechanisms for mitigating and adapting to climate change. In accordance with the provisions of the Bali Action Plan, and in conjunction with China's economic and social development plan and sustainable development strategy, China has formulated and published the National Programme on Climate Change and promulgated a series of laws and regulations. In 2009, at the Copenhagen Climate Conference, China and the United States jointly promoted the Copenhagen Accord.[36] The joint statement on climate by China and other countries covered the core issues of climate negotiations and laid a solid foundation for the conclusion of the Copenhagen Accord. In the negotiation process of the Paris Agreement, China committed to its carbon emissions peaking by 2030 and expending its best efforts to achieve an earlier peak; it further committed to using 20 percent non-fossil energy as its primary energy supply by 2030. In October 2021, China's National Focal Point for the UNFCCC formally submitted to the Convention Secretariat the "China's Achievements, New Goals and New Measures for Nationally Determined Contributions"[37] and "China's Long-Term Low Greenhouse Gas Emissions Development Strategy for the Mid-Century".[38] These initiatives and strategy are major measures adopted by China to implement the Paris Agreement and reflect China's determination and effort to promote green and low-carbon development and actively respond to global climate change. The documents introduced China's NDC policies, measures and achievements since 2015; proposed new NDC goals and essential policies and initiatives; and detailed China's position concerning contribution to and interest in further promoting

[35] Liu and Lo (2021).

[36] Zheng et al. (2016).

[37] "China's Achievements, New Goals and New Measures for Nationally Determined Contributions". (《中国落实国家自主贡献成效和新目标新举措》). unfccc.int/sites/default/files/NDC/2022-06/中国落实国家自主贡献成效和新目标新举措.pdf.

[38] "China's Long-Term Low Greenhouse Gas Emissions Development Strategy for the Mid-Century" (《中国本世纪中叶长期温室气体低排放发展战略》). unfccc.int/documents/307766.

international cooperation with a view to fighting against climate change. The Chinese government also released a White Paper on China's Policies and Actions on Climate Change in October 2021.[39] All these actions demonstrate China's commitment to transparency in climate action and GHG emissions reduction.

China has also sought to address climate concerns through its investment policies in the Green BRI. In jointly building the Belt and Road, China has prioritized green development and issued a series of policy documents, plans, and measures aimed at achieving green growth. The first official document issued in 2015 proposed to "strengthen green and low-carbon infrastructure construction and operation management", "fully consider the impact of climate change in the construction", "highlight the concept of ecological civilization in investment and trade, strengthen cooperation on ecological environment, biodiversity, and climate change, and build a green BRI".[40] Since 2006, the Chinese government has promulgated many sustainable policies and guidelines applicable to overseas ventures to enhance its international reputation and highlight its role in promoting Chinese enterprises' sustainable overseas investment.[41] Various agencies have been involved in the regulatory process, including China's State Council, the National Development and Reform Commission, the Ministries of Commerce and Foreign Affairs, and other state entities such as the Export–Import Bank of China. The various policy documents provide a framework that reveals how the Chinese state intends to shape the environmental performance of all Chinese enterprises overseas. This is a critical demonstration of China's efforts to put the concept of global climate governance into action. China has helped developing countries improve their capacity to cope with climate change, creating exchanges and cooperating with countries along the Belt and Road in green technology, green equipment, green services, and green infrastructure development. Given that Chinese enterprises and financial institutions are increasingly investing in infrastructure projects overseas, in September 2021 President Xi Jinping announced that Chinese enterprises would not make new investments in coal-power projects in other countries.[42] China's commitment to cease building international coal-power projects will help spur the global clean energy transition, generate clean energy jobs, and further promote the transition to a green economy.

Finally, China also financially contributes to institutions and bodies that are responsible for addressing climate change concerns globally as a means of helping developing countries adapt to climate change. Guided by the vision of building CSFM, China has been actively engaged in cooperating with other developing countries to address climate change and providing support for their effective adaptation to climate change. Developing countries face many difficulties in climate change

[39] "White Paper on China's Policies and Actions on Climate Change" (《中国应对气候变化的政策与行动》白皮书). m.thepaper.cn/baijiahao_15094136.

[40] Ibid.

[41] Bernasconi-Osterwalder et al. (2013) and Liu (2021a).

[42] The State Council Information Office of the People's Republic of China, "Responding to Climate Change: China's Policies and Actions" (October 2021), english.www.gov.cn/archive/whitepaper/202110/27/content_WS617916abc6d0df57f98e3f3b.html.

adaptation owing to capital, technology, and human resources limitations. China has promoted South–South climate cooperation and strengthened its capacity to provide foreign climate assistance.[43] In terms of financial assistance, since 2011 the Chinese government has provided funding for climate adaptation in developing countries and proposed the establishment of a South–South Cooperation Fund on climate change. By 2024, China had allocated significant financial resources for South-South cooperation on climate change. Specifically, China has established a 20 billion RMB South–South Climate Cooperation Fund (SSCCF) to support climate change initiatives in developing countries.[44] In addition to financial assistance, China has also supported developing countries by donating climate-related equipment. This includes solar street lamps, photovoltaic power generation systems, electric motorcycles, new energy transportation infrastructure, and environmental monitoring equipment, all aimed at enhancing their capacity to adapt to climate change.[45] By 2024, China had signed 52 climate change cooperation documents and implemented relevant cooperation with 42 developing countries.[46]

5.2.1.2 Private Actors' Engagement in Global Climate Governance

In addition to the Chinese government, multiple stakeholders in China are playing an increasingly large role in climate governance.[47] China's regulatory approach to addressing global climate challenges has tended to rely heavily on top-down, command-and-control regulations that govern behavior through directives regarding emission-control levels or methods. In recent years, however, the role of multi-stakeholder participation in global climate negotiations and governance has expanded substantially. As a consequence, the Chinese government has increasingly called for greater use of market-based instruments to address climate issues.[48] Since the signing of the Paris Agreement, Chinese corporations, financial institutions, and social organizations have increased their enthusiasm for participating in global climate action and shared China's advanced concepts and practices in "ecological civilization" construction and development. The Paris Agreement advocated for a multi-stakeholder engagement approach; hence, social organizations, NGOs, enterprises

[43] UNDP China (2016).

[44] SAIIA (2024).

[45] "Responding to Climate Change: China's Policies and Actions". global.chinadaily.com.cn/a/202110/28/WS6179dfdba310cdd39bc71b86.html.

[46] "China's Policies and Actions Addressing Climate Change (2024).

[47] Schreurs (2017).

[48] The State Council Information Office of the People's Republic of China (2021).

and financial institutions at both the national and the local levels have become important players in combating climate change in China. In line with these multiple stakeholders' new role as crucial non-state actors in carbon neutrality and climate cooperation endeavors, their actions and climate commitments are increasingly valued in the global climate governance system.[49]

The active participation of Chinese enterprises and financial institutions in incentivizing the transition to a low-carbon economy exemplifies China's shift to multi-stakeholder involvement in global climate negotiations and governance. Chinese SOEs are a significant source of GHG emissions owing to their focus on energy-intensive production activities such as cement, iron, and steel production; power generation; machine manufacturing; and petroleum and chemical refining.[50] As discussed before, the ownership structure strongly influences the governance practices of Chinese enterprises. As Chinese SOEs are usually organized around networked hierarchies, they are linked through institutionalized personnel channels and political approaches to state organs.[51] Therefore, Chinese SOEs also bear the additional responsibility of projecting a positive image of the Chinese state and government.[52] Before the cap-and-trade pilot programmes were launched, China's SOEs were actively responding to the government's call to conserve energy and reduce emissions. Measures they adopted included improving energy efficiency, adopting new technologies, substituting a proportion of their fuel consumption with solar, wind, biomass, or other renewable energy sources, and centralizing production in the coal-fired power and steel industries.[53]

Financial institutions are also taking action and demonstrating leadership in addressing climate change. The development of low-carbon finance is beneficial to China's green economic transformation. Climate mitigation is a priority within China's green finance policies, and many Chinese local governments have issued guidance documents on green finance.[54] At the Second Belt and Road Forum held in April 2019, twenty-eight major Chinese financial institutions, including the China Development Bank, the China International Capital Corporation, the China Construction Bank, and the Agricultural Development Bank of China, endorsed the "Green Investment Principles for the Belt and Road Initiative".[55] The Belt and Road Initiative International Green Development Coalition was established in Beijing with the aim of promoting green and sustainable development in countries along the Belt and Road

[49] Pearson (2019).

[50] Marquis et al. (2011).

[51] Ho (2013).

[52] Liu (2021b).

[53] Bergsager (2013).

[54] Climate Bonds Initiative and SynTao Green Finance, "Study on China's Local Government Policy Instruments for Green Bonds". climatebonds.net/files/reports/chinalocalgovt_02_13.04_final_a4.pdf. See also Climate Bonds Initiative and SynTao Green Finance, "China Green Finance Policy", climatebonds.net/files/reports/policy_analysis_report_2021_en_final.pdf.

[55] "Green Belt and Road Principles Receive Industry Backing," City of London (24 April 2019).

to protect the ecological environment and mitigate climate change impacts.[56] The AIIB is also playing an increasingly important role in helping member states improve capacity building to address climate change and promote green development.[57]

The People's Bank of China's Guidelines for Establishing the Green Financial System[58] and other green finance policy documents highlight climate mitigation and low-carbon development. Some financial institutions allocate capital and steer financial flows toward more low-carbon, sustainable activities. Others are taking steps to change corporate behavior; influence policy outcomes; and collect the data, develop the tools and normalize the transparency required to embed climate change in how markets function.[59] The green finance policies adopted by Chinese financial institutions promote investment in a wide range of assets, including renewable energy projects, water treatment plants, recycling facilities and mass transit.[60] Chinese financial institutions have realized the importance of financing support for enterprises implementing energy conservation and emissions reduction initiatives. To improve energy efficiency to reduce carbon emissions, tax exemptions are granted to enterprises. Financial institutions also play an essential role in China's carbon market; their involvement helps to bring greater liquidity to carbon markets. In addition, by developing derivative products and services, financial institutions are helping to accelerate the formation of carbon assets and increase the willingness of enterprises to participate in carbon markets. Additionally, financial institutions are contributing to innovations in business systems and the mechanisms and products of the carbon market, improving the economic and social benefits of China's financial industry, and enhancing the CSR of financial institutions.[61]

5.2.1.3 China's Efforts to Incentive Green Energy Transition

To reach the goal of carbon neutrality and further accelerate the transition to a low-carbon economy, China will take stronger measures to control the consumption of fossil fuels, develop non-fossil fuels, and accelerate the development of renewable energy. In addition, China will also comprehensively promote green and low-carbon activities in key areas, develop low-carbon transportation and green buildings, promote innovation in green and low-carbon technologies, and encourage green and low-carbon lifestyle.[62]

---

[56] UNEP, "The Belt and Road Initiative International Green Development Coalition", org/regions/asia-and-pacific/regional-initiatives/belt-and-road-initiative-international-green.

[57] Chin (2016).

[58] People's Bank of China, "Guidelines for Establishing the Green Financial System" (2 September 2016), at 1(1), pbc.gov.cn/english/130721/3133045/index.html.

[59] UNEP Finance Initiative, "Financial Institutions Taking Actions on Climate Change", unepfi.org/fileadmin/documents/FinancialInstitutionsTakingActionOnClimateChange.pdf.

[60] Gilbert and Lihuan (2017).

[61] Haigh (2011).

[62] "Realizing Carbon Neutrality, the 14th Five-Year Period is the Key". http://www.gov.cn/xinwen/2021-01/18/content_5580590.htm.

Specifically, China's efforts to incentive the transition toward a low-carbon economy are led by the concept of 'Ecological Civilization', which provides a driving force for China's technological transformation of low-carbon economy. The concept of "Ecological Civilization" advocates a shift from the focus on the development of fossil energy to the utilization of renewable energy and low carbon energy, which is the core connotation of low-carbon economy. The renewable energy development such as solar energy, geothermal energy, wind energy, marine energy, nuclear energy, and biological energy are the core elements to realize low-carbon economy.[63]

Accelerating structural adjustment and optimizing industrial structure is also significant to achieve low-carbon economy. The government will continue to give priority to green industries with financial subsidies to reduce dependence on the consumption of high-carbon energy. Specific actions include controlling the rapid growth of industries with high energy consumption and high emissions, speeding up the elimination of backward production capacity, and increasing investment in low-carbon technologies to develop low-carbon products.[64]

The development of low-carbon finance is also conducive to China's green economy transformation. China has been actively developing green finance. Especially, the development of domestic emission trading market can effectively promote the transformation of domestic economic growth mode. Chinese financial institutions have also realized the importance to provide financing support for enterprises implementing energy conservation and emission reduction. Tax exemptions are granted to enterprises for improving energy efficiency to reduce carbon emissions.[65]

5.2.2 *China's Green Finance Cooperation with Africa*

Green cooperation between China and Africa has increasingly become a core issue of China-Africa cooperation and a key element in building a community with a shared future. China-Africa cooperation on green development has been integrated into the BRI. In particular, China and Africa have established a relatively sound policy support system, prioritized clean energy cooperation, and promoted China-Africa green cooperation on climate change through trilateral cooperation on climate finance.[66] China also places great emphasis on cooperation in addressing climate change, committing to strengthening international exchanges and cooperation, and promoting South-South cooperation in the field of climate change by building green cooperation platforms to share experience, provide technical support, and facilitate

[63] General Office of the State Council (2014).

[64] Springer et al. (2019).

[65] Cui et al. (2014).

[66] Yu and Wang (2022).

the transfer of intellectual property rights.[67] The White Paper on China-Africa Cooperation in the New Era clearly states that China and Africa jointly advocate for green, low-carbon, circular, and sustainable development.[68]

In recent years, China and African countries have conducted remarkable cooperation in climate change adaptation and mitigation, energy structure transformation, and green and low-carbon development. As previously mentioned, the AU's Agenda 2063 is a long-term plan for Africa's development over the next 50 years, with tackling climate change and achieving sustainable development being one of its 20 goals. Guided by the Global Development Initiative,[69] China-Africa green development cooperation is not only beneficial to both China and Africa but also conducive to global ecological and sustainable development.

5.2.2.1 Development and Characteristics

Green cooperation has become an integral part of South–South cooperation, with climate change emerging as a crucial area of China-Africa collaboration. Technologies such as clean energy, renewable energy, and green agriculture have become vital for mitigating and adapting to climate change in developing countries. In recent years, to support Africa's green energy transformation and enhance its energy infrastructure, China has prioritized clean energy in China-Africa green cooperation.[70] Currently, clean energy development is not only a core component of China and Africa's development plans but also a significant aspect of their shared cooperative vision. The African renewable energy sector is characterized by abundant resources and a shortage of technologies. Africa is rich in solar, wind, and hydropower resources, yet renewable energy sources like nuclear and hydropower account for less than 10% of Africa's energy supply structure, with renewable energy making up only 2%.[71] China's off-grid photovoltaic power generation technology holds high practical value for African countries. It can address the challenges of laying power grids or constructing large-scale power generation facilities in remote mountainous areas and offshore islands, providing technical support for the utilization and transformation of solar energy in Africa.[72] Historically, China and Africa have laid a solid foundation for cooperation in clean energy technology.[73]

Moreover, China's climate aid to Africa is a significant aspect of China-Africa green cooperation. Due to their relatively weak economic strength, lower levels of

---

[67] Ibid.

[68] "The White Paper on China-Africa Cooperation in the New Era". https://www.gov.cn/zhengce/2021-11/26/content_5653540.htm.

[69] Ministry of Foreign Affairs (2022).

[70] Zhou (2023a).

[71] African Energy Chamber, "Africa Energy Outlook 2021". https://energychamber.org/wp-content/uploads/AEC_Outlook_2021.pdf.

[72] Zhao and Zhang (2021a).

[73] Zhang and Sun (2023a).

science and technology, and limited scientific research personnel, African countries often lag behind in energy efficiency and climate change adaptation. Considering the actual conditions of African countries, under the framework of South-South cooperation and the green BRI, China has provided climate aid and support to help them accelerate the adjustment of their energy structure and the transformation of their economic development model. In 2012, China allocated 200 million RMB for a three-year international cooperation program to assist small island countries, least developed countries, and African countries in coping with climate change.[74] In 2015, China announced an investment of 20 billion RMB to establish the China South–South Cooperation Fund on Climate Change and unveiled the "Ten Hundred Thousand" project on South–South climate cooperation among developing countries.[75] China planned to set up 10 low-carbon demonstration zones in developing countries, launch 100 climate change mitigation and adaptation projects, and provide 1,000 training opportunities on climate change. It also continued to promote international cooperation in clean energy, disaster prevention and reduction, ecological protection, climate-resilient agriculture, and low-carbon and smart city building.[76] In 2024, China announced a renewed US$10 million contribution to the China-IFAD South-South and Triangular Cooperation (SSTC) Facility, which is part of China's broader commitment to South-South cooperation, which also includes the South-South Cooperation Assistance Fund.[77] Additionally, China has upgraded the South-South Cooperation Assistance Fund to the Global Development and South-South Cooperation Fund, increasing its total funding to US$4 billion.[78] By 2024, China had signed 19 memorandums of understanding (MOUs) on South-South cooperation to address climate change with 17 African countries, supporting Africa's climate change response through the implementation of mitigation and adaptation projects, the construction of hydropower stations and solar photovoltaic power stations, and the provision of relevant technical training.[79]

Currently, China is the largest source of public financing in Africa's clean energy sector. According to statistics from the International Renewable Energy Agency, Africa's clean energy sector (including project development, planning, and technology transfer) received a total of US$64.7 billion in public funding support from 2010 to 2019, with China contributing 51% of this amount.[80] This has effectively ensured the smooth implementation of various clean energy projects in Africa and addressed the urgent need for clean energy development in African countries. By undertaking various types of projects, Chinese energy, and power enterprises have

---

[74] Wang and Zhang (2022b).

[75] China International Development Cooperation Agency (2015).

[76] Ibid.

[77] UN China (2024).

[78] CGTN (2024).

[79] The State Council of the PRC (2024).

[80] IRENA, "Renewable Energy Market Analysis: Africa and Its Regions". https://www.irena.org/-/media/Files/IRENA/Agency/Publication/2022/Jan/IRENA_Market_Africa_2022_Summary.pdf?la=en&hash=BA5F72AAA3D5995E42D9B6C10203594E679CD7A6, 108.

enhanced African countries' capabilities in contract construction, engineering operations, technical services, and project financing. They have also gained profits from project development and operation, thereby comprehensively improving their ability to operate on the international stage.[81]

5.2.2.2 Major Platform for China-Africa Climate Cooperation

China-Africa green cooperation has been continuously promoted through the FOCAC, the BRI and multilateral platforms dominated by the UN. The FOCAC, launched in October 2000, marks a starting point for China-Africa relations and the beginning of the substantive development of China-Africa green cooperation, becoming an important platform for China-Africa green cooperation. China-Africa green cooperation not only provides an important perspective of the South-South cooperation for the international community, but also reflects the development trend of international cooperation among developing countries. FOCAC has reached a series of green cooperation plans and projects, which are profoundly shaping the China-Africa green cooperation process, guiding and prompting the implementation of China-Africa green cooperation.[82]

In addition, international cooperation on green development under the BRI has emerged as a significant platform for China-Africa green cooperation. Promoting green development cooperation has become a crucial aspect of the BRI. Currently, China is actively engaging in cooperation with African countries, international and regional organizations under the framework of the BRI Green Development International Alliance and the BRI Ecological and Environmental Protection Big Data Service Platform.[83] The establishment of the China-Africa Environmental Cooperation Center represents an important milestone in implementing the outcomes of the 2018 Beijing Summit of the FOCAC. It has created a new platform for China and Africa to enhance exchanges and dialogue on environmental policies, promote information exchange and cooperation on environmental industries and technologies, and conduct joint research on environmental issues, thereby further advancing China-Africa green cooperation.[84]

Moreover, multilateral platforms led by the UN also serve as vital venues for China and Africa to enhance green cooperation and advance the evolution of international climate and environmental governance. China has placed significant emphasis on strengthening coordination with the African Group in global climate negotiations and deepening China-Africa green cooperation through the G77 and China platform mechanism. Furthermore, during the 2024 Beijing Summit of the FOCAC, China and 53 African countries jointly adopted the Declaration on China-Africa Cooperation

[81] Wang and Liu (2022).

[82] Ibid., 38.

[83] Wang and Zhang (2022a).

[84] The China-Africa Environmental Cooperation Center. https://www.unep.org/regions/africa/regional-initiatives/china-africa-environmental-cooperation-centre.

on Climate Change, committing to actively address climate change.[85] In the field of renewable energy, China, in partnership with the UNDP, has initiated tripartite cooperation projects on biogas and solar energy technology transfer with several African countries, including Ghana, Zambia, and Ethiopia.[86]

5.2.2.3 Backed by Sufficient Policy Support

After years of cooperation, China and Africa have established a relatively solid policy support system for addressing climate change. At the first FOCAC held in 2000, high-level officials of China and Africa reached initial cooperation intentions on environmental protection and addressing climate change. In 2006, China's Policy Paper on Africa officially defined 'South-South cooperation on climate change' for the first time, and the two sides began to cooperate in adapting to climate change. Under the framework of FOCAC, China-Africa cooperation on climate change has gradually deepened. The FOCAC Beijing Action Plan (2007–2009) included environmental protection in the action plan for the first time, proposing that China and Africa should strengthen personnel exchanges and capacity building in the field of environmental protection and promote bilateral cooperation in desertification prevention and control.[87] The FOCAC Sharm el-Sheikh Action Plan (2010–2012) and FOCAC Beijing Action Plan (2013–2015) both emphasize China's need to help African countries enhance their capacity to adapt to climate change and deepen cooperation on climate change monitoring, crisis and vulnerability reduction. Since 2012, China and Africa have jointly held the Ministerial Dialogue on China-Africa Environmental Cooperation to strengthen communication and coordination on environmental policies. The 2015 China Policy Paper on Africa reaffirms and upholds the principles and provisions of the UNFCCC and Kyoto Protocol, and promotes the establishment of a global climate governance system to promote the full, effective, and sustained implementation of the UNFCCC.[88]

On the basis of the above documents, the FOCAC Beijing Action Plan (2019–2021) provides specific measures and technical assistance to jointly address climate change between China and Africa, including joint training of professional and technical personnel and material assistance in the field of climate change mitigation and climate change adaptation.[89] The Vision 2035 for China-Africa Cooperation released in 2021 defines the overall framework for China-Africa cooperation in the next 15 years, describes the prospects for China-Africa cooperation in various fields

---

[85] "Beijing Declaration on Jointly Building an All-Weather China-Africa Community with a Shared Future for the New Era". http://www.china.org.cn/chinese/2024-09/06/content_117412273.htm.

[86] Zhao and Zhang (2021b).

[87] "The Beijing Action Plan Outlines Mutually Beneficial Cooperation between China and Africa in the Next Three Years". https://www.gov.cn/jrzg/2006-11/05/content_433307.htm.

[88] "The 2015 China Policy Paper on Africa". https://www.gov.cn/xinwen/2015-12/05/content_5020197.htm.

[89] "FOCAC Beijing Action Plan (2019–2021)". http://focacsummit.mfa.gov.cn/chn/hyqk/201809/t20180905_5859862.htm.

in 2035, and proposes to jointly build a new model of green development.[90] China will actively develop renewable energy sources such as solar, wind, geothermal, biogas, tidal current, and wave, and provide stable and affordable power supply to remote areas in Africa. At the same time, China and Africa issued the Declaration on China-Africa Cooperation on Climate Change for the first time, proposing to establish China-Africa strategic cooperative partnership on climate change. The FOCAC-Beijing Action Plan (2025–2027) has further set up Green Development Partnership Action. China will support Africa in improving its climate resilience, provide new energy technologies and products, implement 30 clean energy and green development projects, and set up a special fund for China-Africa green industrial chain. China will continue to carry out capacity building and joint research on disaster prevention, mitigation and relief, biodiversity conservation, environmental quality improvement and desertification control, and jointly build a meteorological early warning platform.[91] According to the above policy documents, it is evident that the two parties will prioritize the use of clean energy in their energy cooperation to address the prominent development needs of African countries.

5.2.2.4 Enhanced Capacity Building

During the process of China-Africa green cooperation, China has prioritized capacity building. In the area of personnel training for climate change and green development, China has continuously trained a large number of African personnel. From 2013 to 2018, relevant Chinese government departments held over 200 training programs on climate change and ecological and environmental protection. They also established academic and degree programs in environmental management and sustainable development, training more than 5,000 personnel for relevant countries.[92] By August 2020, China had conducted 45 training courses on South-South cooperation on climate change, training over 2,000 officials and technicians in the field of climate change for more than 120 developing countries, including African countries. This has effectively enhanced the capacity of African countries for green development.[93]

Under the framework of the FOCAC, China has supported Africa in hundreds of clean energy and green development projects. By 2024, twelve African countries had joined the International Alliance for Green Development under the BRI, actively promoting the construction of a green BRI. Under the framework of South-South cooperation, China has signed 15 cooperation documents with 14 African countries, implementing climate change mitigation and adaptation projects, establishing

[90] "The Vision 2035 for China-Africa Cooperation". https://www.yidaiyilu.gov.cn/p/293626.html.

[91] "FOCAC—Beijing Action Plan (2025–2027)". https://www.gov.cn/yaowen/liebiao/202409/content_6972589.htm.

[92] The State Council Information Office of China (2021).

[93] Wang et al. (2020).

low-carbon demonstration zones, and conducting capacity-building training.[94] As a pivotal country, China has taken on the direct responsibility of technology transfer, providing Zambia and Ghana with services such as technical personnel training, technical case sharing, and technical facility construction.[95]

5.3 China's Financial Institutions' Green Finance in Africa

Climate finance is mostly implemented on a voluntary basis by financial institutions. In China, however, climate finance is to a significantly promoted by the government, and its implementation has specific combinations of state-centric regulation and Chinese versions of soft or voluntary policies.[96] This section analyzes China's state-centric approach and its implications on China financial institutions domestic and overseas green finance development.

5.3.1 China's State-Centric Approach in Regulating Financial Institutions

As previously discussed, before a Chinese company invest abroad, it usually needs to get administrative approval from the Chinese government and obtain capital from a financial institution (including Chinese policy banks and state-controlled commercial banks).[97] The Chinese government uses a wide range of substantial state finance to facilitate Chinese enterprises' foreign investment activities. In most cases, the financial institution is a state-owned bank, such as China Exim Bank. With the rise of Chinese enterprises' overseas investment under China's BRI and their potential to exacerbate Chinese enterprises overseas environmental impacts through financial support, it is important to examine the role of Chinese financial institutions in promoting Chinese sustainable investment.

China's development of green finance has several distinctive characteristics that set apart from those of other countries. Green finance development in OECD countries is much more strongly driven by market, shareholder, and stakeholder pressures, and includes a wide spectrum of market-based lending or project financing practices.[98] It relies on the voluntary measures and private standards, for responsible investment

---

[94] Climate Cooperation China, "China and Africa Pledge to Ramp up Cooperation and Call Climate Change Existential Threat". https://climatecooperation.cn/climate/china-and-africa-pledge-to-ramp-up-cooperation-and-call-climate-change-existential-threat/.

[95] UNDP (2014).

[96] Lin and Milhaupt (2017).

[97] Leung and Zhao (2013).

[98] Wagemans et al. (2014).

and credit systems,[99] and less so by governments. Governments play an indirect role in governing the greening of finances, such as through transparency and reporting requirements of banking activities.[100]

However, for Chinese financial institutions, ownership structure asserts a huge influence over the governance practices. As discussed before, China is regarded as the world's leading practitioner of "state capitalism". The relationship between Chinese state-owned financial institutions bears the hallmark of Chinese state capitalism. As discussed in Chapter 2, most Chinese overseas large-scale overseas infrastructure projects are financed by state-owned policy banks. Given that Chinese state-owned policy banks are organized as "networked hierarchies", the Chinese government plays a large role in the supervision and governance of the state-owned banks. Therefore, the interaction among the Chinese government, Chinese overseas SOEs, and state-owned banks provide the condition for the implementation of the state-centric financing.

5.3.2 *China's State-Centric Approach to Promote Green Finance Overseas*

Over sixty governments worldwide have adopted green finance policies.[101] The policies focus on specific types of projects, such as large-scale infrastructure projects, or on certain types of risks, such as climate change. China is the first to adopt a comprehensive green finance strategy, and its green credit policies apply broadly to all commercial lending.[102] This section will discuss the China's state-centric climate finance development in China and Africa to analyze the China's policy support to promote climate finance overseas under the state-centric approach.

5.3.2.1 The State-Centric Policy and Initiative Development in China

The Chinese government is an advocator for green finance. As discussed in Chapter 2, for over a decade, the Chinese government has introduced an array of top-down mechanism and state-centric framework to promote the development of green financial policies. Since 2007, a series of measures have been introduced to support the development of green finance, including the sustainable credit principle and the responsibility investment principle; the promotion of environmental information disclosure

---

[99] UNEP (2014).

[100] Mol (2017).

[101] UNEP (2018).

[102] Ho, Virginia, "Sustainable Finance & China's Green Credit Reforms: A Test Case for Bank Monitoring of Environmental Risk", University of Oslo Faculty of Law Legal Studies Research Paper Series No. 2019-03, 615.

and governance requirements; and the introduction of green loans, green infrastructure investment trusts, and green index funds.[103] Several governmental authorities started collectively releasing a series of directive-based regulations to set principles for investments and lending performances and forced banks to design their own policies.[104] These policies impose tighter regulatory oversight of Chinese financial institutions' lending practices. Chinese financial institutions, especially Chinese banks have further strengthened their processes on environmental and social protection policies in approving loans.[105] Under the state-centric approach, state-owned policy banks and state-owned commercial banks have relatively better green lending performance compared to private-owned banks and fund enterprises.

5.3.2.2 The State-Centric Policy and Initiative Development Overseas

Chinese green finance development was originally proposed and designed to regulate domestic lending practices. In many host developing countries, as the environmental governance are relatively inadequate, simply relying on a local permit may not be sufficient to manage environmental risks. This geographic limitation has already exposed Chinese financial institutions to unpredictable lending risks.[106] With the rapid increase of China's outward foreign investment under the BRI, the Chinese government has gradually made efforts to develop green finance overseas. The preface of China's Constitution has included the concept of "Ecological Civilization". This guiding concept to environmental protection has been translated into not only domestic environmental policies but also foreign sustainable investment measures.[107] The concept has also influenced China's green finance development overseas. For example, on August 2016, 'Guidance on Building Green Finance System' supports Chinese financial institutions and enterprises to issue green bonds abroad.[108] "Guidance on Promoting Green One Belt One Road" was released on April 2017, regarding green finance cooperation as one of the five core principles of the BRI.[109] Subsequently, "Environmental Risk Management Initiative for China's Overseas Investment" was issued on September 2017. It consists of 12 Articles on the disclosure of environmental and social governance information, and environmental and social protection standards overseas to improve financial institutions' capacity

[103] Ecological Finance Research Centre of Renmin University of China (2017).

[104] Bai et al. (2014b). See also, Aizawa and Chaofei (2010).

[105] China Banking Regulatory Commission, WWF and PWC (2013).

[106] Bai et al. (2014a).

[107] UNEP (2016a).

[108] "Guidance on Building Green Finance System" (关于构建绿色金融体系的指导意见). http://www.mep.gov.cn/gkml/hbb/gwy/201611/t20161124_368163.htm.

[109] "Guidance on Promoting Green One Belt One Road" (关于推进绿色"一带一路"建设的指导意见). http://www.mep.gov.cn/gkml/hbb/bwj/201705/t20170505_413602.htm.

for environmental risk management overseas.[110] The regulation especially emphasizes the importance of financial institutions in complying with regulations in China and host countries, and with the adoption of the highest standards where possible. Table 2.3 of the Chapter 2 has already comprehensively introduces the efforts of the Chinese government in promoting green finance to better address overseas investment risks from 2007 to 2021.

In addition to the gradual policy development, the internal green finance policies and initiatives of Chinese financial institutions are also progressively developing. Chinese financial institutions have signed up for a number of international, regional, and industry-specific initiatives, such as by expanding their cooperation with the UN Environment,[111] the World Bank, the ADB, and other multilateral organizations and international NGOs.[112] China and City of London Corporation issued the Green Investment Principles for the Belt and Road, and cooperated to promote the business environment and sustainable development in late 2019.[113] As of September, 2024, the GIP had 44 signatories and 14 supporting institutions from 17 countries and regions, with total assets held or under management exceeding USD 41 trillion, including China's four major state-owned commercial banks and three major policy banks, signed the principles.[114] CBRC has also signed memorandum of cooperation on cooperation with the financial regulatory authorities of 32 countries along the BRI route to promote the implementation of green finance.[115] Table 5.1 presents a summary of the most up-to-date environmental and social governance frameworks of Chinese financial institutions.

5.4 Limitations of China's State-Centric Green Finance Development in Africa

Although there is a considerable development of China's state-centric green finance in Africa, there are still challenges of China-Africa climate finance cooperation, including lacking comprehensive environmental and social safeguard framework, lacking transparency and effective external monitoring mechanism, backward supporting capacity of African countries and insufficient financial support.

---

[110] "Environmental Risk Management Initiative for China's Overseas Investment" (中国对外投资环境风险管理倡议). http://www.greenfinance.org.cn/displaynews.php?id=1472.

[111] United National Environment Programme-Finance Initiative (UNEP 2014).

[112] Ma (2017).

[113] City of London (2018).

[114] "The Green Investment Principle (GIP) for the Belt and Road Initiative". https://green-bri.org/green-investment-principle-gip-belt-and-road-initiative/.

[115] "The China Banking Regulatory Commission has Signed MOU or Exchange Notes with 32 BRI Countries", https://www.yidaiyilu.gov.cn/xwzx/roll/60575.htm.

Table 5.1 Selective environmental and social governance frameworks of Chinese financial institutions

Financial institution	Framework
Asian Infrastructure Investment Bank	Issued its "Environment and Social Security Framework"[116] in 2016. Updated its "Environment and Social Security Framework"[117] in 2024
New Development Bank	Issued its "Environment and Social Security Framework"[118] in 2016
China Development Bank	Joined the UN Environment Financial Initiative (UNEP FI) and required the bank to comply with relevant international norms and national policies.[119] Participated in the UN Global Compact since 2006 and issued its first CSR report in 2008.[120] There is no public disclosure of environmental and social security policies. Established the customer ESG rating system and applied the results of customer ESG rating in customers' credit rating[121]
China Export–Import Bank	No specific safeguard policy. Issued "China Export–Import Bank Environmental and Social Evaluation Guidance on Loans" in 2008 which requires overseas project developers to complete an environmental and social impact assessment before approving the loan.[122] Issued "China Export–Import Bank Green Credit Guideline" in 2015 to provide specific requirements for strengthening environmental and social risk management of credit projects in the aspects of organization and management, policy system, process management, internal control management, and information disclosure.[123] Issued the "Environmental and Social Framework of CEXIM AIIB Green On-lending Facility"[124] in 2022. Updated the "China Export–Import Bank Green Credit Guideline" in 2023[125]

(continued)

116 Asian Infrastructure Investment Bank (2016).

117 Asian Infrastructure Investment Bank (2024).

118 New Development Bank (2016).

119 Friends of the Earth (2012).

120 Ibid.

121 China Development Bank (2024).

122 China Exim Bank (2007).

123 China Exim Bank (2015).

124 China Exim Bank (2022).

125 China Exim Bank. http://english.eximbank.gov.cn/Responsibility/GreenF/.

Table 5.1 (continued)

Financial institution	Framework
Bank of China	No specific safeguard policy. Complies with "Environmental Information Disclosure Guidelines for Listed Companies of Shanghai Stock Exchange"[126] ";Environmental, Social and Governance Reporting of the Hong Kong Stock Exchange"[127]; and the "Global Sustainability Development Report Guideline of International Organization for Standardization".[128] Signed the UN Principles for Responsible Banking (PRB), joined the United Nations Environment Programme Finance Initiative (UNEP FI), and become the Task Force on Climate-related Financial Disclosures (TCFD) supporter in 2021.[129] Formulated "Management Policy on Environmental (Climate), Social, and Governance Risks Associated with Customers of Bank of China"[130]
Industrial and Commercial Bank of China	Joined the Carbon Disclosure Project, UN Global Compact committed to good practice industry initiatives such as the UN Environment Finance Initiative and the UN Principles for Responsible Investment. Implemented the "Green Credit Guidelines" and "Green Credit Evaluation Indicators" to provide a more stringent standard for financial institutions to carry out domestic and overseas infrastructure operations to control environmental and social risks. However, this guideline does not specify whether it also applies to overseas investment lenders. Formulated "Guideline for Greening Investment and Financing of Industrial and Commercial Bank of China (Trial)". Has released green finance reports for six consecutive years since signed the recommendations for upholding the Task Force on Climate-related Financial Disclosure (TCFD) in 2018[131]
China Construction Bank	No specific safeguard policy. Become the Task Force on Climate-related Financial Disclosures (TCFD) supporter in 2021 and issued its first Environmental Information Disclosure (TCFD) Report in 2022. Signed the UN Principles for Responsible Banking (PRB) and joined the UN Environment Financial Initiative (UNEP FI) in 2023. Formulated the "Measures on Environmental, Social and Governance Risk Management for Investment and Financing Businesses"[132]

(continued)

[126] Shanghai Stock Exchange (2008).

[127] The Stock Exchange of Hong Kong Ltd. (2015).

[128] Bank of China (2015).

[129] Bank of China (2022).

[130] Bank of China (2024).

[131] Industrial and Commercial Bank of China (2024).

[132] China Construction Bank (2024).

Table 5.1 (continued)

Financial institution	Framework
Silk Road Fund	Has not yet established a set of comprehensive, systematic environmental social risk assessment and management standards or policies. Its environmental and social risk management can only be analyzed through its investment and financing projects.[133] Formulated "Silk Road Fund Sustainable Investment Policy".[134] Issued its first Sustainable Development Report in 2024[135]
Silk Road Gold Fund	Pays attention to green and sustainable development to actively assume social responsibility. No specific safeguard policy
Green Silk Road Equity Investment Fund	No specific safeguard policy. Committed to the BRI economic zone for green industry investment, promote the Silk Road along the country and region to improve the ecological environment and the development of green economy
China—ASEAN Investment Cooperation Fund	Issued "Environmental and Social Protection Safeguard Reference Guide" in 2014.[136] Focuses on the sustainable development of potential investment projects and uses the environmental and social standards advocated by the World Bank to regulate the environmental performance of its investment projects
China Insurance Investment Fund	No specific safeguard policy
Agricultural Bank of China	Issued Agricultural Bank of China Implementation Guideline on green financial credit.[137] No specific safeguard policy. Signed the UN Principles for Responsible Banking (PRB), joined the UN Environment Financial Initiative (UNEP FI), and become the Task Force on Climate-related Financial Disclosures (TCFD) supporter in 2021. Issued the "Risk Management Measures of Agricultural Bank of China for Environmental, Social and Governance of Credit Business" in 2023[138]
China Investment Co., Ltd	No specific safeguard policy
CITIC Co., Ltd	No specific safeguard policy. Set up multi-layered and multi-category system of risk management policies[139]

Author's Compilation

[133] Silk Road Fund. http://www.silkroadfund.com.cn/cnweb/19854/19878/index.html.

[134] Silk Road Fund, "Silk Road Fund Sustainable Investment Policy". https://www.silkroadfund.com.cn/uiFramework/js/pdfjs/web/viewer.html?file=/enweb/attachDir/2023/01/2023010400145011962.pdf.

[135] Silk Road Fund (2024).

[136] China-ASEAN Investment Cooperation Fund (2014).

[137] Agricultural Bank of China (2015).

[138] Agricultural Bank of China (2024).

[139] CITIC Co., Ltd (2024).

5.4.1 *Lacking Comprehensive Internal Environmental and Social Safeguard Framework*

5.4.1.1 From Chinese Financial Institutions' Perspective

Despite the significant progress of the Chinese government efforts to incorporate social and environmental guidelines into its banks' procedures, Chinese financial institutions' safeguard framework are not yet par with western financial institutions.[140] State-centric green finance policies and initiatives regarding overseas sustainable lending are relatively less developed. In addition, Chinese financial institutions still lack comprehensive environmental and social safeguard frameworks. Particularly, country-specific or continent-specific green credit policies are lacking. The guidelines are usually general and vague without specific requirements on risks assessment in host countries. For the funds affiliated with banks (such as Silk Road Fund, Green Silk Road Equity Investment Fund), have not yet established a set of comprehensive and systematic environmental social risk assessment and management standards or policies.

As shown in Table 2.1, an overview of environmental and social policies of Chinese financial institutions shows that Chinese financial institutions are still in the initial stage of integrating environmental and social considerations into their lending policies. Unlike the international standards, their environmental and social governance instruments do not contain comprehensive and transparent information disclosure mechanisms or grievance mechanisms to ensure affected communities have access to channels to express their concerns and complaints. Moreover, compared to the commercial financial institutions, the policy banks have a relatively developed safeguard framework to protect local environments and social conditions in host countries.

In general, Chinese financial institutions are still lacking comprehensive internal environmental and social safeguard framework, effective external monitoring mechanism, and transparency to implement green finance initiatives. Major Chinese state-controlled financial institutions, such as CDB, China Exim Bank and People's Bank of China, do not have comprehensive and well-established environmental and social protection frameworks. Additionally, their environmental and social governance instruments do not contain comprehensive environmental and social assessment criteria. Although the Chinese government has developed a series of ostensibly regulatory measures to promote green finance, many of these administrative regulations and departmental rules are simply guidelines without enforcement power. The language of the guidelines is also broad and general, essentially taking the form of a rhetoric statement of objectives. Concrete details on how to make financial institutions achieve these objectives, such as specific assessments, follow-up measures, implementation, and enforcement details are absent. In African countries with weak governance and law enforcement, the gap between policy and practice may

[140] Mol (2017).

impede Chinese financial institutions' social responsibility and pursue sustainable development overseas.

In addition, there is generally lacking specific contents regarding the capacity building requirement and the responsibility of directors and senior managers. Many Chinese financial institutions have not established overseas environmental and social protection departments with technical experts to carry out green operations. The immature green finance policies and system development, lax adherence to domestic environmental laws, insufficient public financing information, and language barriers in communicating with affected communities, have all limited effective implementation of Chinese green finance guidelines and policies in African host countries. Due to lack of expertise concerning the evaluation of environmental and social risks, Chinese financial institutions may have difficulties in supervising enterprises' overseas environmental and social performance. Without adequate qualified personnel involved in the lending process, the credibility and quality of China Exim Bank's social and environmental risk assessment is questioned. As discussed previously, the Chinese government's personnel control over Chinese SOEs and financial institutions is an idiosyncratic monitoring system. Without specific contents regarding the responsibility of directors and senior managers, it remains another challenge for Chinese financial institutions to effectively implement green finance policy.

5.4.1.2 From African Countries' Perspective

When Chinese financial institutions invest in Africa, the institutional environment of the host country is an important variable in the effectiveness implementation of green finance and affect Chinese financial institutions' green finance and CSR initiatives. Given the regionalized characteristics of regulations and legislations, and sociocultural contextual conditions of various countries, the implementation of green finance requires cooperation with African governments, domestic financial institutions, and other relevant institutions. Green finance is implemented differently in overseas projects due to varying local conditions. A range of "unwritten" factors such as political connections, low governance capacity, weak law enforcement, and corruption also strongly affect green finance implementation.[141] However, local governments, and the corresponding incentives and subsidies are generally lacking. Most African countries along BRI route have insufficient support for green finance development, and their financial market mechanisms are not well developed. These factors have further hindered the green finance development overseas.

The governance capacity plays a crucial leading role in the development of clean energy. The government needs to coordinate the relationship between traditional domestic energy interest groups and new energy industries, as well as provide legal, institutional, and policy support for attracting investment. However, most of African countries face the issues of poor policy stability and continuity. Under the multiparty electoral system, except for a few African countries that can achieve long-term

[141] Weng and Buckley (2016).

stability of the ruling party, the rest of the countries generally face the problem of frequent changes in the executive, which brings frequent changes in the national development plan. Even at a time when African countries are beginning to develop long-term vision or medium-term action plans to ensure the continuity of development, a change in leadership will still bring about a change of governance, or even a denial of the predecessor's problem.[142]

Specifically, African countries lack effective incentive policies. Although some countries have set clean energy development goals, but most countries have failed to propose a feasible path to promote clean energy development. The Committee of African Heads of State and Government on Climate Change is only a specialized organization for climate governance in Africa, it is still a coordination mechanism among African countries, and its relevant resolutions do not have any mandatory binding force on AU member states.[143] Due to the lack of policies that are compatible with climate governance, clean energy projects that can be actually implemented are relatively limited.[144] Moreover, the profitability and sustainability of the clean energy industry depends on an efficient, orderly, and friendly electricity market. However, many African countries still lack clean energy regulatory policies and have not simplified business licensing procedures. According to the most recent African Development Bank's report, of the 43 African countries, 30 countries have low levels of regulation.[145] The lagging policy support obstacles the green development between China and Africa.

5.4.2 Lacking Transparency and Effective External Monitoring Mechanism

First, Chinese current financial institutions' environmental and social governance instruments do not contain comprehensive and transparent information disclosure mechanisms. The Chinese government and its affiliated institutions have often been criticized for their low transparency in governance and policymaking, resulting in uncertainty about the degree to which Chinese financial institutions follow its own written corporate policies in actual practice.[146] In general, Chinese financial institutions often failed to provide effective communication or sufficient information to the public regarding project selection and assessment criteria, potential negative impacts

[142] Zhang and Sun (2023b).

[143] Deng (2022).

[144] Ibid.

[145] Gatete and Dikko (2024).

[146] Take China Exit Bank as an example, for transactions with higher risk, China Exim may engage with third parties to conduct monitoring and/or site visits. For lower-risk transactions, the in-house environmental and social team usually monitors environmental and social performance and accepts documentary evidence to confirm compliance with environmental and social agreement. For more information, Ma, Jun. *Establishing China's Green Financial System* (China Financial Publication House, 2017).

on affected regions and groups, or dispute resolution. There are already some accusations that the Chinese financial institutions might hide key data concerning their credit practices, especially for the environmentally and socially controversial projects in Africa. Public information regarding Chinese financial institutions' loan amount and the distribution of borrowers are insufficient.[147]

Second, many reports issued by Chinese financial institutions were not audited by an independent third party. It is therefore difficult to determine how national policies are incorporated into lending policies and work plans. The grievance mechanism has emerged as a critical metric for evaluating CSR performance. Significant differences exist between China and the West in the structure and operation of CSR grievance mechanisms, reflecting distinct cultural, legal, and market environments. Under China's state-centric CSR approach, grievance mechanisms in Chinese companies are heavily influenced by government promotion and paternalistic oversight. Chinese companies typically address grievances through internal consultation and informal channels, prioritizing collaborative problem-solving and avoiding adversarial methods.[148] Chinese companies predominantly rely on informal negotiations to resolve CSR disputes and have limited experience collaborating with foreign NGOs. Although informal mechanisms are effective for addressing straightforward disputes, they often lack the authority and credibility needed to handle complex or serious CSR issues.

In contrast, Western companies place greater emphasis on transparency and independent third-party arbitration within their grievance mechanisms, which often incorporate formal legal procedures, independent arbitration, and mediation to resolve disputes. These mechanisms provide formal complaint channels to ensure standardized and transparent handling processes.[149] Through independent investigation and mediation, Western grievance mechanisms aim to deliver fair remedies to complainants. For instance, international financial institutions such as the World Bank and the European Investment Bank have established robust, independent grievance mechanisms. Notable examples include the Inspection Panel of the International Bank for Reconstruction and Development, the Compliance Advisor Ombudsman (CAO) of the IFC, and the EIB Complaints Mechanism (EIB-CM) of the European Investment Bank. These mechanisms enable individuals, organizations, and other stakeholders to file environmental complaints, particularly those related to climate change impacts and sustainability issues.[150] Additionally, transparency in grievance mechanisms also varies significantly between China and the West. Western financial institutions prioritize high transparency and independent third-party arbitration in their CSR grievance mechanisms, ensuring that stakeholders can fully understand and oversee corporate operations. Most multinational financial institutions often use external auditing services to monitor clients for a variety of pre-credit and post-credit activities on a regular or ad hoc basis. This transparency fosters greater

[147] Business Daily (2019); see also, Hudson (2014).

[148] Bian and Liu (2022).

[149] Owen and Kemp (2024).

[150] Bradlow (2024).

stakeholder participation and supervision of CSR practices.[151] Furthermore, the transparency of these mechanisms is bolstered by well-developed citizen complaint systems in Western countries, which have evolved over decades and are supported by mature legal frameworks and practical experience. These systems utilize complaints and mediation to protect citizens' rights by addressing grievances related to corporate decisions or actions.

While informal consultation mechanisms in China are effective for resolving simple disputes, the growing demand for formalized grievance mechanisms has prompted Chinese companies to explore more structured approaches. Despite some companies have established internal grievance platforms to receive complaints from employees and stakeholders through multiple channels, providing timely feedback on resolution outcomes, the transparency of China's grievance mechanisms still lags behind that of Western countries, particularly in terms of public oversight and NGO involvement. Many Chinese companies prefer to collaborate with government regulators rather than NGOs or public oversight bodies. While this approach can enhance the fairness and transparency of the complaint-handling process, it limits broader stakeholder engagement. The "Green Finance Guidelines for the Banking and Insurance Industry" issued by the CBIRC, encourage financial institutions to establish complaint response mechanisms for projects involving significant ESG risks. The guidelines also permit the engagement of qualified independent third parties to verify, evaluate, or audit ESG-related activities.[152] However, most Chinese financial institutions still rely on national regulatory agencies for oversight, rather than adopting fully independent mechanisms. For example, the China Development Bank currently lacks an independent grievance mechanism, and there is no dedicated channel for the public to submit environmental or climate-related complaints.[153] The Export–Import Bank of China has introduced a grievance mechanism under the "China Export–Import Bank–Asian Infrastructure Investment Bank Green Refinancing Cooperation Project", allowing affected parties to submit environmental and social complaints.[154] However, this mechanism still lacks robust stakeholder participation and transparent public engagement processes. Many Chinese financial institutions invite third party assurance only to review their annual CSR reports, but do not use verification from an independent third party for their environmental and social risk management systems.[155] The lack of third-party monitoring of Chinese financial institutions may damage the overall credibility of its ESIA process and impacts the overall transparency of the lending process.

At last, China's state-centric financial investment may aggravate the "neo-colonialism" suspicion in Africa. As discussed above, the pervasiveness of state control over Chinese financial institutions and overseas SOEs that dominate infrastructure and extractive sector projects in Africa has already raised the fear that

151 Rees and Vermijs (2008).

152 CBIRC (2022).

153 Friends of the Earth U.S. (2016).

154 The Export–Import Bank of China. http://english.eximbank.gov.cn/News/highlights/CEXIMAIIB/202302/t20230220_46940.html.

155 Ye (2013).

Chinese investments are to realize China's ambitions. It raises concerns on how China's state-centric financial institutions may be effective to protect disadvantaged local people in Africa where there is a high level of corruption as well.[156] The lack of transparency of China's state-centric green finance could further cultivate corruption and deepen the concern that Chinese foreign investment always goes to African countries with weak rule of law and high level of corruption.

5.4.3 Backward Supporting Capacity

Most African countries have low levels of economic development and insufficient technological reserves, which hinder their ability to cope with the adverse effects of climate change. Africa possesses 60% of the world's solar energy resources and other abundant renewable energy sources such as wind, geothermal, and hydropower. However, the development of clean energy remains limited. This is because African countries generally lack the technological capacity to build hydropower, wind power, and geothermal power stations, often relying on external bidding and foreign technology and experience to construct clean energy facilities.[157] This reliance poses a hidden risk to Africa's pursuit of energy self-sufficiency and sustainable development. The lack of reliable energy supply has constrained Africa's economic and social progress and impeded the use of advanced technologies to mitigate climate change impacts. As Africa is in the early stages of industrialization and urbanization, its future economic and social development will require substantial energy resources. If the current energy structure, dominated by fossil fuels, remains unchanged, it will result in a significant increase in carbon emissions, further exacerbating global climate change.[158]

Access to technology in African countries is hindered by domestic political, economic, and social conditions. While investment primarily flows into renewable energy generation in these countries, the risk of corruption and mismanagement correspondingly rises with the development of investment projects. From bidding to construction, corruption often prevents funds allocated to renewable energy technology projects from enhancing the efficiency and effectiveness of clean power programs. As a result, the people who are the ultimate beneficiaries of these renewable energy projects remain without electricity. This unmet need can accumulate public discontent, potentially leading to political unrest such as demonstrations, which further distracts African countries from effectively addressing climate change.[159] How can China prevent Africa's corruption problem from undermining the effectiveness of China-Africa technical cooperation on climate change is an issue that China needs to consider during its cooperation with Africa.

---

[156] Warf (2017). See also, UN Economic Commission for Africa (2016). See also, Bersselaar (2011).

[157] Zhang and Sun (2023a).

[158] Wang and Liu (2022).

[159] Zhao and Yating (2021).

Moreover, the incomplete development of the low-carbon technology market also poses a significant economic barrier to sustainable technological progress in African countries. Faced with a substantial funding gap, hybrid finance could serve as a dependable avenue for China-Africa technical cooperation on climate change. The Paris Agreement also designates private entities as key participants in the international carbon market. However, in Africa's low-carbon technology markets, private operators frequently encounter substantial entry barriers. In addition to unfair competition caused by corruption, the low-carbon technology market itself is fraught with numerous institutional gaps. The licensing process for private operators to enter the market is often cumbersome and difficult to obtain government support.[160] The more ambiguous the government's criteria for providing credit support and partial risk guarantees for renewable energy, the greater the risks private enterprises may face when entering the market. In the absence of clear regulations, technology developers may be coerced into accepting bribes at the local level, which directly increases the cost of market access for private Chinese investors.[161]

5.4.4 Insufficient Financial Support

The full implementation of climate governance requires substantial and sustained financial and technical support. Africa still faces a significant financial gap in implementing effective climate governance programs. According to the Emissions Gap Report 2020 published by the UNEP, there are significant financial needs for adaptation globally and the challenges faced by developing countries in meeting these needs, including Africa.[162] However, balancing financial support for mitigation and adaptation measures in African countries is challenging.

First, it is difficult for Africa to obtain adequate matching financial support. Africa has the highest proportion of less developed countries globally. According to the Emissions Gap Report 2024 published by the UNEP, the cost of adapting to climate change in developing countries could reach $140 billion to $300 billion per year by 2030 and $280 billion to $500 billion per year by 2050.[163]The cost of adaptation to climate change in developing countries is estimated to be 10–18 times greater than current public financial flows for climate adaptation, and this gap is widening.[164] According to the 2024 Climate Policy Initiative report, Africa needs approximately $250 billion annually from 2020 to 2030 to tackle climate adaptation.[165] However, in 2024, Africa received only $44 billion in climate finance.[166] This significant gap

160 Ibid.

161 Ibid., 94-95.

162 UNEP (2024).

163 Ibid.

164 UNEP (2023).

165 Tyssen (2024).

166 FSDAfrica (2024).

highlights the urgent need for increased funding to support Africa's transition to green technologies and address the impacts of climate change.

The 2010 Cancun Agreement (COP16) established that the international community should provide $100 billion in climate finance per year by 2020 to support developing countries, including Africa, in their efforts to combat climate change. This commitment was extended through 2025 by the 2015 Paris Agreement (COP21). However, the funds that were allocated were often based on the carbon emission reduction rankings of different countries, which left many African countries, with minimal carbon emissions, struggling to access the financial support from the international community. As a result, the international financial support for Africa to address climate change has been far from sufficient. Africa needs at least $33 billion a year to support climate adaptation, but only $6 billion has been delivered.[167] Given the impact of the pandemic and the Russia-Ukraine conflict on the global economy, it is highly unlikely that follow-up funding will come on time. That is the reason that, at the Sharm el-Sheikh 2022 Climate Conference (COP27), the AU once again stressed that practical financial support for Africa should be the focus of the international community.[168]

In addition, the global economic situation and geopolitical conflicts have significantly increased the debt pressure on African countries.[169] According to the World Bank, African governments were projected to spend 16.5% of their revenues on foreign debt in 2021. Of the 38 International Development Association (IDA) countries in Africa, eight were in debt distress and 14 were on the brink of debt distress.[170] A UNDP report released in 2022 indicated that of the 54 low-income countries worldwide facing debt crises, 24 countries were African, including major regional economies like Egypt and Nigeria.[171] The debt of African countries is primarily denominated in US dollars and other foreign currencies, and repeated interest rate hikes in the U.S. have significantly increased the debt repayment burden for African countries. This has left many African countries unable to provide public funding support or sovereign guarantees for large-scale clean energy projects.[172] Moreover, the rigid financing model has posed obstacles for Chinese clean energy investment in Africa. Chinese financial institutions typically use a domestic guarantee and foreign loan model for overseas clean energy projects, requiring Chinese investment enterprises to use domestic assets as collateral. This ties up a large amount of the enterprises' guarantee resources and severely restricts their subsequent financing capabilities.[173] In particular, compared to fossil fuel projects, clean energy projects require

[167] Reuters, "Keep Your Promises on Climate Finance, African Leaders Tell West". https://www.reuters.com/business/environment/keep-your-promises-climate-finance-african-leaders-tell-west-2021-11-02/.

[168] "African Union Pledges Support to Egypt in Hosting COP 27 to Reach 'Concrete Actions' on Climate Change", 2022. https://english.ahram.org.eg/NewsContent/1/1234/452016/Egypt/Foreign-Affairs/African-Union-pledges-support-to-Egypt-in-hosting-.aspx.

[169] Zhou (2023a).

[170] World Bank (2022).

[171] UN (2022).

[172] Zhang and Sun (2023a).

[173] Ibid.

higher capital investment and have longer profit recovery cycles. Most enterprises in the clean energy sector are private and find it difficult to bear the burden of such guaranteed financing. All these factors have increased the difficulty of financing clean energy projects in African countries.

5.5 Conclusion

In recent years, the relationship between foreign investment and environmental protection has garnered increasing attention. This trend is increasingly evident in China's domestic and overseas green finance development. To ensure stability and long-term financial success in overseas financing projects and to enhance its international reputation in environmental and social protection in Africa, the Chinese government is motivated to develop green finance overseas and to establish other environmental and social protection policies and guidelines to regulate and guide Chinese financial institutions. China's green finance development in Africa presents a unique opportunity to explore the state's role in monitoring and driving sustainable lending practices among Chinese financial institutions overseas. Under state guidance, Chinese state-controlled financial institutions have increasingly adopted green finance in response to the environmental and social protection needs of African host countries.

The green finance cooperation between China and Africa offers an effective pathway to achieve the SDGs, particularly in combating climate change. Under the framework of South-South cooperation, China has provided Africa with valuable experience, funding, technology, and personnel training in green development. However, the development of green finance in Africa faces constraints due to the institutional contexts and policy limitations of African countries. In addition to the challenges posed by the domestic political, economic, and social environments of African countries, there are still issues in China-Africa green finance cooperation, such as an insufficient social and environmental framework, an imperfect deployment structure, and inadequate cooperation mechanisms.

References

Agricultural Bank of China (2015) Agricultural Bank of China 2015 Corporate Social Responsibility Report. http://www.abchina.com/cn/AboutABC/CSR/CSRReport/201603/P020160407315742267844.pdf

Agricultural Bank of China (2024) 2023 Green Finance Development (Environmental Information Disclosure Report. https://www.abchina.com/cn/AboutABC/Green_finance/GF_report/202406/P020240606372812108576.pdf

Aizawa M, Chaofei Y (2010) Green credit, green stimulus, green revolution? China's mobilization of banks for environmental cleanup. J Environ Dev 19:119–120

Asian Infrastructure Investment Bank (2016) Environmental and Social Framework. https://www.aiib.org/en/policies-strategies/_download/environment-framework/20160226043633542.pdf
Asian Infrastructure Investment Bank (2024) Environmental and Social Framework. https://www.aiib.org/en/policies-strategies/_download/environment-framework/AIIB-Environmental-and-Social-Framework_ESF-June-2024.pdf
Bai Y et al (2014a) The role of China's banking sector in providing green finance. Duke Environ Law Policy Forum 24:139
Bai Y et al (2014b) The role of China's banking sector in providing green finance. Duke Environ Law Policy Forum 24:89–137
Bank of China (2015) Bank of China 2015 Social Responsibility Report. http://www.boc.cn/investor/ir5/201603/t20160330_6627628.html
Bank of China (2022) Green Finance (TCFD) Report 2022. https://pic.bankofchina.com/bocappd/cbservice/202307/P020230714793800334314.pdf
Bank of China (2024) Corporate Social Responsibility Report of Bank of China Limited for 2023 (Environmental Social Governance). https://pic.bankofchina.com/bocappd/report/202403/P020240328720914424945.pdf
Beattie A, Callan E (2006) China loans create 'New Wave of Africa Debt" (Financial Times)
Bergsager H (2013) China's state-owned enterprises as climate policy actors: the power and steel sectors. Nordic Council of Ministers, Copenhagen, pp 11–25
Bernasconi-Osterwalder N et al (eds) (2013) Chinese outward investment: an emerging policy framework. International Institute for Sustainable Development, Winnipeg
Bersselaar D (2011) No longer at ease: corruption as an institution in West Africa. Int J Public Adm 34(11):741–752
Bian Y, Liu X (2022) Corporate social responsibility with Chinese characteristics: a rivalry of Western CSR? US-China Law Rev 19:167–185
Business Daily (2019) State Become Less Transparent. https://www.businessdailyafrica.com/analysis/columnists/State-becoming-less-transparent/4259356-5178996-10o9atc/index.html
Bradlow DD (2024) Private complaints and international organizations: a comparative study of the independent inspection mechanisms in international financial institutions. Georgetown J Int Law 36:405–437
CBIRC (2022) Green finance guidelines for the banking and insurance industry. Art. 28, https://www.gov.cn/zhengce/zhengceku/2022-06/03/content_5693849.htm
CGTN (2024) 3 Years on, global development initiative continues to build consensus for cooperation. https://news.cgtn.com/news/2024-09-21/3-years-on-GDI-continues-to-build-consensus-for-cooperation-1x4P0lSVpXq/p.html
Chen Y (2018) Silk Road to the Sahel: African ambitions in China's Belt and road initiative. Johns Hopkins SAIS-CARI Policy Brief No. 23
Chin GT (2016) Asian infrastructure investment bank: governance innovation and prospects. Glob Gov 22:11
China-ASEAN Investment Cooperation Fund (2014) China-ASEAN investment cooperation fund issued environmental and social protection safeguard reference guide. http://china-asean-fund.com/sc/news-detail.php?id=20
China Banking Regulatory Commission, WWF and PWC (2013) The sustainable performance of Chinese banking and international financial institutions comparative study. http://www.wwfchina.org/content/press/publication/2015/greenfinanceen.pdf, 24
China Construction Bank (2024) 2024 Semi-annual Sustainable Finance Report. https://en.ccb.com/eng/attachDir/2024/08/2024080917045199677.pdf
China Development Bank (2024) China Development Bank 2023 Sustainability Report. https://www.cdb.com.cn/English/shzr/kcxfzbg/shzr_2023/
China Exim Bank (2007) Guidelines for environmental and social impact assessments of the China export and import bank's loan projects. (中国进出口银行贷款项目环境与社会评价指导意见). https://www.globalwitness.org/sites/default/files/library/Chinese%20guidelines%20EN.pdf

China Exim Bank (2015) China Exim Bank Guidelines for Green Loans. (中国进出口银行绿色信贷指引). http://www.eximbank.gov.cn/tm/medialist/index_26_29111.html

China Exim Bank (2022) Environmental and Social Framework of CEXIM AIIB Green On-lending Facility (中国进出口银行与亚洲基础设施投资银行绿色信贷转贷项目环境社会框架). http://www.eximbank.gov.cn/info/ztzl/lsxdzdhz/202211/P020221118389558060550.pdf

China International Development Cooperation Agency (2015) China South-South climate cooperation fund benefits developing countries. http://en.cidca.gov.cn/2015-11/30/c_262133.htm

China's Policies and Actions Addressing Climate Change (2024). https://english.mee.gov.cn/News_service/news_release/202501/P020250122370358250549.pdf

CITIC Co., Ltd (2024) 2023 Environmental, Social and Governance Report. https://www.citic.com/uploadfile/2024/0422/2024042200535.pdf

City of London (2018) City of London Corporation works with China to green the belt and road initiative. https://news.cityoflondon.gov.uk/city-of-london-corporation-works-with-china-to-green-the-belt-and-road-initiative/. The Green Investment Principles for the Belt and Road aims to ensure that environmental consciousness, climate resilience, and social inclusiveness are integrated into BRI investment projects

Clark GL, Dariusz W (2007) The geography of finance: corporate governance in the global marketplace. Oxford University Press, Oxford

Cui L et al (2014) How will the emissions trading scheme save cost for achieving China's 2020 carbon intensity reduction target? Appl Energy 136:1043–1052

Deng Y-T (2022) Addressing climate change: Africa's exploration and the significance of China-Africa cooperation. J Univ Chin Acad Soc Sci 10:117

Duyck S et al (2018) Human rights and the Paris agreement's implementation guidelines: opportunities to develop a rights-based approach. Carbon Clim Law Rev 12:191–202

Ecological Finance Research Centre of Renmin University of China (2017) Green finance for the belt and road initiative. China Financial Publication House, Beijing, pp 122–136

Engels A (2018) Understanding how China is championing climate change mitigation. Palgrave Commun 4(1)

Foster V (2009) Building bridges: China's growing role as infrastructure financier for sub-saharan Africa. World Bank, Washington

Friends of the Earth (2012) China Development Bank's Outward Investments: An Assessment of Environmental and Social Policies and Practices. http://ef.amazonia.org.br/wp-content/uploads/2012/07/china_development_bank.pdf

Friends of the Earth U.S (2016) Emerging Sustainability Frameworks China Development Bank and China Export-Import Bank. https://foe.org/wp-content/uploads/wpallimport/files/archive/emerging-sustainability-frameworks-CDB-ChinaExim.pdf

FSDAfrica (2024) Landscape of Climate Finance in Africa 2024. https://fsdafrica.org/landscape-of-climate-finance-in-africa-2024/

Gao X (2018) China's evolving image in international climate negotiation: from Copenhagen to Paris. China Q Int Strateg Stud 4(2):213–239

Gatete C, Dikko H (2024) Policy framework and regulations to promote clean energy and renewable energy transition in ECOWAS countries. Energy regulation in Africa: dynamics, challenges, and opportunities. Springer, Cham, pp 131–150

General Office of the State Council (2014) Notice of Issuing the Action Plan on Energy Development Strategy. http://www.gov.cn/zhengce/content/2014-11/19/content_9222.htm.

Gilbert S, Lihuan Z (2017) The knowns and unknowns of China's green finance. Global Commission on the Economy and Climate

Haigh M (2011) Climate policy and financial institutions. Clim Policy 11(6):1367–1385

Ho V (2013) Beyond regulation: a comparative look at state-centric corporate social responsibility and the law in China. Vanderbilt J Transnatl Law 46:408

Hu T et al (2014) Managing environmental impact: international experience and lessons in risk management for overseas investments. World Resources Institute, Washington

Hudson R (2014) Chinese investments in Africa: the ethics of transparency. https://sevenpillarsinstitute.org/chinese-investments-africa-ethics-transparency/
Industrial and Commercial Bank of China (2024) 2024 Interim Special Report on Corporate Social Responsibility and Sustainable Finance of Industrial and Commercial Bank of China Limited. https://v.icbc.com.cn/userfiles/resources/icbcltd/download/2024/esg20240926en.pdf
IRENA. Renewable Energy Market Analysis: Africa and Its Regions. https://www.irena.org/-/media/Files/IRENA/Agency/Publication/2022/Jan/IRENA_Market_Africa_2022_Summary.pdf?la=en&hash=BA5F72AAA3D5995E42D9B6C10203594E679CD7A6, 108
Kono DY, Montinola GR (2019) Foreign aid and climate change policy: what can('t) the data tell us? Polit Govern 7(2):68
Leung D, Zhao Y (2013) Environmental and social policies in overseas investments: progress and challenges for China. World Resources Institute, Washington
Li Z et al (2021) China's 30-year participation in international climate governance in retrospect. China Popul Resour Environ 31(9):202–210
Lindenberg N (2014) Definition of green finance. German Development Institute, Bonn
Lin L, Milhaupt C (2017) Bonded to the state: a network perspective on China's corporate debt market. J Financ Regul 3(10):1–39
Liu B (2021a) China's state-centric approach to corporate social responsibility overseas: a case study in Africa. Transnatl Environ Law 10(1):66
Liu B (2021b) China's state-centric approach to corporate social responsibility overseas: a case study in Africa. Transnatl Environ Law 10(1):72
Liu Y, Feng Z (2011) South-South cooperation: a new strategy for climate aid. China Econ Weekly 9:18
Liu M, Lo K (2021) Pathways to international cooperation on climate governance in China: a comparative analysis. J Chin Govern 6(3):417–434
Liu R, Wang S (2023) Evolution logic and implications of the US climate security strategy. Pac J 1:10
Ma J (2017) Green finance leads green one belt one road initiative. China Financial Publication House, Beijing
Marquis C et al (2011) Regulatory uncertainty and corporate responses to environmental protection in China. Calif Manag Rev 54(1):39
Ministry of Foreign Affairs (2022) Chair's statement of the high-level dialogue on global development. https://www.mfa.gov.cn/eng/zy/jj/GDI_140002/xw/202206/t20220624_10709812.html
Mol APJ (2017) China's policies on greening financial institutions: assessment and outlook. Routledge handbook of environmental policy in China, Routledge, pp 208–222
Munson P, Zheng R (2011) Feeding the dragon: managing Chinese resource acquisition in Africa. Seattle J Environ Law 2:373–376
New Development Bank (2016) Environmental and Social Framework. https://www.ndb.int/wp-content/uploads/2017/02/ndb-environment-social-framework-20160330.pdf
Owen JR, Kemp D (2024) Corporate responses to community grievance: voluntarism and pathologies of practice. J Bus Ethics 1:55–68
Pearson MM (2019) China and global climate change governance. In: Zeng K (ed) Handbook on the International Political Economy of China. Edward Elgar, Cheltenham, pp 411–423
Qin T, Liu B (2024) China and global climate change governance: a union of top-down governance and multistakeholder engagement. In: De La Rasilla I, Cai CY (eds) The Cambridge handbook of China and International Law. Cambridge University Press, Cambridge
Rees C, Vermijs D (2008) Mapping grievance mechanisms in the business and human rights arena. Corporate Social Responsibility Initiative Report
Richardson B (2019) Socially and environmentally responsible investment. In: Kate M (ed) Research handbook on environment and investment law. Edward Elgar, Cheltenham, pp 504–524
SAIIA (2024) China's Climate and Energy Partnerships in the Global South. https://saiia.org.za/wp-content/uploads/2024/07/SAIIA_PB_297_ChinaClimateEnergy.pdf.
Schreurs M (2017) Multi-level climate governance in China. Environ Policy Gov 27(2):163–174

Shanghai Stock Exchange (2008) Environmental information disclosure guidelines for listed companies of Shanghai Stock Exchange. http://www.sse.com.cn/lawandrules/sserules/listing/stock/c/c_20150912_3985851.shtml
Shinn D (2016) The environmental impact of China's investment in Africa. Cornell Int Law J 25:25–65
Silk Road Fund (2024) Silk Road Fund Sustainability Report. https://www.silkroadfund.com.cn/enweb/20241031/Silk%20Road%20Fund%20Sustainability%20Report.pdf
Springer C et al (2019) Low carbon growth in China: the role of emissions trading in a transitioning economy. Appl Energy 235:1118–1125
Sun T (2021) How to deliver international aid to climate change: mitigation, adaptation and mainstreaming. Low Carbon World 12
Teng F, Wang P (2021) The evolution of climate governance in China: drivers, features, and effectiveness. Environ Polit 30(1):141–161
The State Council Information Office of China (2021) China's International development cooperation in the new era. People's Publishing House, 45
The State Council Information Office of the People's Republic of China (2021) Respond to climate change: China's policies and actions. cciced.net/ccicedPhoneEN/NewsCenter/LEaDN/202111/t20211104_130073.html
The State Council of the PRC (2024) Stronger Cooperation Sought on Climate Change. https://english.www.gov.cn/news/202409/03/content_WS66d679c6c6d0868f4e8ea82b.html
The Stock Exchange of Hong Kong Ltd. (2015) Environmental, Social and Governance Reporting of the Hong Kong Stock Exchange. http://www.ngocn.net/column/2015-12-23-a3ec9ad0e79abf5b.html
Toetzke M et al (2022) Consistent and replicable estimation of bilateral climate finance. Nat Clim Chang 12:897
Trombetta MJ (2019) Securitization of climate change in China: implications for global climate governance. China Q Int Strateg Stud 5(1):97–116
Tyssen TS (2024) Unlocking Climate Finance in Africa: Breaking Down the Barriers. https://www.nrc.no/expert-deployment/2016/2024/climate-finance---accessing-the-green-climate-fund/
UN (2022) UN Development Programme Calls for Debt Relief Now for 54 Countries
UN China (2024) China contributes US$10 million to scale up South-South and Triangular Cooperation with IFAD
UN Economic Commission for Africa (2016) Measuring Corruption in Africa: The International Dimension Matters. https://repository.uneca.org/handle/10855/23012
UNDP (2014) China-Zambia South-South cooperation on renewable energy technology transfer. https://www.undp.org/china/projects/china-zambia-south-south-cooperation-renewable-energy-technology-transfer
UNDP China (2016) More money, more impact? China's climate change South–South cooperation to date and future trends. https://bit.ly/456PYCw.
UNEP (2014) Aligning the financial system with sustainable development. https://www.unep.org/resources/report/aligning-financial-system-sustainable-development-coming-financial-climate
UNEP (2016a) Green is gold. The strategy and actions of China's ecological civilization. https://reliefweb.int/sites/reliefweb.int/files/resources/greenisgold_en_20160519.pdf.
UNEP (2016b) GEO-6: Regional Assessment for Africa. https://www.unep.org/resources/assessment/geo-6-regional-assessment-africa#:~:text=The%20GEO%2D6%20regional%20assessment,well%2Dbeing%20are%20continuously%20enhanced
UNEP (2018) UN environment inquiry annual overview. https://www.unep.org/resources/un-environment-2018-annual-report
UNEP (2020) Emissions Gap Report 2020. https://www.unep.org/emissions-gap-report-2020
UNEP (2023) As Climate Impacts Accelerate, Finance Gap for Adaptation Efforts at least 50% Bigger than Thought. https://www.unep.org/news-and-stories/press-release/climate-impacts-accelerate-finance-gap-adaptation-efforts-least-50

UNEP (2024) Emissions Gap Report 2024. https://www.unep.org/resources/emissions-gap-report-2024
United National Environment Programme-Finance Initiative (UNEP 2014)
Wagemans FAJ et al (2014) The effectiveness of socially responsible investment. J Integr Environ Sci 10:235–252
Wang H, Liu Z (2022) China-Africa cooperation on climate change: implications, challenges and strategies. J Zhejiang Norm Univ 6:37–43
Wang W, Zhang Y (2022a) China-Africa green cooperation from the perspective of global ecological civilization construction. China Afr J 4:128–141
Wang W, Zhang Y (2022b) China-Africa green cooperation from the perspective of global ecological civilization construction. China Afr J 4:138
Wang W, Zhang Y (2022c) China-Africa green cooperation from the perspective of global ecological civilization construction. China Afr J 4:130–133
Wang X et al (2020) Analysis and countermeasures for South-South cooperation on climate change in the 14th five-year plan. Environ Prot 16:65
Warf B (2017) Geographies of African corruption. PSU Res Rev 1(1):20–38
Weng X, Buckley L (eds) (2016) Chinese businesses in Africa. Perspectives on corporate social responsibility and the role of Chinese government policies (IIED)
World Bank (2022) African Governments Urgently Need to Restore Macro-economic Stability and Protect the Poor in a Context of Slow Growth. https://www.worldbank.org/en/news/press-release/2022/10/04/african-governments-urgently-need-to-restore-macro-economic-stability-and-protect-the-poor-in-a-context-of-slow-growth
Ye Y et al (2013) The sustainable performance of Chinese banking and international financial institutions comparative study. China Banking Regulatory Commission, WWF and PWC
Yu H, Wang W (2022) African issues and China-Africa cooperation in the context of climate geocompetition. West Asia Afr 1:93–110
Zhang R, Sun T (2023a) China-Africa clean energy cooperation under the global development initiative. China Afr J 1:62–82
Zhang R, Sun T (2023b) China-Africa clean energy cooperation under the global development initiative. China Afr J 1:70
Zhao B, Yating Z (2021) China-Africa technical cooperation on climate change in the post-Paris era. China Afr J 3:80–97
Zhao B, Zhang Y (2021a) China-Africa technical cooperation on climate change in the post-Paris era. China Afr J 3:86
Zhao B, Zhang Y (2021b) China-Africa technical cooperation on climate change in the post-Paris era. China Afr J 3:88–91
Zhao B, Zhang Y (2021c) China-Africa technical cooperation on climate change in the post-Paris era. China Afr J 3:80–97
Zheng G et al (2016) Paris climate change conference: a fresh start of international climate governance in the new era. Chin J Urban Environ Stud 4(1)
Zhou Y (2023a) China-Africa green development cooperation under the global development initiative. China Afr J 1:46–61
Zhou Y (2023b) China-Africa green development cooperation under the global development initiative. China Afr J 1:61

Chapter 6
Policy Recommendations to Promote China's Sustainable Investment Overseas

6.1 Introduction

Chapter 2 and Chinese companies and financial institutions' sustainable investment in Chapter 3 and 4 have demonstrated that state-centric CSR has the potential of influencing Chinese investors' environmental and social behavior overseas. The Chinese government has attempted to endorse, facilitate, and mandate CSR to promote China's sustainable overseas investment. However, the current state-centric approach has many weaknesses and limitations. Therefore, this chapter offers policy recommendations to enhance the state-centric approach's effectiveness in regulating Chinese foreign investment. The recommendations address the problems reflected in the SGR case study and China's green finance cooperation with Africa, as well as the limitations of the general CSR policies analyzed in Chapter 2. The policy recommendations are as follows: improve the regulatory framework, enhance transparency, strengthen capacity building, improve international cooperation, and establish effective communication with local and international NGOs and media.

6.2 Improve the Regulatory Framework

6.2.1 Improve the Effectiveness of Broad and Vague Guidelines

As discussed in Chapter 2, the Chinese government has developed a series of laws and guidelines to regulate Chinese corporate activities overseas. The rules are often very broad and vague without implementation details. When the guidelines are broad, it is difficult for companies to know how to implement them. It is important to consider how to turn the broadly stated principles into practical measures.

B. Liu, *China's Green Investment in Africa: A State-Centric Corporate Social Responsibility Perspective*, Modern China and International Economic Law,
https://doi.org/10.1007/978-981-95-2157-9_6

First, on the corporate side, a corporate template sensitive to local needs is very helpful. Companies should convert the broad policy guidelines into detailed internal operation plans. It helps enhance the implementation of CSR policies during daily operations of Chinese companies overseas. In the case of the SGR, core elements of Chinese policies are already incorporated into CRBC's internal procedures to influence CRBC's daily operations in Kenya. CRBC made efforts to add details to the government's broad policies. For instance, CRBC formulated internal quality management measures, quality assurance plans, and administrative measures to investigate and manage environmental and social activities and to urge local subcontractors to comply with CRBC's internal environmental requirements. CRBC's experience in converting the Chinese government's related guidelines and initiatives into the CRBC's internal policies and measures could be shared with other Chinese infrastructure companies to more effectively implement Chinese guidelines in host countries in Africa. The information sharing could be facilitated by the information platform created by the Chinese embassy or local industrial associations. With CRBC's experience as a template, other Chinese companies operating in Kenya may find it easier to turn the broad policies into practice sensitive to local demands.

Second, on the governmental side, the Chinese government's agencies in host countries should make country-specific guidelines. Different host countries may pose different challenges for foreign investors. As an interviewee reported, one of the difficulties to implement the existing guidelines is that the guidelines are usually very general and vague without conducting particular conditions of host countries.[1] The country-specific guidelines help Chinese companies address investment risks specific to the host country. Chinese embassies in host countries may employ their local knowledge to promulgate country-specific guidelines. For example, in Kenya, land disputes were noted as a key business risk for Chinese companies. Chinese general policies and guidelines have not given much attention to this issue, despite the fact that it is a common problem faced by Chinese companies in Kenya and other African countries with complex land-tenure regimes. Under China's state-centric approach, specialized guidance on this topic may be provided in Chinese policy documents and through training and information-sharing platforms offered by Chinese embassies.

Furthermore, Chinese government agencies' political oversight over Chinese companies' operations in host countries is important to monitor the implementation of the guidelines. Even if the head offices of Chinese companies adopt these guidelines and principles, there is often a lack of supervision and transparency at the project implementation level in host countries. The political oversight may include administrative oversight, such as regular training and reporting mechanism compulsorily required by Chinese embassies and government affiliated economic and trade agencies in host counties. These government agencies have direct administrative control over Chinese companies operating overseas, especially Chinese SOEs; thus, they can

[1] Interview with project coordinator of Centre for Training and Integrated Research for ASAL Development.

better monitor, regulate, and facilitate Chinese companies' CSR policy implementation in host countries. In the SGR project, the development of the CRBC's internal management policies also benefits from the informal governance oversight and guidance from the Chinese embassy and the ECCO in the host country. The compulsory training and reporting mechanism, combined with the close guidance and supervision from the Chinese embassy and local ECCO office, ensures an effective monitoring role for Chinese SOEs operating in Kenya. The Chinese government's agencies in host countries should play a role in ensuring that Chinese companies comply with country-specific guidelines.

Third, local industrial associations in host countries may release CSR reports and guidelines sensitive to local business needs and open to input by local companies. Several SOEs in Kenya found the CSR report released by the KCETA useful, as it described localized experiences that could be shared and applied in Kenya. Industrial associations in host counties, such as the KCETA, are familiar with practical issues arising from business practices and in a good position to issue practical guidelines sensitive to local needs. The KCETA and the ECCO in Kenya offered an opportunity for the Chinese companies in Kenya to provide feedback on the CSR report, which further increased the usefulness of the report for Chinese companies. The KCETA's good practice of engagement with CSR advancement in Kenya could be continued by engaging with more companies in the future to promote Chinese companies' sustainable investment practice in Kenya and beyond. Such kind of partnership is also helpful to enhance the Chinese government's dialogues with other stakeholders and partnerships on CSR issues.

6.2.2 *Improve the Environmental and Social Safeguard Framework*

6.2.2.1 Improve the Protection Framework

An overview of environmental and social policies of Chinese financial institutions, as discussed in Chapter 2, shows that Chinese financial institutions are still in the initial stage of integrating environmental and social considerations into their lending policies. Major Chinese state-controlled financial institutions, such as CDB, China Exim Bank and People's Bank of China, do not have comprehensive and well-established environmental and social protection frameworks. In addition, their environmental and social governance instruments do not contain comprehensive environmental and social assessment criteria. They also do not come with adequate information disclosure mechanisms or grievance mechanisms to ensure that affected communities have access to channels to express their concerns and complaints.

Chinese financial institutions could adapt and learn from the environment and social protection frameworks of multinational financial institutions. Over the decades, multinational financial institutions have developed detailed environmental and social risk management rules for project financing as well as supervision mechanisms, such as the grievance mechanism and third-party auditors. Global sustainable investment guidelines, such as the Equator Principles, the UN Global Compact, and GRI also provide a reference for Chinese financial institutions to develop internal, project-based environmental and social risk management systems.[2]

Specifically, the World Bank has a complete operational policy for the projects it supports, which is intended to ensure the economic, financial, social, and environmental viability of its projects and activities. The World Bank Group Environmental, Health, and Safety Guidelines are "technical reference documents with general and industry-specific examples of good international industry practice".[3] The World Bank's guidelines include policies designed to prevent unintended negative impacts on third parties and the environment. It deals with natural habitats, corruption, cultural property, involuntary migration, ethnic minorities, dam safety, projects in international waterways, and projects in disputed areas in its four environmental social security requirements.[4] In terms of combating climate change and guiding sustainable investment, the World Bank Group has launched a climate change action plan to further integrate climate change elements into their lending projects.[5] As a member of the World Bank Group, the IFC developed its own sustainability framework, which has become an integral part of its approach to risk management.[6] The sustainability framework comprises the "IFC's Policy and Performance Standards on Environmental and Social Sustainability" and the "IFC's Access to Information Policy". The performance standards cover the "assessment and management of environmental and social risks and impact", "labor and working conditions", "resource efficiency and pollution control"; "community health, safety and security", "land acquisition and involuntary migration"; "biodiversity conservation", and the "sustainable management of biological resources, indigenous peoples, and cultural heritage"[7].The environmental and social management of IFC-financed projects is required to include policies, identifications of risks and impacts, management plans, organizational capabilities and qualifications, early warning and response measures, stakeholder participation, monitoring, and reviews.[8] The ADB has also developed detailed environmental and social policy framework with information disclosure, complaint, and accountability mechanisms.[9] With regard to environmental and social risk management, the ADB details its involuntary migration policy, aboriginal policy, and environmental protection policy. The ADB divides projects into four categories,

[2] The three global initiatives set out standard guidance and requirements for incorporating environmental and social-related covenants into loan documentation and for monitoring the environmental and social performance of project finance transactions throughout the life of the loan.

[3] IFC (2007).

[4] World Bank (2002).

[5] World Bank (2016a). See also, World Bank (2016b).

[6] IFC (2012a).

[7] IFC (2012b).

[8] IFC (2007).

[9] ADB (2009).

depending on the type, location, size, and impact they may have on the environment, setting different policies for each category.[10] The ADB also publicizes the social environmental impact and assessment documents of all projects or activities they fund. Both the IFC and the ADB have provided mechanisms to enable people adversely affected by financed projects can file complaints to the financial institutions.[11]

By learning from the environmental and social risk management policies of these above-mentioned multinational financial institutions, Chinese financial institutions may develop and improve their environmental and social safeguard frameworks throughout their lending process to address the potential environmental and social risks of the projects they finance. These frameworks should account for a comprehensive range of potential concerns, such as assessment and management of environmental and social risks and impact, land acquisition and involuntary migration, labor and working conditions, and climate change, etc. A social and environmental protection framework based on different project characteristics such as location, size, and impact can help Chinese financial institutions better identify potential environmental and social risks of financed projects. In addition, Chinese financial institutions may cooperate with multilateral development banks such as the World Bank and the ADB to gain better insights into how to design and implement the policies.

6.2.2.2 Refining Investor's Obligation Clauses

To better regulate investors' environmental and social behavior overseas, there is an increasing demand to establish binding obligations for investors. A constructive starting point would be refining specific obligation clauses and jointly applying binding and nonbinding obligation clauses in light of the mandatory character of binding obligations for investors and the flexibility of nonbinding obligations. Furthermore, systematically optimizing investment agreements and enhancing the coordination between international investment law and domestic law can better promote the fulfillment of climate change obligations by transnational investors.

Establishing or increasing the minimum mandatory obligations of investors and providing enforcement mechanisms for incentives or penalties can effectively fill the regulatory gap.[12] Refining investor obligation clauses is crucial to ensuring their effective implementation. In addition to the general requirement that investors comply with their host state's law, the content of climate-change-related binding investor obligation clauses should follow these improvement paths. First, optimize CSR clauses in international investment agreements. On one hand, the binding nature

---

[10] Ibid.

[11] IFC, "IFC Grievance Mechanism". https://www.ifc.org/wps/wcm/connect/4d94aa80488559ed849cd66a6515bb18/PartOne_GrievanceManagement.pdf?MOD=AJPERES. CAO Operational Guidelines. http://www.cao-ombudsman.org.

[12] Yan (2019).

of CSR standards should be strengthened. For example, Article 18(1) of the Belgium–Luxembourg Economic Union Model BIT (2019) requires investors to act in accordance with internationally accepted standards applicable to foreign investors to which the contracting parties are a party. This provision increases the possibility of transforming voluntary, nonbinding CSR standards into legally binding mandates for investors.[13] On the other hand, the scope of CSR should be expanded as much as possible, including to explicitly stipulate climate-related requirements. For example, Article 30 of the Revised Investment Agreement for the COMESA Common Investment Area contains a requirement that investors and their investments shall proceed in ways that do not conflict with the climate change mitigation and adaptation obligations of host states in pursuit of their economic objectives, and moreover, investors shall be sensitive to changes in the social and economic goals of the host states.

Second, there is a necessity to refine the climate obligation rules for investors during both the pre- and post-establishment stages. On one hand, stricter standards could be imposed on investors' pre- and post-entry environmental impact assessment obligations and environmental management system maintenance obligations, in line with Articles 14 and 18 of the Morocco–Nigeria BIT and Article 13 of the SADC BIT Model. Further, incorporate the precautionary principle into pre-establishment obligations to provide host states with more favorable solutions for addressing causation issues in climate change claims.[14] On the other hand, to support potential counterclaims by the host state, the greenhouse gas emission standards for investors should be negotiated and established based on the nationally determined contributions under the UNFCCC that the contracting parties actually undertake. Investors' corresponding obligations for emissions monitoring and reporting should be clarified, and they should be required to periodically disclose climate change information during both the pre- and post-establishment stages, with disclosures including but not limited to net-zero targets and commitments, carbon emissions profiles, portfolio risk and opportunity assessments, and climate-related financial information.[15]

To effectively implement the rules on investor obligations, it is also necessary to continuously promote the improvement of domestic laws regarding investor responsibility, driven by both external pressure from the international community and the internal needs of home states. States are increasingly expressing their significant concerns regarding sustainable development on the international stage, and sustainable development issues in investment agreements are also interacting at the international and domestic levels.[16] In the interaction between international and domestic laws, a trend has emerged where states leverage international law to achieve the objectives of domestic law in terms of protecting national interests, as evidenced by many states to incorporate investor obligations into the texts of a new generation of IIAs to regulate subjects traditionally governed by domestic law. The legal framework of climate change has the distinctive characteristics that international law precedes and

[13] Krajewski (2020).

[14] Scherer and Reichenbach (2024).

[15] The Investor Agenda (2021).

[16] Ratner (2020).

also guides the development of domestic law. At the same time, although IIAs provide a pathway for regulating investor misconduct, ensuring that investors assume social responsibility still requires a strong rule of law guarantee at the national level.[17] From the formulation of comprehensive regulations by the host state of investor obligations to the resolution of obstacles to accountability in the system of court remedies in the investor's home state, the effective implementation of investor obligation clauses in IIAs primarily depends on the improvement of domestic legal systems in both the host and home states. To address the practical challenges of investor obligation clauses under IIAs, domestic legislation should appropriately develop rules for transnational investor responsibility in the field of climate change, further fostering a basic consensus among states on attributing climate change responsibility to transnational investors and thereby reducing legal obstacles to regulating investors' climate responsibilities.

Promoting domestic regulatory measures to enforce investor responsibilities can further advance the development of investor obligations, particularly binding obligations, in the substantive rules of international investment law. While it remains to be seen whether the documents issued at the UN level regulating the activities of transnational corporations can be effectively translated into binding domestic laws or regulations, they can provide guidance for states to establish domestic legal frameworks to hold transnational investors accountable for their climate responsibilities. International policies on supply chain responsibilities are influencing legislation within individual states and at the EU level. Some states and regions have already adopted, or are in the process of adopting, regulatory documents that transform human rights due diligence principles into binding obligations.[18] For example, the EU officially published the Corporate Sustainability Due Diligence Directive in July 2024, which imposes higher due diligence requirements on EU and non-EU companies of a certain size in terms of human rights and the environment.[19] Germany also passed the Act on Corporate Due Diligence in Supply Chains in 2021, which mandates human rights and environmental due diligence obligations for large companies regarding environmental and labor rights issues within their supply chains, detailing procedures for risk prevention, remediation, and complaints.[20] The coordinated development of domestic regulations on investor behavior and investor obligation clauses in IIAs highlights the obligation of states to protect the climate, environment, and human rights through legal norms and judicial remedies, while also emphasizing the binding or nonbinding obligations of investors to respect human rights and assume CSR, thus establishing a "protect, respect, and remedy" legal framework that overcomes the international policy deadlock caused by the debate between mandatory and voluntary methods.[21]

[17] Feo (2020).

[18] Tang (2022).

[19] Official Journal of the European Union (2024).

[20] Germany Federal Ministry of Labour and Social Affairs (2021).

[21] Ruggie (2013).

6.3 Improve Transparency

6.3.1 Enhance Internal Transparency

The Chinese government and its affiliated institutions have often been criticized for their low transparency in governance and policymaking. This transparency problem can also be observed in China's state-centric approach to CSR. The Chinese government disclosed very limited information on the implementation of its CSR policies. In particular, China Exim Bank as a critical gatekeeper of CSR performance in the SGR project, did not make its assessment report on the environmental and social impact of the SGR project available to the public. China Exim Bank is not the only Chinese financial institution that fails to publish such reports.

Chinese financial institutions normally do not actively report their activities in the same way as other international financial institutions.[22] In general, Chinese financial institutions do not provide effective communication or sufficient information regarding project selection and assessment criteria, potential negative impacts on affected regions and groups, or dispute resolution. The disclosure of information on business activities and their associated environmental impact is an important step in building public confidence in sustainable infrastructure construction. For overseas loans, documents on the projects they finance should be made available to affected communities before project approval. The types of information that should be documented and disclosed include the project's name, location, and sector; environmental impact assessments; social impact assessments; indigenous peoples' plans; and resettlement action plans, etc.

For the SGR project, CRBC published China's first overseas project CSR report, which included details on the implementation of CSR practices throughout the construction process. This was an encouraging step forward. This type of CSR publication helps other stakeholders learn about CRBC's CSR performance and more effectively monitor CSR compliance throughout the project. However, the report was not audited by an independent third party. Moreover, although the CRBC did release CSR reports for the SGR project, the SOE's internal social and environmental policies are not available to the public. It is difficult to determine how national policies are incorporated into CRBC's corporate policies and work plans. There is also uncertainty about the degree to which CRBC follows its own written corporate policies in actual practice.

To ensure the transparent enforcement of Chinese overseas companies' internal policies, Chinese policymakers should require the public disclosure of such policies on corporate websites. To better strengthen environmental information disclosure, it is necessary for Chinses regulatory authorities to strengthen legislation in order to better regulate listed companies to disclose environmental and social information. Since 2003, Chinese regulatory authorities and stock exchanges have issued a series of policy documents and guidelines to force or encourage domestic enterprises

[22] China Banking Regulatory Commission, WWF and PWC (2013a).

to disclose environmental information. "The Overall Reform Plan for Ecological Civilization" in 2015 proposes to establish a mandatory environmental information disclosure mechanism for Chinese listed companies.[23] In August 2016, "Guideline on Building a Green Financial System" clearly proposes that China should establish a mandatory environmental information disclosure system for listed companies step by step. Shenzhen Stock Exchange and the Shanghai Stock Exchange have issued corresponding guidance and relevant documents on Environmental and Social Governance (ESG) Information Disclosure.[24] This lays a foundation for China to introduce mandatory ESG information disclosure requirements through legislation. China Securities Regulatory Commission requires that all Chinese listed companies shall disclose environmental information by the end of 2020.[25]

In this way, stakeholders can scrutinize overseas companies and hold them accountable for their behavior. Chinese companies should fully disclose environmental and social information through CSR reports and strengthen public participation to ensure accountability to affected communities, especially in countries where regulatory agencies are not well developed. The information should be comprehensive and concrete to reflect the economic, social, and environmental impact of overseas operations and CSR performance. The information should also fully disclose the company's CSR principles and frameworks, and the company's CSR systems, measures, and performance. Such information should be provided in Chinese, English, and the local language(s). The information may relate to a wide range of topics: the company annual CSR report, social and environmental policies, sustainable development reports, operational details and business development plans, environmental protection initiatives, job opportunities, employee policies, employee benefits, employee codes of conduct, health and safety management, or social welfare funds and projects. In countries with less access to the Internet and social media, Chinese companies should communicate through radio, brochures, and press conferences to ensure stakeholders' accessibility to the information.

6.3.2 Enhance External Monitoring

In addition to internal monitoring, external monitoring is also of great significance. While China's grievance mechanisms are gradually becoming more formalized, significant gaps remain, particularly in terms of public oversight and NGO involvement, China has yet to establish a CSR grievance mechanism comparable to those in OECD countries. In the SGR project, there was no third-party monitoring or grievance mechanism for affected people to file complaints to China Exim Bank during construction. According the project manager of the China Exim Bank, for

---

23 State Council (2015).

24 Shanghai Stock Exchange (2008).

25 "Guidance on Building Green Finance System" (关于构建绿色金融体系的指导意见). http://www.mep.gov.cn/gkml/hbb/gwy/201611/t20161124_368163.htm.

transactions with higher risk, China Exim may engage with third parties to conduct monitoring and/or site visits. For lower-risk transactions, the in-house environmental and social team usually monitors environmental and social performance and accepts documentary evidence to confirm compliance with environmental and social agreement.[26] The lack of third-party monitoring of China Exim Bank damaged the overall credibility of its ESIA process and impacts the overall transparency of the lending process.

Several monitoring mechanisms could be used to ensure the effectiveness of regulatory tools, including "monitoring by the meta-regulator, peer monitoring by the members, or third-party monitoring by an independent evaluator".[27] The establishment of cooperation mechanisms with third-party institutions has the advantage of using private standards and intermediaries as a complement to legal and policy approaches. External verification requires extensive engagement with the companies and stakeholders to verify companies' CSR performance and risk exposure.[28] Chinese financial institutions should introduce external verification to their environmental and social risk management systems. For high-risk subprojects, it should be compulsory for Chinese financial institutions to hire professional third-party auditing organizations to conduct environmental and social risks. Under the current CSR reporting regime in China, independent third-party assurance performed by a major accounting organization is already a standard practice among large companies.[29] Most multinational financial institutions often use external auditing services to monitor clients for a variety of pre-credit and post-credit activities on a regular or ad hoc basis. However, many Chinese financial institutions invite third party assurance only to review their annual CSR reports, but do not use verification from an independent third party for their environmental and social risk management systems.[30]

External monitoring should focus on four key areas: First, it should ensure that environmental and social risk management obligations are implemented in accordance with the terms of the contract. Second, it should confirm that project construction and operations comply with host countries' environmental and social standards as well as industry and loan agreements. Third, financial institutions should ensure that the project developer is in compliance with the project finance management rules by regularly submitting environmental and social risk management reports. Finally, monitors should verify that the project developer is in compliance with the designated requirement to report negative environmental and social impact in environmental and social risk management report. At Citibank, for example, environmental and social covenants are monitored either by an independent consultant or internally by the client's environmental team members. In addition, portfolio managers at Citibank

---

[26] Interview with project manager of China Exim Bank.

[27] Cafaggi (2016).

[28] Aalders and Wilthagen (1997).

[29] KPMG (2015).

[30] Ma (2017).

conduct annual credit reviews of all transactions, which ensure client compliance with environmental and social covenants.[31]

In addition to third-party auditing, Chinese financial institutions should establish grievance mechanisms to enhance external monitoring to ensure sustainable lending. A grievance mechanism is an independent oversight authority that reports directly to the president of a financial institution and ascertains the application of environmental and social protection standards. It aims to promote dispute resolution through dialogue, fact finding, or advice. It is a formal mechanism to protect individuals, employees, and communities that are adversely affected by commercial issues.[32] Any person, group, or community affected or likely to be affected is eligible to file a complaint related to any aspect of the planning, implementation, or impact of the financed project. Complaints that are filed through the grievance mechanism are continuously monitored and disclosed after project approval in order to resolve disputes or conduct compliance surveys.

Having a grievance mechanism in place has become a standard practice for international financial organizations such as the World Bank and the ADB. In the SGR project, China Exim Bank did not have a grievance mechanism for affected communities to file complaints regarding the SGR project. To better ensure sustainable lending that can benefit local communities, Chinese financial institutions should set up independent complaint and accountability mechanisms to protect local communities and residents. As an example, the IFC, a corporate arm of the World Bank, has established a grievance mechanism through which people or entities affected by Chinese-financed projects can file complaints with a compliance ombudsman. This office is an independent oversight authority that reports directly to the president of the World Bank Group. It ascertains the application of IFC standards and manages complaints through dispute resolution, compliance investigation, and consultancy.[33] The ADB has set up a separate accountability mechanism, which has two offices: a Special Projects Promotion Office (responsible for solving disputes) and a Compliance Audit Office (responsible for compliance audits).[34]

In addition to resolving issues for affected individuals, grievance mechanisms can provide financial institutions with policy advice on environmental and social behavior through environmental and social audits and reviews. An ombudsman's team conducts field visits to contested project sites and interviews a company's staff, local authorities, affected community representatives, and other relevant local organizations. Complaints reports of field missions, and recommendations are all published on the compliance ombudsman's website with updates on ongoing investigations.

[31] China Banking Regulatory Commission, WWF and PWC (2013b).

[32] ADB and IFC have set up Compliance Audit Office and Compliance Advisor/Ombudsman, responsible for compliance audits and dealing specifically with complaints with three functions of dispute resolution, compliance investigation and consultancy. Database of Complaints Mechanism Cases. http://www.eib.org/about/accountability/complaints/cases/index.htm.

[33] IFC Grievance Mechanism. https://www.ifc.org/wps/wcm/connect/4d94aa80488559ed849cd66a6515bb18/PartOne_GrievanceManagement.pdf?MOD=AJPERES.

[34] More detailed information on the specific procedure can be found in the CAO Operational Guidelines. http://www.cao-ombudsman.org.

After considering complaints, the compliance ombudsman formulates recommendations for the financial institution and company involved. In this mechanism, financial institutions are required to appoint independent personnel to oversee projects and report on social and environmental matters, and investment companies must report on social and environmental issues to financial institutions on a quarterly and annual basis. If a project's impact violates the project's safeguard policy and other relevant criteria, financial institutions can then revoke the project's funds. Continued efforts to enhance transparency, stakeholder engagement, and independent oversight will be critical to advancing China's grievance mechanisms and aligning them with international best practices.

6.4 Enhance Capacity Building

6.4.1 Enhance the Responsibility of Directors and Senior Managers

Vertical oversight within the corporate hierarchy is vital to monitor the implementation of the guidelines. In the SGR case, while the head office issued internal CSR rules, it did not exercise sufficient monitoring over how overseas subsidiaries implemented the rules. The head office should not only issue rules but also install enforcement mechanisms within the corporate group by enhancing the responsibility of directors and senior managers.

In the SGR project, managers' social and environmental performance records were linked with their career development. CRBC project managers who violate Kenyan regulations and cause negative environmental and social impact would be warned or criticized by the Chinese embassy and reported to the CCCC. In serious cases that cause major financial losses or reputational damage to Chinese SOEs, the political careers of project managers or even senior managers in the CCCC could be affected accordingly. In the meantime, affected officials would face administrative disciplinary actions including demotion, termination, or even criminal prosecution. These disciplinary sanctions imposed by the Chinese government play an important role in driving managers' behavior.

The Chinese government's personnel control over Chinese SOEs and financial institutions is an idiosyncratic monitoring system, rather than a usual supervisory system seen in modern business organizations. In the SGR case, there seemed very limited involvement by the board of directors, the central governing institution of a modern corporation. The board of directors who act as the formal authority of corporate decision-making play significant roles in bringing about organizational reform.[35] The board's commitment is crucial to the successful implementation of environmental and social risk management. A prevailing practice of CSR at the board

[35] Weaver et al. (1999).

level of Western companies is to set up a CSR special committee. The committee is in charge of reviewing and enacting the company's CSR policies. Chinese companies may borrow the Western practice to enhance internal environmental monitoring systems and to better promote Chinese companies' sustainable investment in the future.

Chinese companies and financial institutions should ensure that their board of directors or senior management continuously monitor and evaluate their company's sustainability policies, and approve sustainability policies with frequent reviews and updates.[36] They should also conduct an annual review and update of environmental and social risk management strategies and development direction. For example, the board of ICBC has authorized the President of the bank to review and approve the bank's sustainability policy annually.[37] Particularly, senior managers and directors ought to be required to conduct due diligence on the adequacy of their companies' environmental and social risks management system and the accuracy of the reported environmental and social risks data. Senior managers and directors should be responsible for the assertions and claims made in the CSR report, the integrity of information on environmental and social risks, and oversight procedures and internal CSR management systems. Transactions that pose significant environmental, social, or reputational risks should be reported to the board for review. Directors who fail to consider the impact of environmental and social risks on their business could be held personally liable for breaching the duty of due diligence they owe to their companies.

In addition, managerial compensation and promotions could be linked with social and environmental performance. More specifically, the directors and senior managers of Chinese financial institutions could be evaluated for their performance in carrying out sustainable development goals. A relevant performance indicator in this regard could be "environmental and social contribution per share".[38] Chinese companies and financial institutions could retain a certain percentage of senior management's performance-based income as a risk fund to be realized in the future based on the evaluation results.[39] These measures are designed to help management hold long-term sustainable development visions rather than focusing on short-term performance.

Indeed, some Chinese SOEs and financial institutions have already evaluated and compensated their managers partly based on CSR performance.[40] For example, Industrial Bank incorporates sustainable development performance into senior management performance evaluation and compensation.[41] Senior management of ICBC is evaluated by indicators such as "social contribution per share", to uphold social responsibility and pursue sustainable development.[42] However, CSR performance only accounts for a very small portion of the evaluation. The evaluation criteria

---

[36] Center for Policy Development (2016).

[37] China Banking Regulatory Commission, WWF and PWC (2013c).

[38] Ibid., 9.

[39] Ibid.

[40] Qi (2018).

[41] China Banking Regulatory Commission, WWF and PWC (2013d).

[42] Ibid.

are typically vague and lack operation details.[43] The CSR performance indicators should be specific and should be disclosed to the public in corporate annual reports.

6.4.2 *Enhance Chinese Financial Institutions' Assessment Capacity*

CSR practices require considerable resources input by participating institutions. As seen in Chapter 4, China Exim Bank assigned three staff members in charge of reviewing and approving the SGR project. The SGR project was only one of the many infrastructure projects handled by the limited staff. With such limited human resources, the quality of the social and environmental risk assessment was in doubt. According to a project manager of China Exim Bank, the banks' greatest challenges in carrying out internal audits were the high costs of acquiring information on environmental and social risks and the lack of qualified professional auditors.[44] With a growing number of projects waiting to be approved, China's Exim Bank's Approval and Management Department with fewer than thirty staff members is under great pressure. Without adequate qualified personnel involved in the lending process, the credibility of China Exim Bank's social and environmental risk assessment is questioned.

It is necessary to enhance the capacity of Chinese financial institutions to carry out risk identification, monitoring, and evaluation to effectively control, mitigate, and reduce overseas investment risks. A lack of professionals with backgrounds in environmental and social risk assessment limits a bank's professional capability in this area. There should be more research and training as well as more technical environmental and social management teams in order to strengthen environmental and social management capacity. In particular, Chinese financial institutions should create specialized teams for assessing environmental and social risks in their credit and lending businesses. Also, as will be discussed at greater length below, third-party monitoring is important to enhance transparency and credibility of Chinese financial institutions' green lending process. As green finance requires specialized technological and environmental knowledge, the special teams should undertake a series of training programs. For example, Hong Kong and ShangHai Banking Corporation (HSBC) offers a diverse range of environmental and social risks-related training programs, including a senior on-boarding training program, risk management program, and senior risk management program. HSBC also launched a climate business learning program designed to educate its commercial banking relationship managers on renewable energy technologies and relevant financing structures.[45]

---

[43] Interview with director of WWF-China.

[44] Interview with project manager of China Exim Bank.

[45] China Banking Regulatory Commission, WWF and PWC (2013e).

The team or department in charge of credit risk management or sustainable finance should be based either at the headquarters or in branches of financial institutions. Each branch's sustainable finance department formulates evaluations based on the information it receives from the bank's operations department. The evaluations should then be delivered to headquarters for review. This is particularly important for reviewing high-risk transactions and investments. Financial institutions should periodically undertake internal verifications to evaluate the consistency of environmental and social risk policy and analysis. Financial institutions may employ external audit services to support the development and improvement of internal controls for environmental and social analysis.[46]

6.5 Improve International Cooperation

6.5.1 Deepen Strategic Cooperation Between China and Africa

The China-Africa cooperation strategy on climate change should continue to align with multilateral climate change conventions, such as the UNFCCC, the Kyoto Protocol, and the Paris Agreement, as well as with the UN SDGs and the AU Agenda 2063. It should emphasize low-carbon and green development in the context of the BRI and provide policy guidance for China-Africa cooperation in addressing climate change. Chinese and African government departments and industry organizations should deepen policy exchanges on national frameworks related to clean energy. Both parties should develop long-term energy transformation strategies to encourage commercial investment, establish electricity market mechanisms conducive to clean energy consumption, and promote green finance policies.

Strengthening political mutual trust, strategic coordination, and experience sharing on climate governance is also crucial. China should continue to share successful practices and experiences in climate governance with Africa, enhancing alignment of ideas and concepts to secure more development benefits for both sides. China and Africa must advocate for green and low-carbon development, actively promote renewable energy sources like solar and wind, and ensure the effective implementation of the Paris Agreement. This will enhance their capacity for sustainable development. Under the FOCAC framework, the China-Africa Cooperation Committee on Climate Change can serve as a high-level coordination body for climate change cooperation. Additionally, China and Africa should leverage platforms such as the China-Africa Climate Change Cooperation Forum, side events at the United Nations Climate Change Conference, the China-Africa Think Tank

[46] Ecological Finance Research Centre of Renmin University of China (2017).

Forum, and the China-Africa Youth Roundtable Dialogue, as well as bilateral cooperation frameworks between China and the AU or African sub-regions, to build a partnership addressing climate change and promoting green investment.

To address climate change through climate aid, financing is crucial for accelerating the development of clean energy in Africa. Clean energy projects, particularly those involving photovoltaic and wind power, require additional incentives from existing financing mechanisms. China's state-led development financial institutions should continue to set higher standards for green investment by offering more green bonds, green insurance, and other financial products, and by directing more public funds toward the clean energy sector. Furthermore, exploring tripartite cooperation is essential for expanding climate aid resources. Tripartite cooperation represents an expansion and innovation of the traditional foreign aid model. Its ability to fully mobilize resources from multiple parties, create strong synergies between developed countries and emerging donors, and offer flexible forms has garnered increasing attention and participation from countries and international organizations worldwide.[47] China has already engaged in tripartite cooperation with developed countries and international institutions and can further leverage this approach to expand its climate foreign assistance resources. Strengthening cooperation among financial institutions is also significant, especially with regional financial institutions like the African Development Bank, to enhance China-Africa climate investment and financing cooperation. Additionally, learning from the experiences of multilateral financial institutions can improve project financing at the early stages of development.

6.5.2 Enhance Global Cooperation with Other Major Partners

The global green and low-carbon development trend is ubiquitous, and the global race to lead in green and low-carbon technologies has become intense. Likely, competition for international climate leadership will intensify among the major global powers; yet, climate change action represents a point of major convergence of interests and the best entry point for cooperation among countries.[48] With the rise of its economy, China has become a climate superpower on par with the EU and the United States. In the new context of climate governance aimed at achieving the goal of carbon neutrality, enhancing global cooperation with leading partners and further enhancing coordination mechanisms between levels of governance will be essential. Additionally, improving global climate change partnerships and enhancing the coordination mechanism between levels of governance actors and sectors will require a mixed approach.

Climate change is a matter of environmental policy as well as industrial policy and social policy; it is a central geopolitical issue today. It has also prompted protectionist

[47] Zuo et al. (2021).

[48] Yan (2017).

national trade policies, which has led to economic conflict during climate governance negotiations. Yet, cooperation among states under the top-down governance approach could serve as a solid basis for better relations between China, the EU, the United States and other leading partners on climate issues. Cooperative relationships on climate change between China and other countries have the potential for both positive and negative outcomes, with the nature of the relationships influencing the trends in international politics and economics.

The U.S. and the EU have continued to increase their assistance to Africa in the field of clean energy in recent years, aiming to pursue their own strategic interests in clean energy development cooperation in Africa. Under this background, China seeks to establish an inclusive cooperation framework with the international community, including Western countries. China, the U.S., and the EU may strengthen strategic dialogue on various issues such as African affairs, climate governance and energy governance, explore trilateral or multi-party cooperation paths for climate aid. China, the U.S., and the EU can also integrate each other's resources and advantages, carry out capacity-building activities for African countries under multilateral mechanisms such as the UN and the International Renewable Energy Agency, and promote clean energy infrastructure investment and planning under the framework of the AU.

In the meanwhile, China can also undertake cooperation with other developing countries under the South–South Cooperation Framework. Many developing countries still lack the capacity or resources to combat climate change effectively. As analyzed before, China recognizes that climate change is a common challenge for humanity and advocates for international cooperation to address the crisis. In practice, China has been actively collaborating with African countries and Small Island Developing States through providing technical support, technology transfer, and capacity building.[49] China has also partnered with other countries and organizations to establish the Global South–South Cooperation on Climate Change mechanism, which focusses on policy coordination, capacity building, and information sharing among developing countries.[50] Additionally, China has launched several initiatives, such as the BRI and the South–South Cooperation Fund, which aim to promote green infrastructure and low-carbon development in developing countries. The provided funding, equipment, human resources, technical support, and capacity building further promote exchange and cooperation between China and other developing countries in the fight against the climate crisis.[51]

As many developing countries, including China, have been accelerating their domestic green transition, there will be opportunities for mutual learning to ensure successful achievement of the Paris Agreement. Many developing countries can learn from China's experience in successfully adapting to the adverse effects of climate change. Developing countries have identified priority areas, such as energy efficiency, renewable energy, and education and public awareness, where China can focus on

[49] UNDP (2016).

[50] Ibid.

[51] Ibid.

capacity-building projects.[52] Education and public awareness activities, particularly, can help fill the capacity gaps in developing countries. Also, China could continue to share ecological security and climate law enforcement cases, improve international and regional climate policies and legislation, share its experience in low-carbon emissions reduction, and seek to enhance inter-agency coordination in the fight against climate change.[53] Another possible way to increase the expertise provided to developing countries and improve communication with partner governments is through the expansion of trilateral cooperation involving both bilateral cooperation agencies and intergovernmental organizations. This could be facilitated through various means, such as leveraging UN country offices and other established channels.[54]

In addition, China's broader foreign development cooperation and international trade and investment have significant impacts on the developing countries' ability to address climate change. Green investment can help countries cope with climate change impacts through improved infrastructure projects. Development banks like the AIIB and the New Development Bank's recent pledge to focus on green infrastructure can also enhance mitigation efforts.[55] Continued financial support, including climate change funds, can create innovative opportunities to further help developing countries' clean energy transition and to further promote China's green investment overseas. As China's national ETS came online in 2021, China could also introduce its experience in establishing a carbon market to support other developing countries in establishing carbon trading systems and promote global international cooperation to combat climate change. China can also cooperate with other countries in carbon trading and explore the possibility of linking China's carbon market with an international market.

The rapid development of the energy structure, economic decarbonization, and green finance have brought global climate change governance to a new developmental stage. Addressing climate change is a point of convergence for the interests of all states and a constructive entry point for promoting multilateralism and cooperation among states. When competition among major powers intensifies and global cooperation seems impossible, China should continue trying to mitigate the tension and create a more favorable international environment from within which to better fight against the climate crisis. Combating the climate change crisis requires international collaboration and solidarity. Although divergent economic and political interests in global climate governance still exist among states, states nevertheless have a common interest in international collaboration for the greater good. Further, enhancing the capacity of other developing countries by sharing and exchanging information and practice is a desirable initiative. Despite there being competition owing to the pursuit of self-interested national economic and political gains, the deepening understanding of the significance of climate change and the recognition of the common interests of

[52] UNDP China (2016).

[53] UNCTAD (2022).

[54] UNDP China (2016).

[55] Ibid.

all mankind will make global climate cooperation possible under the idea of building a Common Shared Future for the Mankind.

6.6 Build Effective Communication with Local and International NGOs and Media

Traditional global climate governance has several weaknesses, namely deficient participation, implementation, and funding from sovereign states. The regular involvement of multiple stakeholders, chiefly social organizations, corporations and financial institutions, is thus considered necessary to address the shortcomings of traditional climate governance regimes. Against this background, as an important player in global climate governance, the Chinese government must continue to adhere to its overall national plan and leverage the top-down approach to design climate policies. But, further, the Chinese government should also pay attention to the rise in participation of multiple stakeholders, especially the active involvement of Chinese companies and financial institutions, in combating climate change and incentivizing the transition to a low-carbon economy.

The combination of the top-down governance approach and the multi-stakeholder engagement approach, guided by the concepts of 'ecological civilization' and building a CSFM, will help to lead the shift of China's climate governance from a state-led climate governance system to a co-governance system with participation from multiple stakeholders. Further, increasing investment in the private sector and enhancing the status of corporations and financial institutions in the climate negotiation and rule-making process can help address the insufficiencies of traditional climate change governance. Strengthening the consultation, collaboration and sharing between non-state participants and governments is necessary to enable the global climate governance partnership network to combat climate change collectively,[56] and strengthening collaboration among the multiple stakeholders and leveraging all available collaborating entities, including the public sector, civil society and the private sector, will further help China implement climate initiatives and meet targets.

The state is only one albeit an important stakeholder in promoting CSR. Exclusive reliance on the state without significant input from other stakeholders remains ineffective to CSR development. While the Chinese government may exert tight control over domestic civil society, its administrative influence over overseas civil society is much more limited. China's political powers cannot constrain public participation and civil society's involvement in CSR in democratic host countries. Media and NGOs in foreign countries, especially democratic ones, could play significant roles in monitoring companies' behavior as external observers, representing disadvantaged voices and reflecting real and urgent needs at the local level. Without the sufficient engagement with the civil society of the host country, Chinese companies may face

[56] Dirix et al. (2013).

difficulties communicating with local communities about their true needs regarding CSR programs. As discussed previously, to better reduce potential conflicts and litigation risks, Chinese government agencies and companies in host countries should enhance their communications with local NGOs and media.

Effective partnerships with stakeholders are therefore crucial to building a healthy operational environment overseas. Chinese companies should work to foster trust, social interaction, and communication with local communities and NGOs in the host country. As discussed in Chapter 2, one of the greatest limitations of the state-centric CSR approach is its potential to weaken the balancing role of stakeholders and limit the space for civil society. In the SGR project, although liaison officers were hired to help communicate with the local community for the SGR project, CRBC's collaboration with local NGO researchers and media professionals remained very limited. The lack of effective communication with local media and NGOs in the SGR project resulted in misunderstandings between CRBC and local communities on land compensation issues. Conversely, direct and effective communication with local NGOs and media would help enhance mutual understanding and trust, reduce local resistance to operations, and gain positive public image.

Like CRBC, many Chinese companies operating overseas do not understand the importance of local media, NGOs, and communities in determining the success of their investment projects.[57] This is probably because Chinese companies do not experience active civil activities domestically as civil society and the media in China are strongly controlled by the government. However, China's political powers cannot constrain public participation and civil society's involvement in CSR in democratic host countries. When operating overseas, Chinese companies should recognize that civil society has significant influence on the operation of business. Civil society could play significant roles in monitoring companies' behavior as external observers, in representing disadvantaged voices, and in reflecting real and urgent needs at the local level. Civil society can also impose great pressure on companies to change behavior. This is evident in that in the face of social and environmental campaigns, Western companies have relied on public relations agencies and in-house public relations professionals to deflect criticism from NGOs and the media.[58] There is no reason to expect that Chinese overseas companies can escape the civil society pressure faced by Western companies.

Accustomed to their domestic political culture, many Chinese overseas companies prefer to foster good relationships with local and central governments in host countries, rather than dealing with NGOs.[59] As the program officer of China House pointed out: "Chinese companies do not want to deal with institutions other than the government, including civil organizations. It is a matter of culture and awareness".[60]

[57] Interview with project manager of Centre for Training and Integrated Research for ASAL Development.

[58] Sharam (2013).

[59] Tang and Sun (2016).

[60] Interview with program officer of China House.

Paying attention to relationships with the government while ignoring the engagement with local NGOs and media will not only make it difficult to win the support of local people, but may also pose huge political risks to investment projects, especially in less developed areas with more turbulent political environments. Ignoring or avoiding communication with non-governmental actors causes misunderstandings and complications for Chinese companies. As seen in the SGR project, CRBC complained that its voice was not heard by local communities, while local communities struggled to convey their own messages to Chinese companies. During the process of project investment and operations, it is necessary for Chinese companies to develop a platform to improve communication with local communities, labor unions, ethnic and religious groups, and local and international NGOs and media to avoid potential misunderstandings.

CSR programs should be based on the sentiments of local people and the consideration of their community's long-term development needs.[61] Local NGOs play an important mediating role between Chinese companies and local communities. Chinese overseas companies should effectively strengthen communication with the local community with the help of NGOs. These organizations can aid Chinese overseas companies in creating CSR policies sensitive to the local demands through objective and impartial monitoring and evaluation, open sharing of experiences, and adequate and practical capacity-building initiatives. Building good relationships with local media is important too as they have great influence on projecting a positive or negative image of Chinese companies to local people. Close engagement with local NGOs and media could help companies build trust and social capital. Early and active engagement with local NGOs and media could also help companies identify potential environmental conflicts and promote cooperation with host countries. In addition, taking the initiative to cooperate with local NGOs and media could help Chinese companies enhance transparency, avoid unnecessary conflicts, and gain the understanding of local residents and the international community.

As environmental governance varies in each country due to different social and cultural environments, Chinese overseas companies sometimes face complex challenges in understanding local laws and regulations in host countries. With the help of local NGOs and media, Chinese overseas companies can more easily learn about local laws, norms, and cultures. The WWF's help to Chinese companies in Gabon is a good example.[62] Chinese companies in Gabon faced many barriers including language and culture in communicating with the local communities there. Local NGOs in Gabon and the WWF helped translate local regulations into Chinese and introduced Gabon's forest management guidelines to Chinese companies. As a result, the Chinese companies, local government, and Chinese government agreed to establish the Gabon-China Sustainable Forestry Roundtable facilitated by WWF in June 2014. This collaboration helped communication between Chinese companies and local stakeholders.[63]

---

[61] Visser (2008).

[62] WWF (2016).

[63] Ibid.

In climate cooperation, enterprises, NGOs and the public could achieve better results in terms of gaining public trust, promoting cultural exchanges, and coordinating intergovernmental negotiations. China-Africa climate cooperation should further increase the participation of enterprises, NGOs and the public, expand investment by enterprises, enrich business models, stimulate market vitality, accelerate technology transfer, and give full play to the role of NGOs to actively mobilize diverse social forces to participate in climate cooperation. While strengthening China-Africa cooperation, China can also strengthen cooperation with international institutions such as the World Bank, Asian Development Bank, UNEP and other UN organizations in tackling climate change, gradually expand the participation of social funds, and guide the support for developing economies in Africa through existing international cooperation platforms.

6.7 Conclusion

This chapter offers policy recommendations to address the limitations of China's state-centric approach to CSR. Specifically, it proposes measures to enhance the effectiveness of the Chinese government's broad guidelines and its environmental and social safeguard framework, to improve information disclosure mechanisms, and to strengthen Chinese investors' capacity for internal and external monitoring. To further improve international cooperation with Africa, the chapter suggests that both parties deepen strategic cooperation and enhance global collaboration with other major partners. It also recommends that Chinese investors establish effective communication with local and international NGOs and media. These practical policy suggestions may help shape Chinese companies' CSR behavior abroad. In turn, improving the environmental and social performance of Chinese companies and financial institutions would promote sustainable overseas investment by China.

References

Aalders M, Wilthagen T (1997) Moving beyond command-and-control: reflexivity in the regulation of occupational safety and health and the environment. Law Policy 19(4):417–445

ADB (2009) The Safeguard Policy Statement. https://www.adb.org/documents/safeguard-policy-statement

Cafaggi F (2016) Transnational private regulation: regulating global private regulators. In: Cassese S (ed) Research handbook on Global Administrative Law. Edward Elgar, Cheltenham, p 220

Center for Policy Development (2016) Legal opinion: directors' duties and climate risk. http://cpd.org.au/2016/10/directorsduties/Newlegalopinionandbusinessroundtableonclimaterisksanddirectors'duties

China Banking Regulatory Commission, WWF and PWC (2013a) The sustainable performance of Chinese banking and international financial institutions comparative study. http://www.wwfchina.org/content/press/publication/2015/greenfinanceen.pdf

China Banking Regulatory Commission, WWF and PWC (2013b) The sustainable performance of chinese banking and international financial institutions comparative study, 21. http://www.wwfchina.org/content/press/publication/2015/greenfinanceen.pdf
China Banking Regulatory Commission, WWF and PWC (2013c) The sustainable performance of Chinese banking and international financial institutions comparative study. 10. http://www.wwfchina.org/content/press/publication/2015/greenfinanceen.pdf
China Banking Regulatory Commission, WWF and PWC (2013d) The sustainable performance of Chinese banking and international financial institutions comparative study. 9. http://www.wwfchina.org/content/press/publication/2015/greenfinanceen.pdf
China Banking Regulatory Commission, WWF and PWC (2013e) The sustainable performance of Chinese banking and international financial institutions comparative study. 24. http://www.wwfchina.org/content/press/publication/2015/greenfinanceen.pdf
Dirix J et al (2013) Strengthening bottom-up and top-down climate governance. Clim Policy 13(3):363–383
Ecological Finance Research Centre of Renmin University of China (2017) Green finance for the belt and road initiative. China Financial Publication House, Beijing
Feo VD (2020) Corporate social responsibility through the lens of investment law: will any solution work without the rule of law. McGill Human Rights Internships Working Paper Series 8:27
Germany Federal Ministry of Labour and Social Affairs (2021) Act on corporate due diligence in supply chains. https://www.csr-in-deutschland.de/SharedDocs/Downloads/EN/act-corporate-due-diligence-obligations-supply-chains.pdf?__blob=publicationFile. section 6.5–6.8
IFC (2007) General environmental, health, and safety guidelines. https://www.ifc.org/wps/wcm/connect/topics_ext_content/ifc_external_corporate_site/sustainability-at-ifc/publications/publications_policy_ehs-general
IFC (2012a) IFC sustainability framework. https://www.ifc.org/wps/wcm/connect/b9dacb004a73e7a8a273fff998895a12/IFC_Sustainability_+Framework.pdf?MOD=AJPERES
IFC (2012b) IFC performance standards on environmental and social sustainability. https://www.ifc.org/wps/wcm/connect/c8f524004a73daeca09afdf998895a12/IFC_Performance_Standards.pdf?MOD=AJPERES
KPMG (2015) The KPMG survey of corporate responsibility reporting 2015. https://www.kpmg.com/CN/en/IssuesAndInsights/ArticlesPublications/Documents/kpmg-survey-of-corporate-responsibility-reporting-2015-O-201511.pdf
Krajewski M (2020) A nightmare or a noble dream? Establishing investor obligations through treaty-making and treaty-application. Bus Hum Rights J 5:116
Ma J (2017) Establishing China's green financial system. China Financial Publication House, Beijing
Official Journal of the European Union (2024) Directive (EU) 2024/1760 of the European Parliament and of the Council of 13 June 2024 on corporate sustainability due diligence and amending Directive (EU) 2019/1937 and Regulation (EU) 2023/2859. https://eur-lex.europa.eu/legal-content/EN/TXT/PDF/?uri=OJ:L_202401760
Qi A (2018) Relationship between corporate manager compensation and corporate social responsibility. Front Theory 1:117–119
Ratner SR (2020) International investment law and domestic investment rules: tracing the upstream and downstream flows. J World Invest Trade 21:7–33
Ruggie JG (2013) Just business: multinational corporations and human rights. W.W. Norton & Company, pp 87–89, 120
Scherer M, Reichenbach C (2024) Climate-related counterclaims in international investment arbitration. In: Ipp A, Magnusson A (eds) Investment arbitration and climate change. Wolters Kluwer, p 124.
Shanghai Stock Exchange (2008) Guidelines for environmental information disclosure of listed companies in Shanghai stock exchange. (上海证券交易所上市公司环境信息披露指引). http://www.sse.com.cn/lawandrules/sserules/listing/stock/c/c_20150912_3985851.shtml;

"Social responsibility instructions to listed companies" (深圳证券交易所上市公司社会责任指引). http://www.szse.cn/aboutus/online/infonotice/t20151203_557713.html
Sharam B (2013) Contextualizing CSR in Asian: corporate social responsibility in asian economics and the drivers that influence its practices. http://ink.library.smu.edu.sg/cgi/viewcontent.cgi?article=1004&context=lien_reports
State Council (2015) Overall reform plan for ecological civilization. (生态文明体质改革总体方案). http://www.gov.cn/guowuyuan/2015-09/21/content_2936327.htm.
Tang X (2022) Research on the considerations and typology of mandatory human rights due diligence legislation. Chin J Hum Rights 39:43
Tang X, Sun Y (2016) Social responsibility or development responsibility-what is the environmental impact of Chinese investments in Africa: what are its drivers, and what are the possibilities for action. Cornell Int Law J 49(1):69–99
The Investor Agenda (2021) Investor Climate Action Plan (ICAPS) Ladder of Expectations. https://www.aigcc.net/wp-content/uploads/2021/11/expectations-ladder-english-1.pdf
UNCTAD (2022) South–South cooperation for climate adaptation and sustainable development. unctad.org/system/files/official-document/tcsgdsinf2022d1_en.pdf
UNDP (2016) China's climate change South–South cooperation: history and future trends. https://bit.ly/44ja0Zy
UNDP China (2016) More money, more impact? China's climate change South-South cooperation to date and future trends. https://www.undp.org/china/publications/more-money-more-impact-chinas-climate-change-south-south-cooperation-date-and-future-trends
Visser W (2008) Corporate social responsibility in developing countries. In: Crane A et al (eds) The Oxford handbook of corporate social responsibility. Oxford University Press, Oxford, pp 473–499
Weaver G et al (1999) Integrated and decoupled corporate social performance: management commitments, external pressures, and corporate ethics practices. Acad Manag J 42(5):539–552
World Bank (2002) The World Bank Policy on disclosure of information. http://siteresources.worldbank.org/OPSMANUAL/Resources/DisclosurePolicy.pdf
World Bank (2016a) World Bank Group climate change action plan. http://pubdocs.worldbank.org/en/677331460056382875/WBG-Climate-Change-Action-Plan-public-version.pdf
World Bank (2016b) World Bank Group sets new course to help countries meet urgent climate challenges. http://www.worldbank.org/en/news/feature/2016/04/07/world-bank-group-sets-new-course-to-help-countries-meet-urgent-climate-challenges.
WWF (2016) Partnership approaches beginning to Bear Fruit in Gabon's forest. http://wwf.zxzx.me/content/press/publication/2016/WWF英文版单页.pdf
Yan B (2017) Divergences and convergences between the EU and China on post-2020 global climate governance. In: Telò M et al (eds) Deepening the EU-China partnership in an unstable world. Routledge, Abingdon, pp 193–203
Yan M (2019) Corporate social responsibility versus shareholder value maximization: through the lens of hard and soft law. Northwest J Int Law Bus 40:76
Zuo J et al (2021) A new model of global cooperation on climate change: an analysis of 'tripartite cooperation on climate change. Adv Clim Chang Res 1:98

Chapter 7
Conclusion

7.1 Concluding Remarks

This book examines the benefits and limitations of China's state-centric CSR approach in promoting China's sustainable investment overseas through the qualitative and quantitative analysis of Chinese CSR policies, an empirical study of the SGR project in Kenya and China's green finance cooperation with Africa. It pays close attention to the development of China's CSR in Africa—the major investment destination of the Belt and Road Initiative. The book offers a comprehensive and critical analysis of China's green investment in Africa, including current development status, practices, challenges, and reforms. Theoretically, it analyzes the advantages and limitations of the application of China's state-centric approach to CSR in Africa. Empirically, it takes China's SOEs and financial institutions' investment as examples to examine how the state-centric CSR approach promotes China's green investment in Africa. After analyzing the challenges of green investment, the book proposes innovative and detailed proposals on reforms of China's sustainable investment framework.

The findings of this book show that the state-centric approach can have positive impact on promoting CSR. Under the state-centric approach, the Chinese government is not only a regulator but also an important stakeholder of Chinese SOEs in advancing CSR. The Chinese government can influence the behavior of Chinese SOEs and state-controlled financial institutions through the power to appoint their board members and senior managers. The Chinese government uses its various institutional connections to the SOEs and financial institutions to create a stronger awareness of policy objectives and provide incentives for policy implementation. In addition, under the state's guidance, Chinese companies and financial institutions are increasingly following global trends in adopting socially responsible business practices. Hence, state-centric CSR presents a complementary regulatory approach that can address the potential limitations of conventional CSR approaches that rely on market logic, altruism, or active civil society as motivational factors. However,

B. Liu, *China's Green Investment in Africa: A State-Centric Corporate Social Responsibility Perspective*, Modern China and International Economic Law,
https://doi.org/10.1007/978-981-95-2157-9_7

the state-centric approach does possess its own limitations. These include the lack of engagement with civil society actors, the lack of sufficient transparency and its inability to influence privately-owned Chinese companies and financial institutions outside of the Chinese state's control in host countries.

This book specifically examines how China's state-centric approach has been applied in Africa. In particular, the book uses the case study of the SGR project in Kenya to reveal the strengths and limitations of the state-centric approach in advancing Chinese companies' overseas CSR. This is done mainly through the analysis of the key actors in the implementation of the SGR project, including the Chinese government, China Exim Bank and the CRBC, the Kenyan government and local NGOs and media. It shows that the CSR commitments made in the SGR project were a result of coordination among the Chinese government and its affiliations, with very limited input from local NGOs and media.

Additionally, given that green finance has the potential to shape the CSR behavior of borrowing companies, which may in turn lead to more socially acceptable business practices, the book uses China's green finance cooperation with Africa as a case study to further examine the promise and limitations of the state-centric CSR approach. China's green finance development in Africa offers a unique opportunity to consider the potential for the state to monitor and drive sustainable lending by Chinese financial institutions overseas. Under state guidance, Chinese state-controlled financial institutions have increasingly adopted green finance in response to the environmental and social protection needs of African host countries. The book provides a comprehensive and critical analysis of the current status, practices, challenges, and reforms of China's green investment in Africa. It highlights that, in addition to the constraints posed by the domestic political, economic, and social environments of African countries, there are still challenges in China-Africa green finance cooperation, such as an insufficient social and environmental framework, an imperfect deployment structure, and inadequate financial support.

Based on the review of Chinese CSR policies, the empirical case of the SGR project and Chinese financial institutions' green finance in Africa, this book proposes policy suggestions to improve the state-centric approach. The policy recommendations include: improve the regulatory framework, enhance transparency, strengthen capacity building, improve international cooperation, and establish effective communication with local and international NGOs and media. Hopefully, the policy recommendations may improve Chinese investors' overseas CSR performance and in turn improve relations between Chinese investors and African peoples, and eventually improve environmental justice.

However, it should be noted that this book only examined the role of the state-centric SGR in one Chinese SOE engaged in infrastructure construction in Kenya. Given different governance cultures between Chinese SOEs and privately-owned companies, the state-centric approach may not be equally effective in influencing the practices of Chinese privately-owned companies that are relatively autonomous from the Chinese government. Moreover, given the varying economic and social conditions in different African countries, whether the state-centric regulatory approach is applicable to other Chinese investment projects in other African contexts requires further empirical examination.

7.2 Future Research Agenda

This book is a starting point for further research on China's state-centric approach to CSR overseas. It has laid a foundation for future empirical work to analyze the strengths and limitations of the state-centric approach in promoting Chinese sustainable overseas investment. As many internal and external factors can influence a Chinese investors' CSR behavior, including the political, economic, regulatory environment in host countries, the ownership type of Chinese investment entity, and the characteristics of the industrial sector. Future research may develop in three directions as suggested below to understand China's sustainable investment overseas.

1. Many internal and external factors can influence a Chinese investors' CSR behavior, including the political and economic environment in which the corporation operates, the existing regulatory condition, the size of investment, the ownership type of investing entity, the characteristics of the industrial sector, etc. Whether the empirical findings of the Kenyan case study are equally applicable to other Chinese companies in other African countries merits further study.
2. As infrastructure investment projects have long lifecycles, post-operation monitoring on their social and environmental impact is important and warrants future academic attention. This ongoing oversight probably plays a more significant role in protecting host countries' interests and influencing foreign investors' economic, social, and environmental practices than the entry screening of foreign investment.
3. While Chinese infrastructure investment in Africa is mainly dominated by SOEs, private companies are playing an increasingly important role through "aggressively investing and reinvesting their capital, filling critical market niches, and employing locals and conducting skills training at a higher rate than SOEs".[1] With governmental support, private Chinese investors could be an even more powerful force in Africa's development. While Chinese embassies and government commercial offices located in African countries have easy access to Chinese SOEs, they have limited resources to track environmental and social behavior of Chinese privately-owned companies. More attention should be paid to Chinese private companies and financial institutions operating overseas and how their governance structures can be improved. It remains unclear how their overseas CSR behavior is influenced by China's state-centric approach.

[1] McKinsey and Co. (2017).

Reference

McKinsey and Co. (2017) Dance of the Lions and Dragons: how are Africa and China engaging, and how will the partnership evolve? 70. https://www.mckinsey.com/global-themes/middle-east-and-africa/the-closest-look-yet-at-chinese-economic-engagement-in-africa

Appendix 1
List of Interviews

No.	Organization	Interviewee	Source of Recruitment
1	UN Environment	Official	Personal Contact
2	UN Environment	Official	Personal Contact
3	China Council for International Cooperation on Environment and Development	Staff	Personal Contact
4	National Development and Reform Commission	Official	Personal Contact
5	International Cooperation Centre of National Development and Reform Commission	Researcher	Personal Contact
6	Kenya Wildlife Service	Staff	Personal Contact
7	Ministry of Environmental Protection, China	Deputy Director	Personal Contact
8	WWF-Africa	Project Manager	Personal Contact
9	WWF-China	Director	Personal Contact
10	WWF-China	Project Manager	Personal Contact
11	Institute of International Development Cooperation at the Chinese Academy of International Trade and Economic Corporation, MOFCOM	Director	Personal Contact
12	Institute of International Development Cooperation at the Chinese Academy of International Trade and Economic Corporation, MOFCOM	Deputy Director	Personal Contact
13	China Civil Engineering Construction Corporation	Former General Counsel	Personal Contact

(continued)

B. Liu, *China's Green Investment in Africa: A State-Centric Corporate Social Responsibility Perspective*, Modern China and International Economic Law,
https://doi.org/10.1007/978-981-95-2157-9

(continued)

No.	Organization	Interviewee	Source of Recruitment
14	Chinese Embassy in Kenya	Officer	Personal Contact
15	Ministry of Environmental Protection to UN Environment	Representative	Personal Contact
16	Economic and Commercial Counselor's Office of the Chinese Government to Kenya	Counselor	Personal Contact
17	China Export–Import Bank	Project Manager	Personal Contact
18	China-Africa Excellency Foundation	Project Manager	Personal Contact
19	China House	Program Officer	Personal Contact
20	Kenya Coalition for Wildlife Conservation and Management	Staff	Personal Contact
21	The Kenya China Economic and Trade Association (KCETA)	Vice Secretary	Personal Contact
22	Centre for Training and Integrated Research for ASAL Development (CETRAD)	Project Coordinator	Personal Contact
23	African Station, China Central Television	Head	Personal Contact
24	African Station, China Daily	Head	Personal Contact
25	China Road and Bridge Company (Kenya)	Project Manager	Personal Contact
26	China Road and Bridge Company (Kenya)	Public Relations Officer	Personal Contact
27	China Road and Bridge Company (Kenya)	Engineer	Cold Email
28	China Road and Bridge Company (Kenya)	Engineer	Cold Email
29	China Road and Bridge Company (Kenya)	Liaison Officer	Cold Email
30	China Road and Bridge Company (Kenya)	Liaison Officer	Cold Email
31	Great Wall Drilling Company of China National Petroleum Corporation	Project Manager	Personal Contact
32	China Wu Yi Co., Ltd. (Kenya Branch)	Project Manager	Personal Contact
33	SinoHydro Corporation Limited (Kenya)	Project Manager	Personal Contact
34	Power China (Kenya)	Project Manager	Personal Contact
35	China Gezhouba Group Company Limited (Kenya)	Project Manager	Personal Contact

(continued)

(continued)

No.	Organization	Interviewee	Source of Recruitment
36	Kajiado County Government	Officer	Cold Email
37	Kajiado County Government	Officer	Cold Email
38	Mombasa County Government	Officer	Cold Email
39	Mombasa County Government	Officer	Cold Email

Appendix 2
Interview Guideline for Chinese Infrastructure SOEs in Kenya

Perception of Chinese companies' environmental risk during foreign investment

1. What is the status of your company's investment in Kenya? What is the impact of "Going Out" policy on your company's investment in Kenya? What is Africa's strategic significance and impact with regard to Chinese foreign investment?
2. What is the environmental performance of Chinese companies like in Kenya?
   2.1 Are there any existing environmental risks?
   2.2 How do you respond to the existing criticism on the environmental performance of Chinese companies and their exportation of bad behavior? (Neocolonialism, corruption, environmental pollution, human rights violations, etc.)
3. What are the differences between your company's current and previous environmental performance? If the change is positive, what has improved? What are the reasons for this improvement?
4. How do environmental, economic, and social risks interact with one another during foreign investments?
5. Why and how do Chinese companies need to pay attention to environmental risks when making foreign investments? What kind of environmental and social protection measures has your company taken to reduce environmental risks?

Perception of corporate social responsibility

1. What is your perception of corporate social responsibility (CSR)?
2. Are there any CSR programs in your company?
   Are there any reasons behind the establishment of this CSR program? How have the programs gained attention from corporate management?
3. What specific measures do your company's CSR programs include?
   What is your perception of western criticism regarding window dressing of Chinese companies' CSR programs in Kenya?

B. Liu, *China's Green Investment in Africa: A State-Centric Corporate Social Responsibility Perspective*, Modern China and International Economic Law,
https://doi.org/10.1007/978-981-95-2157-9

4. What functional and operational adjustments has your company made to reflect CSR in its environmental and social behavior?
5. What are the strategies your company uses to implement CSR standards effectively?

   (How you communicate with local people, how you communicate and cooperate with external agencies, how you comply with international environmental standards)
6. How does the scale of a company affect its CSR programs?

   (Central SOEs versus provincial SOEs; large-scale SOEs versus small and medium private companies)
7. What are the similarities and differences between the environmental policies of Chinese companies and those of the headquarters and branch offices?

Factors impacting Chinese companies' environmental performance in Kenya

1. What regulatory tools and factors influence the environmental behaviors of Chinese companies?
2. What are the implications of Chinese domestic environmental policy for foreign investment overseas and environmental protection?

   2.1 The Chinese government has adopted a number of policies. However, most of them provide guidance without being legally binding. What is the impact of these guidelines and regulations on Chinese companies' environmental performance in Africa?

   2.2 In addition to traditional legal mechanisms, which financial institutions influence Chinese companies' environmental and social behaviors?

Companies' perception of infrastructure projects' impact on local communities

1. What do you think your companies' infrastructure projects' impact on the environment and social interests (like forest, pasture, farmland, livelihood, transportation) of local communities is?
2. Do you think construction will affect the local community's land or make them the community move from its current land? Who will be responsible for the compensation?
3. Does the affected community know the construction project and the impact of your company? Are there any meetings or discussions being held with local communities about the possible impact of the construction?
4. Has your company tried to consult with local environmental organizations about the construction plan?
5. What are Chinese companies' current and potential contributions to African environmental governance?

Appendix 3
Interview Guideline for Government Officials

The status of China's investment in Kenya

1. What is the status of Chinese companies' investment in Africa? What is the impact of the going abroad policy on Chinese companies in Kenya?
2. What is your response to existing criticism on Chinese companies' exportation of bad behavior? (corruption, environmental pollution, human rights violation, etc.)

Perception of Chinese companies' environmental risk during foreign investment

1. What is the environmental performance of Chinese companies like in Africa? Are there any existing environmental risks?
2. What are the differences between Chinese companies' current and previous environmental performance? If the change is positive, what has improved? What are the reasons behind this change?
3. How do environmental risk, economic risk and social risk interact during foreign investment?
4. Why and how do Chinese companies need to pay attention to environmental risk when making foreign investments? What kind of environmental protection measures have Chinese companies taken to reduce environmental risk?
5. Are there any differences in the environmental standards between SOEs and private companies?

Factors influencing Chinese companies' environmental performance in Africa

1. What regulatory tools and factors influence the environmental behaviors of Chinese companies?
2. What are the implications of Chinese domestic environmental policy for foreign investment overseas and environmental protection?

   2.1 The Chinese government has adopted a number of policies. However, most of them provide guidance without being legally binding. What is the impact

B. Liu, *China's Green Investment in Africa: A State-Centric Corporate Social Responsibility Perspective*, Modern China and International Economic Law,
https://doi.org/10.1007/978-981-95-2157-9

of these guidelines and regulations on Chinese companies' environmental performance in Africa?

2.2 In addition to traditional legal mechanisms, which financial institutions influence Chinese companies' environmental and social behaviors?

3. What can the Chinese government do to better regulate Chinese SOEs' environmental and social behavior in Kenya? Are there any models from other countries?

Appendix 4
Interview Guideline for China Exim Bank

Sustainable lending policies and practices of China Exim Bank

1. What type of capacity-building activities does China Exim Bank undertake with regards to Environmental and social risk management
2. What is China Exim Bank's approach to managing environmental and social risk in its lending activities?
3. Has the bank committed to any other sustainable finance initiatives?
4. Please describe the bank's sustainability policies for managing environmental and social risks?
5. Does China Exim Bank publicly disclose its sustainability policies?
6. Who has ultimate oversight of sustainability issues within the bank?
7. Who is responsible for approving the bank's sustainability policies, and how often are these reviewed and updated?
8. Are the ratings and remuneration of directors/senior management linked to performance with regards to sustainability? If so, how?
9. Does the bank have a dedicated team, or teams, responsible for assessing potential environmental and social risk of lending activities? If yes, how many employees work in this team?
10. When environmental and social risks have been identified, what risk mitigation measures does the bank apply?
11. Does China Exim Banks' internal audit team review the bank's environmental and social risk management performance?
12. Does China Exim Bank obtain external assurance on the environmental and social risk management performance? If so, are the results of the assurance disclosed publicly? If not, why not? Are there currently any plans to develop external assurance in future?

B. Liu, *China's Green Investment in Africa: A State-Centric Corporate Social Responsibility Perspective*, Modern China and International Economic Law,
https://doi.org/10.1007/978-981-95-2157-9

Appendix 5
Interview Guideline for Staff Members of Environmental NGOs and UN Environment

Perception of Chinese companies' environment risk during foreign investment

1. Outlook on China's investment in Africa: What is the status of Chinese investment in Africa?
2. What is the environmental performance of Chinese companies like in Kenya and in other countries? How do you respond to existing criticism on the environment situation of Chinese companies in Africa? (Neocolonialism, lack of environmental impact assessment and implementation, etc.)
3. What are the differences between Chinese companies' environmental conservation practices in Africa compared to other countries?
4. What was Chinese companies' current and previous environmental performance like? If there have been positive changes, what are the improvements? What are the reasons behind these improvements?
5. How do environmental, economic, and social risks interact?

Your organization's role in regulating companies' environmental performance

1. Have the environmental risks during foreign investment begun to receive your organization's attention? Why and how does your organization need to pay attention to environmental risk during foreign investments?
2. What is the role of your organization in improving the environmental performance of Chinese companies?

    2.1 What kinds of environmental protection measures has your organization taken to reduce environmental risks?
    2.2 Are there any successful cases?
    2.3 How does your organization interact with other local environmental NGOs and communities?

B. Liu, *China's Green Investment in Africa: A State-Centric Corporate Social Responsibility Perspective*, Modern China and International Economic Law,
https://doi.org/10.1007/978-981-95-2157-9

3. Are there legal difficulties in regulating multinationals' environmental performance effectively in Africa? Which regulatory tool most affects companies' environmental performance?
4. What efforts has your organization made to regulate companies' environmental performance? What's the future contribution of your organization in this regard?
5. What further efforts has your organization made to improve Chinese companies' environmental performance overseas and prevent environmental risks in the future?

Appendix 6
Policies, Plans and Strategies Involved in Environmental and Social Impact Assessments for the Project

National Environmental Policies	1. The Constitution of Kenya (2010) 2. Environment Policy (2013) 3. Environmental Management and Coordination (Impact assessment and audit) Regulations (2003) 4. Wildlife (Conservation and Management) Act Cap 376 of 1976, 1989 and Bill, 2013 5. National Land Policy (2009) 6. Environment Management and Coordination (Noise and excessive vibration Pollution Control) Regulations, 2009 7. National Water Policy (2012 Draft) 8. The Prevention, Protection and Assistance to Internally Displaced Persons and Affected Communities Act (2012) 9. National Policy for the Sustainable Development of Arid and Semi-Arid Lands of Kenya (2012) 10. Draft National Policy on wetlands Conservation and Management (2013)
National Environmental Plans and Strategies	1. "Vision 2030"-Second Medium Term Plan (2013–2017) 2. National Environment Action Plan (2009–2013) 3. National Biodiversity Strategy and Action Plans (2000) 4. National Climate Change Response Strategy (2010) 5. National Climate Change Action Plan (2013)

(continued)

B. Liu, *China's Green Investment in Africa: A State-Centric Corporate Social Responsibility Perspective*, Modern China and International Economic Law,
https://doi.org/10.1007/978-981-95-2157-9

(continued)

Affected Communities' Plans and Strategies	1. Nairobi County Integrated Development Plan (2013–2017) 2. Mombasa County Integrated Development Plan (2013–2017) 3. Kajiado Integrated Development Plan (2013–2017) 4. Narok County Integrated Development Plan (2013–2017)

Author's Compilation

Appendix 7
Kenya China Economic and Trade Association Members

The list is extracted from 2017 Chinese Overseas Companies in Kenya Social Responsibility Report (As of May 31, 2017)

1. Ever-do International Logistics Supply Chain Co., Ltd.
2. Bank of China, Nairobi Representative Office
3. China Railway Construction Corporation International Limited (EastAfrica)
4. China Road and Bridge Corporation (Kenya)
5. China Wu Yi Co., Ltd. (Kenya Branch)
6. China Sichuan International Cooperation Co., Ltd. (Kenya Office)
7. ZTE Kenya Limited
8. CNPC Great Wall Drilling Company
9. Sinopec Shengli Engineering & Construction Co., Ltd.
10. China Jiang Xi International Kenya Limited
11. Stanbic Bank (Kenya)
12. Sinopec International Petroleum Service Corporation
13. Zhongmei Engineering Group Ltd.
14. Guangxi Hydroelectric Construction Bureau Kenya Limited
15. Kenya Office, China Railway Seventh Group Co., Ltd.
16. China North Industries Corp. (NORINCO Kenya)
17. China Overseas Engineering Group Co., Ltd. (East Africa)
18. China Petroleum Pipeline Bureau (CPP) Limited
19. GCL New Energy Kenya Limited
20. AVIC International Holding Corporation
21. Nanchang Foreign Engineering Company (Kenya) Limited
22. Sichuan Huashi Overseas companies
23. Corporation East Africa (E.A) Limited
24. AHCOF Investments (Kenya) Company Limited
25. Huawei Technologies Kenya Co., Ltd.
26. Weihai Construction Group Co., Ltd. (Kenya)

B. Liu, *China's Green Investment in Africa: A State-Centric Corporate Social Responsibility Perspective*, Modern China and International Economic Law,
https://doi.org/10.1007/978-981-95-2157-9

27. BETT Company (K) Ltd.
28. Hunan Road & Bridge Construction Group Corporation Ltd.
29. China CAMC Engineering Co., Ltd.
30. China Electric Co., Ltd.
31. China Railway No.5 Engineering Group Co., Ltd.
32. SANY Heavy Industry Co., (Kenya) Ltd.
33. China Railway No.10 Engineering Group Co., Ltd.
34. China Jiangsu International Economic and Technical Cooperation Corp. East Africa Branch
35. Jiangxi Water and Hydropower Construction Co., Ltd.
36. Zhonghao Overseas Construction Engineering Co., Ltd.
37. China State Construction Engineering Corporation Kenya Limited
38. The Third Engineering Bureau of China City Construction Group Co., Ltd.
39. SINOTEC Co., Ltd. (Kenya)
40. China Zhongxing Construction Co., Ltd.
41. Weihai International Economic & Technical Cooperative Co., Ltd.
42. China Henan International Cooperation Group Co., Ltd. (Kenya)
43. China International Water & Electric Corp.
44. Fushun Construction Corporation
45. China Communications Services Corporation Limited (Kenya)
46. China Electric Power Equipment and Technology Co., Ltd. (Kenya)
47. China Dalian Economic & Technical Cooperation Group Co., Ltd. (Kenya)
48. Goldsail Asia Africa Logistics Ltd.
49. Jiangsu Entern Co., Ltd.
50. Sinotruck Machinery and Equipment Co., Ltd. (Kenya)
51. Shanxi Dikuang Overseas Engineering Construction (Kenya) Limited
52. China Railway 21st Bureau Group (Kenya) Co., Ltd.
53. Chongqing International Construction Corporation (CICO)
54. CRJE (East Africa) Ltd.
55. China Telecom (Kenya) Ltd.
56. Foton Motor Kenya Ltd.
57. StarTimes Media (Kenya) Company Limited
58. China Machinery Engineering Corporation
59. CGCOG Group Co., Ltd.
60. NARI Group Corporation
61. Jiangxi Transportation Engineering Group Corporation Kenya Ltd.
62. Danafu Co., Ltd. (Kenya)
63. Greenroad Kenya Ltd.
64. TBEA International Kenya Limited
65. Afasia Express Kenya Ltd.
66. China Gezhouba Group Company Limited (Kenya)
67. China Southern Airlines Co., Ltd. Nairobi Office
68. HouseMart (Sunda International) Co., Ltd.
69. China Civil Engineering Construction Corporation (Kenya) Limited
70. Songying Industrial Company

71. Jiangxi Youse Construction (Group) Co., Ltd.
72. Central Southern China Electric Power Design Institute Co., Ltd. (Kenya)
73. Yocean Group
74. SinoHydro Corporation Limited
75. China Jiang Xi International Kenya Limited

Glossary

China Banking and Insurance Regulatory Commission A Chinese government body that is responsible for formulating supervisory rules and regulations governing banking institutions and for administering the supervisory boards of the major state- owned banking institutions.[1]

Chinese Policy Banks This term refers to three banks in China: Agricultural Bank of China (ABC), China Development Bank (CDB), and the Export-Import Bank of China (China Exim Bank). China's policy banks are charged with policy lending in areas such as infrastructure projects, and with promoting foreign trade and diplomacy. These banks participate in a variety of foreign economic activities, including lending to Chinese SOEs to finance projects abroad and lending directly to foreign governments or projects.[2]

Chinese State-Owned Enterprises Public overseas companies that are majority-owned by the government are called SOEs. Different levels of government may own SOEs. There are central-government-owned SOEs and provincial-government-owned SOEs.[3] The type of SOEs discussed in this book is central-government-owned SOEs.

Development Project A project intended to increase a developing country's ability to produce in the future. Such projects are most commonly additions to the country's capital stock, but they may involve improvements in infrastructure, educational facilities, discovery, or development of natural resources, and so on.[4]

---

[1] CBIRC, online: < https://www.nfra.gov.cn/en/view/pages/ > .

[2] ABC, online: < http://www.abchina.com/en/ > . China Development Bank, online: < http://www.cdb.com.cn/English/ > . China Exim Bank, online: < http://english.eximbank.gov.cn/en/ > .

[3] Lin, Liwen and Milhaupt, J. Curtis (2013). "We Are the (National) Champions: Understanding the Mechanisms of State Capitalism in China" 65 *Stanford Law Review* 697–759.

[4] Leung, Denise and Zhao, Yingzhen. *Environmental and Social Policies in Overseas Investments: Progress and Challenges for China* (World Resources Institute, 2013), online: < http://www.wri.org/publication/environmental-and-social-policies-overseas-investments > .

B. Liu, *China's Green Investment in Africa: A State-Centric Corporate Social Responsibility Perspective*, Modern China and International Economic Law,
https://doi.org/10.1007/978-981-95-2157-9

Foreign Direct Investment An investment involving a long-term relationship and reflecting a lasting interest and control by a resident entity in one economy (foreign direct investor or parent enterprise) in an enterprise resident in an economy other than that of the foreign direct investor (FDI enterprise or affiliate enterprise or foreign affiliate)[5]

Investment Risk Investment risk can be defined as the probability or likelihood of occurrence of losses relative to the expected return on any particular investment. The risk of companies' operation is influenced by internal and external environment, with the characteristics of complexity and changeability.[6]

Ministry of Commerce A Chinese government body that is responsible for administering China's foreign trade, economic cooperation, and foreign investment.[7]

Ministry of Ecology and Environment A Chinese government body that is responsible for developing and implementing national policies, laws, and regulations for environmental protection.[8]

National Development and Reform Commission A Chinese government body that is responsible for formulating and implementing national economic and social development and for analyzing domestic and international economics, including overseas investments.

State-owned Assets Supervision and Administration Commission A Chinese government body that is responsible for managing SOEs, appointing top officials, creating laws governing SOEs, and guiding the reform and restructuring of SOEs.[9]

Transnational Companies Economic agents generally led by a parent company that does business in its home country and operates in other countries through subsidiaries or subcontractors.[10]

---

[5] UNCTAD(2017), "UNCTAD Methodological Note", online: < http://unctad.org/en/PublicationChapters/wir2017chMethodNote_en.pdf > .

[6] The Economic Times, "Definition of 'Investment Risk'", online: < https://economictimes.indiatimes.com/definition/investment-risk > .

[7] MOFCOM, online: < http://english.mofcom.gov.c > .

[8] MEE, online: < http://english.mep.gov.cn > .

[9] SASAC, online: < http://en.sasac.gov.cn > .

[10] UNCTAD (2017), "UNCTAD Methodological Note", online: < http://unctad.org/en/PublicationChapters/wir2017chMethodNote_en.pdf > .

Bibliography

Aizawa M, Yang C (2010) Green credit, green stimulus, green revolution? China's mobilization of banks for environmental cleanup. J Environ Dev 19:119–20
Alogna I et al (2021) Climate change litigation: comparative and international perspectives, British Institute of international and perspectives. Br Inst Int Comp Law 2
Asian Development Bank (2009) The safeguard policy statement. https://www.adb.org/documents/safeguard-policy-statement
Adeyeye A (2011) Universal standards in CSR: are we prepared? Corp Govern 11(1):107–119
Adolph C et al (2017) The Shanghai effect: do exports to China affect labor practices in Africa? World Dev 89:1–18
African Development Bank Group (2014) AfDB announces US$2 billion fund with China. https://www.afdb.org/en/news-and-events/afdb-announces-us-2-billion-fund-with-china-13165/
African Development Bank Group. Climate Change Action Plan (2011–2015). https://www.afdb.org/fileadmin/uploads/afdb/Documents/Policy-Documents/Climate%20Change%20Action%20Plan%20%28CCAP%29%202011-2015.pdf
Agricultural Bank of China (2024) 2023 Green finance development (Environmental information disclosure report). https://www.abchina.com/cn/AboutABC/Green_finance/GF_report/202406/P020240606372812108576.pdf
Agricultural Bank of China (2015) Agricultural Bank of China 2015 corporate social responsibility report. http://www.abchina.com/cn/AboutABC/CSR/CSRReport/201603/P020160407315742267844.pdf
Aklilu N (2014) Greening Africa-China relations: African agents punching below their weight?. J China Int Relat 2
Albareda L et al (2008) The changing role of governments in corporate social responsibility: drivers and responses. Bus Ethics 17:347–363
Alden C (2007) China in Africa: partner, competitor or hegemon? Zed Books, London
Alden C (2009) China and Africa's natural resources: the challenges and implications for development and governance. SAIIA Occasional Paper No. 41. http://www.voltairenet.org/IMG/pdf/China_and_Africa_s_Natural_Resources.pdf
Alden C, Hughes C (2009) Harmony and discord in China's Africa strategy: some implications for foreign policy. China Q 563–584
Al-Aameri N et al (2012) Environmental impact of China's outward foreign direct investment. https://oaktrust.library.tamu.edu/bitstream/handle/1969.1/152080/Final%20Bush%20School%20Report_2012.pdf?sequence=1

B. Liu, *China's Green Investment in Africa: A State-Centric Corporate Social Responsibility Perspective*, Modern China and International Economic Law,
https://doi.org/10.1007/978-981-95-2157-9

AmeWiig I (2011) Better the devil you Know? Chinese foreign direct investment in Africa. J Afr Bus 12(1):31–50

Andiva YM (2015) The impact of Chinese led infrastructure development on Sino-African relations: the case of Kenya. http://erepository.uonbi.ac.ke:8080/xmlui/handle/11295/102651

Anghie A (2005) Imperialism, sovereignty and the making of International Law. Cambridge University Press, Cambridge

Arewa O (2016) Constructing Africa: Chinese investment, infrastructure deficits, and development. Cornell Int Law J 49:101–139

Arsene Codrin (2014) Chinese employers and their Ugandan workers: tensions, frictions and cooperation in an African city. J Curr Chin Aff 43(1):139–176

Asian Infrastructure Investment Bank (2016) Environmental and social framework. https://www.aiib.org/en/policies-strategies/_download/environment-framework/20160226043633542.pdf

Bai Y et al (2014) The role of China's banking sector in providing green finance. Duke Environ Law Policy Forum 24:89–137

Baah A, Jauch H (eds) (2009) Chinese investment in Africa: a labour perspective. Africa Labour Research Network. https://www.fnv.nl/site/over-de-fnv/internationaal/mondiaal-fnv/documenten/english/publications/Chinese_investments_in_Africa_final_report1.pdf

Bank of China (2024) Corporate Social Responsibility Report of Bank of China Limited for 2023. Environmental Social Governance. https://pic.bankofchina.com/bocappd/report/202403/P020240328720914424945.pdf

Bank of China (2024) Bank of China: the financial bridge for China-Africa economic and trade cooperation. https://www.bankofchina.com/aboutboc/bi1/202409/t20240904_25147682.html

Bank of China (2022). "Green Finance (TCFD) Report 2022", online:<https://pic.bankofchina.com/bocappd/cbservice/202307/P020230714793800334314.pdf>.

Bank of China (2015) Bank of China 2015 social responsibility report. http://www.boc.cn/investor/ir5/201603/t20160330_6627628.html

Banerjee SB (2008) Corporate social responsibility: the good, the bad and the ugly. Crit Sociol 34(1):51–79

Bavier J (2018) China overloading poor nations with debt though infrastructure projects. Reuters. https://news.abs-cbn.com/focus/07/16/18/china-overloading-poor-nations-with-debt-though-infra-projects

Bernasconi-Osterwalder N et al (eds) (2013) Chinese outward investment: an emerging policy framework. International Institute for Sustainable Development, Winnipeg

Bergsager H (2013) China's state-owned enterprises as climate policy actors: the power and steel sectors. Nordic Council of Ministers, Copenhagen, pp 11–25

Beattie A, Callan E (2006) China loans create 'New Wave of Africa Debt. Financial Times. https://www.ft.com/content/640a5986-863a-11db-86d5-0000779e2340

Benner T et al (2004) Multi-sectoral networks in global governance: towards a pluralist system of accountability. Govern Oppos 39(2):191–210

Bernasconi-Osterwalder N et al (eds) (2013) Chinese outward investment an emerging policy framework. International Institute for Sustainable Development, Winnipeg

Bersselaar D (2011) No longer at ease: corruption as an institution in West Africa. Int J Public Adm 34(11):741–752

Besada H, Sewankambo N (2009) Climate change in Africa: adaptation, mitigation and governance challenges. The Center for International Governance Innovation Special Report. https://www.unicef.org/esaro/Climate_Change_in_Africa.pdf. Accessed on 8 Aug 2018

Beyer A et al (2014) Study on how investment horizon and expectations of shareholder base impact corporate decision-making. National Investor Relations Institute and The Rock Center for Corporate Governance. https://www.gsb.stanford.edu/sites/default/files/2014_Investment-Horizon-Final_0.pdf

Biukovic L, Potter P (2014) Local engagement with international economic law and human rights. University of British Columbia Press, Vancouver

Bian Y, Liu X (2022) Corporate social responsibility with Chinese characteristics: a rivalry of Western CSR? US-China Law Rev 19:167–185

Blacconiere W, Pattenb D (1994) Environmental disclosures, regulatory costs, and changes in firm value. J Acc Econ 18(3):357–377

Bloomberg Brief (2015) One belt, one road assessing the economic impact of China's new silk road. https://issuu.com/davidhallusbct/docs/assessing_the_economic_impact_of_ch

Blue Book of Outbound Investment and Risks (2017) Annual report on China's outbound direct investment and host country risk. Social Science Academic Press China, Beijing

Bosshard P (2008) China's environmental footprint in Africa. China in Africa Policy Briefing. https://www.internationalrivers.org/sites/default/files/attached-files/saiia_policy_briefing_508.pdf

Bourdieu P (1987) The force of law: toward a sociology of the juridical field. Hastings Law J 38:805–853

Bradlow DD (2004) Private complaints and international organizations: a comparative study of the independent inspection mechanisms in international financial institutions. Georgetown J Int Law 36:405–437

Brautigam D (2018) U.S. politicians get China in Africa all wrong. The Washington Post. https://www.washingtonpost.com/news/theworldpost/wp/2018/04/12/china-africa/?noredirect=on&utm_term=.1c64caa6983b

Brautigam D et al (2010) China's investment in African special economic zones: prospects, challenges, and opportunities. World Bank. http://siteresources.worldbank.org/INTPREMNET/Resources/EP5.pdf

Brautigam D (2009) The dragon's gift: the real story of China in Africa. Oxford University Press, London

Brautigam D, Gallagher K (2014) Bartering globalization: China's commodity- backed finance in Africa and Latin America. Glob Policy 5(3):346–352

Brautigam D, Hwang J (2016) Eastern promises: new data on Chinese loans in Africa, 2000–2014. China-Africa Research Initiative Working Paper No. 4. https://static1.squarespace.com/static/5652847de4b033f56d2bdc29/t/58ac91ede6f2e1f64a20d11a/1487704559189/eastern+promises+v4.pdf

Broyles P (1998) The impact of shareholder activism on corporate involvement in South Africa during the reagan era. Int Rev Mod Sociol 28(1):1–19

Burke C (2007) China's entry into construction industries in Africa: Tanzania and Zambia as case studies. China Report. http://journals.sagepub.com; https://doi.org/10.1177/000944550704300304

Butler T (2005) Growing pains and growing alliances: China, timber and Africa. Afr Renaissance 2(4):42–46

Buxbaum P (2016) What in the world is China doing in Kenya?. http://www.globaltrademag.com/global-trade-daily/commentary/what-in-the-world-is-china-ng-in-kenya

Cafaggi F (2016) Transnational private regulation: regulating global private regulators. In: Cassese S (ed) Research handbook on Global Administrative Law. Edward Elgar, Cheltenham

Carroll A (2008) A history of corporate social responsibility: concepts and practice. In: The Oxford handbook of corporate social responsibility. Oxford University Press, Oxford, pp 19–46

Carroll A, Shabana K (2010) The business case for corporate social responsibility: a review of concepts, research and practice. Int J Manag Rev 12(1):85–105

Calabrese L (2017) Chinese investment and knowledge transfer in Africa. Growth Research Programme. https://dl.orangedox.com/Brief-China-Africa-investment-1

CAO Operational Guidelines. http://www.cao-ombudsman.org

Chen Y (2018) Silk road to the Sahel: African ambitions in China's belt and road initiative. Johns Hopkins SAIS-CARI Policy Brief No. 23

China Construction Bank (2024) 2024 Semi-annual Sustainable Finance Report. https://en.ccb.com/eng/attachDir/2024/08/2024080917045199677.pdf

China Exim Bank (2022) Environmental and social framework of CEXIM ALIB green on-lending facility. 中国进出口银行与亚洲基础设施投资银行绿色信贷转贷项目环境社会框架. http://www.eximbank.gov.cn/info/ztzl/lsxdzdhz/202211/P020221118389558060550.pdf

China Exim Bank (2017) China Exim Bank issues White Paper on Green Finance. http://www.eximbank.gov.cn/tm/Newlist/index_343_29878.html

China Council for International Cooperation on Environment and Development (2016) China's ecological civilization and the world. Issues Paper. 8827.pdf

China Banking and Insurance Regulatory Commission (2022) Green Finance Guidelines for the Banking and Insurance Industry. Art. 28. https://www.gov.cn/zhengce/zhengceku/2022-06/03/content_5693849.htm

City of London (2018) City of London corporation works with China to green the belt and road initiative. https://news.cityoflondon.gov.uk/city-of-london-corporation-works-with-china-to-green-the-belt-and-road-initiative/

City of London (2019) Green Belt and Road Principles Receive Industry Backing. https://news.cityoflondon.gov.uk/green-belt-and-road-principles-receive-industry-backing/

Clark GL, Wójcik D (2007) The geography of finance: corporate governance in the global marketplace. Oxford University Press, Oxford

Climate Policy Initiative (2022) The state of climate finance in Africa: climate finance needs of African countries. https://www.climatepolicyinitiative.org/wp-content/uploads/2022/06/Climate-Finance-Needs-of-African-Countries.pdf

Climate Bonds Initiative and SynTao Green Finance. Study on China's Local Government Policy Instruments for Green Bonds. climatebonds.net/files/reports/chinalocalgovt_02_13.04_final_a4.pdf

Climate Bonds Initiative and SynTao Green Finance. China Green Finance Policy. climatebonds.net/files/reports/policy_analysis_report_2021_en_final.pdf

Council of European Union (2022) Agreement in principle on the modernization of the energy charter treaty

Chin GT (2016) Asian infrastructure investment bank: governance innovation and prospects. Glob Govern 22:11

CDB (2017) CDB has financed over US$5 Billion for Africa. http://www.cdb.com.cn/xwzx/khdt/201709/t20170927_4616.html

CDB (2016) Special loan product for small and medium-sized African businesses. http://www.cdb.com.cn/cpfw/gjyw/zxfw_440/201602/t20160222_2675.html

Center for Policy Development (2016) Legal opinion: Directors' Duties and Climate Risk. http://cpd.org.au/2016/10/directorsduties/Newlegalopinionandbusinessroundtableonclimaterisksanddirectorsduties

Chan-Fishel M (2007) Environmental impact: more of the same. In: Manji F, Marks SM (eds) African perspectives on China in Africa, pp 139–152

Chen H (2016) China's 'one belt, one road' initiative and its implications for Sino-African investment relations. Transnatl Corp Rev 8(3):178–182

Chen W et al (2015) Why is China investing in Africa? Evidence from the firm level. Brookings Institution. https://www.brookings.edu/wp-content/uploads/2016/06/Why-is-China-investing-in-Africa.pdf

Chen Y (2018) Silk road to the Sahel: African ambitions in China's belt and road initiative. Johns Hopkins SAIS-CARI Policy Brief No. 23. https://static1.squarespace.com/static/5652847de4b033f56d2bdc29/t/5b67f63b562fa7f5d579f835/1533539945322/Yunnan+Belt+and+Road+-+Final+Version.pdf

Cheng C (2018) Blood cell finance and the belt and road initiative: new model for China Africa development cooperation. Renmin University Press, Beijing

China Africa Research Initiative. Data: Chinese Contracts in Africa. http://www.sais-cari.org/data-chinese-contracts-in-africa

China-Africa Trade Research Center (2016) The practitioner of China-Africa finance: a collection of Bank of China branches in Africa. http://toutiao.manqian.cn/wz_58005fb9e4b0f812e551ac13.html

China-Africa Research Initiative. Chinese Loans to Africa (2000–2014). http://www.sais-cari.org/data-chinese-loans-and-aid-to-africa/

China-ASEAN Investment Cooperation Fund (2014) China-ASEAN investment cooperation fund issued environmental and social protection safeguard reference guide. http://china-asean-fund.com/sc/news-detail.php?id=20

China Banking Regulatory Commission, WWF and PWC (2013) The sustainable performance of chinese banking and international financial institutions comparative study. http://www.wwfchina.org/content/press/publication/2015/greenfinanceen.pdf

China Construction Bank (2015) China Construction Bank and South Africa industrial development company signed a strategic corporation agreement to support the industrialization of Africa. http://ccb.com/cn/ccbtoday/newsv3/20151204_1449191625.html

China Construction Bank (2024) 2024 semi-annual sustainable finance report. https://en.ccb.com/eng/attachDir/2024/08/2024080917045199677.pdf

China Council for International Cooperation on Environment and Development (2016) China's Ecological Civilization and the World. Issues Paper. <http://www.cciced.net/cciceden/POLICY/rr/Issuespaper/201612/P020161214521507778827.pdf

China Development Bank (2024) Deepening financial cooperation and building a high-level China-Africa community with a shared future. https://www.cdb.com.cn/xwzx/khdt/202409/t20240903_11886.html

CITIC Co., Ltd (2024) 2023 Environmental, social and governance report. https://www.citic.com/uploadfile/2024/0422/20240422200535.pdf

China Development Bank (2017) China Development Bank contributes to BRI projects. http://www.cdb.com.cn/rdzt/ydyl/201705/t20170525_4318.html

China Exim Bank (2017) The Export-Import Bank of China contribution on the BRI closing summit forum. http://www.eximbank.gov.cn/tm/newlist/index_343_30120.html

China Exim Bank (2015) China Exim Bank guidelines for green loans. 中国进出口银行绿色信贷指引. http://www.eximbank.gov.cn/tm/medialist/index_26_29111.html

China Exim Bank (2007) Guidelines for environmental and social impact assessments of the China Export and Import Bank's Loan projects. 中国进出口银行贷款项目环境与社会评价指导意见. https://www.globalwitness.org/sites/default/files/library/Chinese%20guidelines%20EN.pdf

Chan-Fishel M (2017) Time to go green: environmental responsibility in the Chinese banking sector. Friends of the Earth–US and Bank Track. https://www.banktrack.org/download/time_to_go_green_environmental_responsibility_in_the_chinese_banking_sector/0_0_070509_chinese_bank_public_report_final.pdf

China WTO Tribune (2017) The 2017 Golden Bees Chinese Companies' Corporate Social Responsibility Report. http://images.mofcom.gov.cn/csr/201712/20171219174229375.pdf

Chhibber A (2017) China's one belt one road strategy: the new financial institutions and India's options. Institute for International Economic Policy Working Paper Series. https://www2.gwu.edu/~iiep/assets/docs/papers/2017WP/ChhibberIIEPWP2017-7.pdf

CIA World Factbook (2018) Kenya Demographics Profile 2018. https://www.cia.gov/library/publications/the-world-factbook/geos/ke.html

Cissé D et al (2014) State-directed multi-national enterprises and transnational governance: Chinese investments in Africa, corporate responsibility and sustainability norms. http://scholar.sun.ac.za/bitstream/handle/10019.1/95493/CCS_DP_Corporate_Responsibilities_Cisse_Grimm_Nolke_20141.pdf?sequence=1&isAllowed=y

Clapp J (2005) Global environmental governance for corporate responsibility and accountability. Global Environ Polit 5(3):23–34

Compagnon D, Alejandro A (2013) "China's external environmental policy: understanding China's environmental impact in Africa and how it is addressed. Environ Pract 15(3):220–227

Consulate General of the People's Republic of China in Lagos (2018) United Bank for Africa obtained US$100 million special loans from CDB. http://www.mofcom.gov.cn/article/i/jyjl/k/201803/20180302716926.shtml

Corkin L et al (2008) China's role in the development of Africa's infrastructure. SAIS Working Papers in African Studies. https://www.sais-jhu.edu/sites/default/files/China%27s-Role-in-the-Development-of-Africa%27s-Infrastructure.pdf

CRI Africa (2018) Chinese ambassador to Kenya accepted CGTN interview on anniversary of SGR operation. https://www.sohu.com/a/233508865_99934374

Cui X (2016) China's 'belt and road': where is Africa?. The Diplomat. https://thediplomat.com/2016/06/chinas-belt-and-road-where-is-africa/

Database of Commerce of the People's Republic of China. http://www.mofcom.gov.cn/article/tongjiziliao

Database of Complaints Mechanism Cases. http://www.eib.org/about/accountability/complaints/cases/index.htm

Davies M et al (2008) How China delivers development assistance to Africa. Center for Chinese studies. http://www0.sun.ac.za/ccs/wp-content/uploads/2009/04/dfid_fa_final.pdf

Davies J (2009) Parliamentarians and corruption in Africa: the challenges of leadership and the practice of politics. African Parliamentarians Network Against Corruption. https://agora-parl.org/resources/library/parliamentarians-and-corruption-africa-challenge-leadership-and-practice-politics

Deloitte (2016) Kenya, Africa's Grounding Growth. https://www2.deloitte.com/content/dam/Deloitte/za/Documents/africa/DeloitteAfrica_Kenya_Country_Report_Africa_Nov2016.pdf

Deutsch J (2010) Partnering with SINOPEC in Loango National Park, Gabon. Wildlife Conservation Society & the African Biodiversity Collaborative Group. http://www.frameweb.org/adl/en-US/5345/file/756/Deutsch%20ABCG%20-20WCS%20Sinopec%20in%20Loango%20NP%20Gabon.pdf

DiMaggio P, Powell W (1983) The iron cage revisited: institutional isomorphism and collective rationality in organizational fields. Am Sociol Assoc Rev 48:147–160

Dine S (2012) Climate-resilient development financing for Africa: a prospective evaluation and strategic framework for action. In: Hanson KT et al Rethinking development challenges for public policy. Macmillan Publisher Limited, New York, pp 260–284

Dolzer R, Schreuer C (2008) Principles of international investment law. Oxford University Press, Oxford, pp 352–385

Dowell G et al (2000) Do corporate global environmental standards create or destroy market value? Manag Sci 46(8):1059–1074

Duyck S et al (2018) Human rights and the Paris agreement's implementation guidelines: opportunities to develop a rights-based approach. Carbon Clim Law Rev 12:191–202

Dupuy P-M, Viñuales J (eds) (2013) Harnessing foreign investment to promote environmental protection: incentives and safeguards. Cambridge University Press, Cambridge

Eaton J (1997) Nigerian tragedy, environmental regulation of transnational corporations, and the human right to a healthy environment. Boston Univ Int Law J 15:261–307

Ecological Finance Research Centre of Renmin University of China (2017) Green finance for the belt and road initiative. China Financial Publication House

Eden L, Miller S (2004) Distance matters: liability of foreignness, institutional distance and ownership strategy. Adv Int Manag 16:187–221

EITI International Secretariat (2016) Chinese companies reporting in EITI countries. 4. https://eiti.org/document/eiti-brief-chinese-companies-reporting-in-eiti-implementing-countries

Embassy of the People's Republic of China in the Republic of Kenya (2018) Interview with the Ambassador of Chinese Embassy in Kenya. http://www.fmprc.gov.cn/ce/ceke/chn/xw/t1564247.htm

Eom J et al (2016) Looking back and moving forward: an analysis of China-Africa economic trends and the outcomes of the 2015 forum on China Africa cooperation. China-Africa Research Initiative. http://static1.squarespace.com/static/5652847de4b033f56d2bdc29/t/56aa3a95a12f44bc3732d26e/1453996965486/CARI_PolicyBrief_9_Jan2016
Esposito M et al (2014) Recolonizing Africa: a modern Chinese story?. (CNBC). https://www.cnbc.com/2014/12/30/recolonizing-africa-a-modern-chinese-story.html
Esterhuyse W et al (2014) African regional economic communities engagement with China. China-Africa relations policy briefing. http://urban-africa-china.angonet.org/content/african-regional-economic-communities-engagement-china
Engels A (2018) Understanding how China is championing climate change mitigation. Palgrave Commun 4(1)
ETC East Africa Ltd (2006) Country Environmental Profile of Kenya. https://europa.eu/capacity4dev/public-environment-climate/document/country-environmental-profile-kenya
Farrell J (2016) How do Chinese contractors perform in Africa? Evidence from World Bank Projects. Johns Hopkins SAIS-CARI Working Paper 3. https://static1.squarespace.com/static/5652847de4b033f56d2bdc29/t/573c970bf8baf3591b05253f/1463588620386/Working+Paper_Jamie+Farrell.pdf
Falk T (2013) China identifies Kenya as its next continental industrial hub why China is investing $5 billion in Kenya's infrastructure. ZDNet. https://www.zdnet.com/article/why-china-is-investing-5-billion-in-kenyas-infrastructure/
Feo VD (2018) Corporate social responsibility through the lens of investment law: will any solution work without the rule of law. McGill Human Rights Internships Working Paper Series 8:27
Foster V (2009) Building bridges: China's growing role as infrastructure financier for Sub-Saharan Africa. World Bank, Washington
Friends of the Earth (2012) China development Bank's overseas investments: an assessment of environmental and social policies and practices. https://foe.org/resources/china-development-banks-overseas-investments-an-assessment-of-environmental-and-social-policies-and-practices/
Fields S (2005) Continental divide: why Africa's climate change burden is greater. Environ Health Perspect 113(8):534–537
Francioni F (2013) The private sector and the challenge of implementation. In: Dupuy P-M, Viñuales J (eds) Harnessing foreign investment to promote environmental protection: incentives and safeguards. Cambridge University Press, Cambridge
Frank B, Pattberg P (2013) Global environmental governance: taking stock, moving forward. Annu Rev Environ Resour 33:277–294
Freeman E (1984) Strategic management: a stakeholder approach. Pitman, Boston, p 46
Friends of the Earth U.S. (2016) Emerging sustainability frameworks China development Bank and China export-import Bank. https://foe.org/wp-content/uploads/wpallimport/files/archive/emerging-sustainability-frameworks-CDB-ChinaExim.pdf
Friends of the Earth (2012) China Development Bank's outward investments: an assessment of environmental and social policies and practices. http://ef.amazonia.org.br/wp-content/uploads/2012/07/china_development_bank.pdf
Friedman L (2006) The place of legal culture in the Sociology of Law. In: Freeman L (ed) Law and sociology: current legal issues. Oxford University Press, Oxford. Chapters 11–12
Frynas J (2005) The false developmental promise of corporate social responsibility: evidence from multinational oil companies. Int Aff 81(3):581–598
Foreign Affairs Department of Shenzhen Government (2016) Ecological Conservation Dialogue Conference on the BRI. http://www.sz.gov.cn/wsbgs/xxgkml/gzdt/201612/t20161212_5669488.htm
Forstater M et al (2010) Corporate responsibility in African development: insights from an emerging dialogue. The Institute of West-Asian Studies of the Chinese Academy of Social Science. https://sites.hks.harvard.edu/m-rcbg/CSRI/publications/workingpaper_60.pdf
Forum on China-Africa Cooperation (2006), China's African Policy (2006). http://www.fmprc.gov.cn/zflt/eng/zxxx/t230479.htm

Forum on China-Africa Cooperation (2016) Africa is an important investment direction and foothold of BRI- interview with Lin Songding, China's director-general of African Affairs of the Ministry of Foreign Affairs. http://www.fmprc.gov.cn/zflt/chn/zxxx/t1393977.htm

Foster V (2009) Building bridges: China's growing role as infrastructure financier for Sub-Saharan Africa. World Bank. https://openknowledge.worldbank.org/handle/10986/2614

Foster V et al (2008) China's emerging role in Africa: part of the changing landscape of infrastructure finance. World Bank. https://documents.worldbank.org/en/publication/documents-reports/documentdetail/888291468029095977/chinas-emerging-role-in-africa-part-ofthe-changing-landscape-of-infrastructure-finance

Fox T et al (2002) Public sector roles in strengthening corporate social responsibility: a baseline study. World Bank. http://pubs.iied.org/pdfs/16017IIED.pdf

Gao X (2018) China's evolving image in international climate negotiation: From Copenhagen to Paris. China Q Int Strat Stud 4(2):213–39

G20 Green Finance Study Group (2017) 2017 G20 Green Finance Synthesis Report. http://unepinquiry.org/wp-content/uploads/2017/07/2017_GFSG_Synthesis_Report_EN.pdf

Ge C et al (2010) Environmental policies on China's investment overseas. China Environmental Science Press, Beijing

Gilbert S, Lihuan Z (2017) The knowns and unknowns of China's green finance. Global Commission on the Economy and Climate

Gielen D et al (2019) The role of renewable energy in the global energy transformation. Energ Strat Rev 24:38–50

Greenoaviton Hub (2016) Financial institutions under the BRI. http://www.ghub.org/wp-content/uploads/2017/04/BRI_201608_cn.pdf

González-Vicente R (2011) China's engagement in South America and Africa's extractive sectors: new perspectives for resource curse theories. Pac Rev 24(1):65–87

Griffin P (2017) The carbon majors database CDP carbon majors report 2017. Climate Accountability Institute. 8

G20 Green Finance Study Group (2017) The 2017 G20 Green Finance Synthesis Report. http://unepinquiry.org/wp-content/uploads/2017/07/2017_GFSG_Synthesis_Report_EN.pdf

Garriga E, Melé D (2004) Corporate social responsibility theories: mapping the territory. J Bus Ethics 53:51–71

Gallagher N, Shan W (2009) Chinese investment treaties: policies and practice. Oxford University Press, Oxford

Gallagher K et al (2016) The globalization of Chinese development finance. Boston University, Global Economic Governance Initiative. https://www.bu.edu/pardeeschool/files/2016/06/Globalization.Final_.pdf

Ge C et al (2010) Environmental policies on China's investment overseas. China Environmental Science Press, Beijing

Geall S (2015) Interpreting ecological civilization. China Dialogue. https://www.chinadialogue.net/article/show/single/en/8018-Interpreting-ecological-civilisation-part-one

Global Markets-EY Knowledge (2015). Riding the silk road: china sees outbound investment boom: outlook for China's outward foreign direct investment. http://www.ey.com/Publication/vwLUAssets/ey-china-outbound-investment-report-en/$FILE/ey-china-outbound-investment-report-en.pdf

Global Report Initiative (2002) Sustainability Reporting Guidelines. https://www.epeat.net/documents/EPEATreferences/GRIguidelines.pdf

Global Sustainable Investment Alliance (2016) 2016 Global Sustainable Investment Review. http://www.gsi-alliance.org/wp-content/uploads/2017/03/GSIR_Review2016.F.pdf

González-Vicente R (2011) China's engagement in South America and Africa's extractive sectors: new perspectives for resource curse theories. Pac Rev 24(1):65–87

Graham D, Woods N (2006) Making corporate self-regulation effective in developing countries. World Dev 34(5):868–883

Granovetter M (1985) Economic action and social structure: the problem of embeddedness. Am J Sociol 19(3):481–510

Greenovation Hub (2016) China's development financing under. "The Belt and Road" initiative. http://www.ghub.org/wp-content/uploads/2017/04/NDB_201610.pdf

Greenovation Hub (2014) China's mining industry at home and overseas: development, impact and regulation. http://www.ghub.org/cfc_en/wp-content/uploads/sites/2/2014/11/China-Mining-at-Home-and-Overseas_Main-report2_EN.pdf

Gunningham N (2008) Environmental regulation and non-state law. In: Schooten H, Verschuuren J (eds) International governance and law: state regulation and non-state law. Edward Elgar, Cheltenham

Gutman J, Zhang C (2015) Who wins world bank-financed government contracts?. Brookings Institution. https://www.brookings.edu/blog/africa-in-focus/2015/06/24/who-wins-world-bank-financed-government-contracts-four-things-we-learned-from-the-data-1-lingering-question/

Gu J et al (2016) Chinese state capitalism? Rethinking the role of the state and business in Chinese development cooperation in Africa. World Dev 81:24–34

Gu J (2015) China's new silk road to development cooperation: opportunities and challenges. United Nations University Centre for Policy Research. https://collections.unu.edu/eserv/UNU:3324/unu_cpr_china_dev.pdf

Guo P (2008) Socially responsible investment emerges in China. China Dialogue. https://www.ChinaDialogue.net/article/2020-Socially-responsible-investment-emerges-in-China

Gwilliam K (2011) Africa's transportation infrastructure: mainstreaming maintenance and management. World Bank. http://www-wds.worldbank.org/external/default/

Haglund D (2008) Regulating FDI in weak african states: a case study of Chinese copper mining in Zambia. J Mod Afr Stud 46(4):547–575

Han X (2013) Study on Chinese companies on environmental protection during overseas investment. Law Press China, pp 121–127

Haigh M (2011) Climate policy and financial institutions. Clim Policy 11(6):1367–1385

Hu T et al (2014) Managing environmental impact: international experience and lessons in risk management for overseas investments. World Resources Institute, Washington

Hudson R (2014) Chinese investments in Africa: the ethics of transparency. https://sevenpillarsinstitute.org/chinese-investments-africa-ethics-transparency/

Hertel S (2010) The paradox of partnership: assessing new forms of NGO advocacy on labor rights. Ethics Int Aff 24(2):171–189

Hilson G (2013) Corporate social responsibility in the extractive industries: experiences from developing countries. Resour Policy 37(2):131–137

Ho V (2019) Sustainable finance & China's green credit reforms: a test case for bank monitoring of environmental risk. University of Oslo Faculty of Law Legal Studies Research Paper Series No.3, 615

Ho V (2013) Beyond regulation: a comparative look at state-centric corporate social responsibility and the law in China. Vanderbilt J Transnatl Law 46:375–422

Ho V (2012) Corporate governance as risk regulation in China: a comparative view of risk oversight, risk management, and accountability. Eur J Risk Regul 3(4):463–475

Hohnen P (2007) Corporate social responsibility an implementation guide for business. International Institute for Sustainable Development. http://www.iisd.org/pdf/2007/csr_guide.pdf

Holme R, Watts P (2000) Corporate social responsibility: making good business sense. World Business Council for Sustainable Development. http://www.ceads.org.ar/downloads/Making%20good%20business%20sense.pdf

Howit N (2013) Chad suspends CNPC's oil operations after oil spill. China Dialogue. https://www.ChinaDialogue.net/blog/6315-Chad-suspends-CNPC-s-oil-opera-tions-after-oil-spill/en

Hu T et al (2014) Managing environmental impact: international experience and lessons in risk management for overseas investments. World Resources Institute. www.wri.org/managing-environmental-impact-international-experience-and-lessons-in-risk-management-for-overseas-investments

Hu T, Wang Y (2015) Environmental and social risk management of Chinese transnational corporations. Yale School of Forestry and Environmental Studies and WWF. http://www.wwfchina.org/content/press/publication/2015/Yale-WWF_final.pdf

Hu T et al (eds) (2015) Analysis of key players in China's Outward foreign direct investment based on the conceptual matrix-part I: case study in Latin America. In: Hu T, Wang Y (eds) Environmental and social risk management of Chinese transnational corporations. http://www.wwfchina.org/content/press/publication/2015/Yale-WWF_final.pdf

Human Rights Watch (2011) Labor abuses in Zambia's Chinese state-owned copper mines. Human Rights Watch. https://www.hrw.org/sites/default/files/reports/zambia1111ForWebUpload.pdf

Hwang J et al (2016) How Chinese money is transforming Africa: it's not what you think. China Africa Research Initiative, Policy Brief No. 11. http://www.africa-platform.org/resources/how-chinese-money-transforming-africa-its-not-what-you-think

Idemudia U (2011) Corporate social responsibility and developing countries: moving the critical CSR research agenda in Africa forward. Prog Dev Stud 11(1):1–18

IRENA, Renewable Energy Market Analysis: Africa and Its Regions. https://www.irena.org/-/media/Files/IRENA/Agency/Publication/2022/Jan/IRENA_Market_Africa_2022.pdf

Industrial and Commercial Bank of China (2024) The Industrial and Commercial Bank of China and Standard Bank Group jointly hosted a China-Africa Economic and Trade Investment Forum. https://www.icbc.com.cn/page/1022090829038731264.html

Industrial and Commercial Bank of China (2024) 2024 Interim Special Report on Corporate Social Responsibility and Sustainable Finance of Industrial and Commercial Bank of China Limited. https://v.icbc.com.cn/userfiles/resources/icbcltd/download/2024/esg20240926en.pdf

International Rivers (2015) Benchmarking the policies and practices of international hydropower companies. https://www.internationalrivers.org/files/attached-files/benchmarking_report_english_part_a.pdf

International Rivers (2012) The new great walls: a guide to China's overseas dam industry. http://www.internationalrivers.org/files/attached-files/intlrivers_newgreatwalls_2012_2.pdf

Ite U (2004) Multinationals and corporate social responsibility in developing countries: a case study of Nigeria. Corp Soc Responsib Environ Manag 11:1–11

Jamali D et al (2008) Corporate governance and corporate social responsibility synergies and interrelationships. Corp Govern 16(5):443–459

Joshua E (1997) Nigerian tragedy, environmental regulation of transnational corporations, and the human right to a healthy environment. Boston Univ Int Law J 15:261–307

Johnston L (2016) Africa, and China's one belt, one road initiative: why now and what next. International Centre for Trade and Sustainable Development. https://www.ictsd.org/bridges-news/bridges-africa/news/africa-and-china%E2%80%99s-one-belt-one-road-initiative-why-now-and-what

Jin X (2017) The financial engine assist China-Africa comprehensive corporation. People's Daily. http://paper.people.com.cn/rmrb/html/2017-12/07/nw.D110000renmrb_20171207_3-14.htm

Jian J (2017) Africa in the maritime silk road: challenges and prospects. In Mayer M (ed) Rethinking the silk road: China's belt and road initiative and emerging eurasian relations. Springer, New York.

Judy D (1986) Hazardous substances in developing countries: who should regulate foreign corporations? Virginia J Nat Resour Law 6:143–177

Kanie N, Haas P (eds) (2004) Emerging forces in environmental governance. United Nations University Press, New York

Kaminski I (2021) Climate litigation up in 2021, with private sector now exposed, China dialogue. https://chinadialogue.net/en/climate/climate-litigation-up-in-2021-with-private-sector-now-exposed/

Kelly R (2017) How China's soft power is building a new-colonial system in Africa. (Ketagalan Media). http://www.ketagalanmedia.com/2017/10/09/how-chinas-soft-power-is-building-a-neo-colonial-system-in-africa/

Kenya China Economic and Trade Association (2017) 2017 Chinese overseas companies in Kenya social responsibility report. http://ke2.mofcom.gov.cn/17en.pdf

Kenya National Bureau of Statistics (2018) 2018 Economic Survey Report. https://www.knbs.or.ke/economic-survey-2018-launched/

KenyaForum (2016) Tribunal Halts Construction of SGR Through National Park. http://www.kenyaforum.net/2016/09/20/environmental-tribunal-halts-construction-of-sgr-through-national-park/

Keeton C (2011) Sharing sustainability: preventing international environmental injustice in an age of regulation. Houston Law Rev 48:1194

Kibugi R al (2016) Large scale land acquisitions for investment in Kenya: is the participation, and benefits of affected local communities meaningful, and equitable?. http://profiles.uonbi.ac.ke/rmkibugi/publications/large-scale-land-acquisitions-investments-kenya-participation-and-benefits-aff

Kivuitu M et al (2005) How can corporate social responsibility deliver in Africa? Insights from Kenya and Zambia. International Institute for Environment and Development. http://pubs.iied.org/pdfs/16006IIED.pdf

Kono DY, Gabriella RM (2019) Foreign aid and climate change policy: what can('t) the data tell us? Polit Govern 7(2):68

Krajewski M (2020) A nightmare or a noble dream? Establishing investor obligations through treaty-making and treaty-application. Bus Hum Rights J 5:116

KPMG (2015) Currents of change: the KPMG survey of corporate responsibility reporting 2015. https://assets.kpmg.com/content/dam/kpmg/pdf/2016/02/kpmg-international-survey-of-corporate-responsibility-reporting-2015.pdf

Kragelund P, Van Dijik M (2009) China's investments in Africa. In: Van Dijik M (ed) The new presence of China in Africa. Amsterdam University Press, Amsterdam

Kuo M, Tang A (2016) China's Africa strategy: going global with infrastructure investment. The Diplomat. https://thediplomat.com/2016/01/chinas-africa-strategy-going-global-with-infrastructure-investment/

Lee CK (2017) The specter of global China: politics, labor and foreign investment in Africa. University of Chicago Press, Vancouver

Lekorwe M et al (2016) China's growing presence in Africa wins largely positive popular reviews. Afrobarometer Dispatch No. 122. http://afrobarometer.org/sites/default/files/publications/Dispatches/ab_r6_dispatchno122_perceptions_of_china_in_africa1.pdf

Leung D, Zhao Y (2013) Environmental and social policies in overseas investments: progress and challenges for China. World Resources Institute, Washington

Levy D, Kaplan R (2008) Corporate social responsibility and theories of global governance. In: Crane A et al (eds) The Oxford handbook of corporate social responsibility. Oxford University Press, Oxford, pp 432–451

Li Z et al (2021) China's 30-year participation in international climate governance in retrospect. China Popul Resour Environ 31(9):202–10

Liang Y (2020) The human rights obligations of multinational companies' home countries. Law Press, 2

Liu M, Kevin L (2021) Pathways to international cooperation on climate governance in china: a comparative analysis. J Chin Govern 6(3):417–34

Liu Y, Zhijun F (2011) South-South cooperation: a new strategy for climate aid. China Econ Wkly 9:18

Liu R, Shuhua W (2023) Evolution logic and implications of the US climate security strategy. Pac J 1:10

Li X, Shaw T (2013) The political economy of Chinese state capitalism. J China Int Relat 1(1):91–113

Lin L, Milhaupt C (2017) Bonded to the state: a network perspective on China's corporate debt market. J Financ Regul 3(10):1–39

Lin L (2015) China's national champions: governance change through globalization? Univ Pennsylvania Asian Law Rev 11(1):82–126

Lin L, Milhaupt C (2013) We are the (National) champions: understanding the mechanisms of state capitalism in China. Stanford Law Rev 65:697–759
Lin L (2010) Corporate social responsibility in China: window dressing or structural change. Berkeley Int Law J 28:64–100
Lindenberg N (2014) Definition of Green Finance. German Development Institute. https://www.cbd.int/financial/gcf/definition-greenfinance.pdf
Liu B, Ai S (2025) Establishing binding climate-change-related investor obligation clauses in international investment agreements: obstacles and pathways. Rev Eur Comp Int Environ Law 4(1):136–154
Liu B (2024) Investment arrangements for climate governance: tracing, evolution and new approaches. Stud Law Bus 4:55–70
Liu B (2021) China's state-centric approach to corporate social responsibility overseas: a case study in Africa. Transnatl Environ Law 10(1):66–72
Liu B (2017) Strengthening the regulation and management of forest biodiversity conservation by multinationals during foreign investment. In: Ed C (eds) et al Protecting forest and marine biodiversity: the role of law. Edward Elgar, Cheltenham
Liu M (2015) Is corporate social responsibility China's secret weapon?. Eco-Business. https://www.weforum.org/agenda/2015/03/is-corporate-social-responsibility-chinas-secret-weapon/
Lu A (2017) The RMB Business of the Bank of China Johannesburg Branch Covers 29 African Countries. CHINAFRICA. http://www.chinafrica.cn/chinese/mrxw/201705/t20170526_800097103.html
Lynch G (2013) The politics of ethnicity. In: Cheeseman N et al (eds) Routledge handbook of African politics. Routledge, Oxon
Liu Q (2016) How to build environmental protection into 'new silk road'. China Dialogue. https://www.chinadialogue.net/article/show/single/en/9247-How-to-build-environmental-protection-into-New-Silk-Road
Liu Q (2015) China's most polluting manufacturers likely to shift to Africa. China dialogue. https://www.chinadialogue.net/culture/7719--Book-China-s-most-polluting-manufacturers-likely-to-shift-to-Africa/en
Ma J (2017) Establishing China's green financial system. China Financial Publication House, Beijing
Ma J (2017) Green finance leads green one belt one road initiative. China Financial Publication House, Beijing
Maljean-Dubois S, Richard V (2013) The application of international environmental law to private enterprises. In: Dupuy P-M, Viñuales J (eds) Harnessing foreign investment to promote environmental protection: incentives and safeguards. Cambridge University Press, Cambridge, pp 69–96
Manero E (2017) Chinas investment in Africa: the new colonialism?. Harvard Political Review. http://harvardpolitics.com/world/chinas-investment-in-africa-the-new-colonialism/
Martyn D (2011) How China is influencing Africa's development. In: Men J, Barton B (eds) China and the European Union in Africa: partners or competitors? College of Europe, Belgium, pp 187–205
Lindenberg N (2014) Definition of green finance. German Development Institute, Bonn
Manero E (2017) Chinas investment in Africa: the new colonialism?. Harvard Political Review
Marquis C et al (2011) Regulatory uncertainty and corporate responses to environmental protection in China. Calif Manag Rev 54(1):39
McBarnet D (2009) Corporate social responsibility beyond law, through law, for law: the new corporate accountability. In: McBarnet D et al (eds) The new corporate accountability: corporate social responsibility and the law. Cambridge University Press, Cambridge
McKenna K (2016) Corporate social responsibility and natural resource conflict. Routledge, Oxon
McKinsey & Co. (2017) Dance of the lions and dragons: how are Africa and China engaging, and how will the partnership evolve?. https://www.mckinsey.com/global-themes/middle-east-and-africa/the-closest-look-yet-at-chinese-economic-engagement-in-africa

McGuire W (2016) The role of ISO 14001 in China's environmental crisis. https://aede.osu.edu/sites/aede/files/!import/McGuire-The%20Role%20of%20ISO%2014001%20in%20China's%20Environmental%20Crisis.pdf
Mclntyre J (2018) 'Game of loans: how china uses 'Debt-trap Diplomacy' to extend its military reach. Examiner. https://www.washingtonexaminer.com/policy/defense-national-security/how-china-uses-debt-trap-diplomacy-to-extend-its-military-reach.
Mele D (2008) Corporate social responsibility theories. In: The Oxford handbook of corporate social responsibility. Oxford University Press, Oxford, pp 47-82
Mol APJ (2017) China's policies on greening financial institutions: assessment and outlook. Routledge Handbook of Environmental Policy in China. Routledge, London, pp 208–222
Ministry of Foreign Affairs (2022) Chair's statement of the high-level dialogue on global development. https://www.mfa.gov.cn/eng/zy/jj/GDI_140002/xw/202206/t20220624_10709812.html
Munson P, Ronghui Z (2011) Feeding the dragon: managing Chinese resource acquisition in Africa. Seattle J Environ Law 2:373–376
Ministry of Commerce of China (2016) 2016 China foreign direct investment statistical bulletin. http://fec.mofcom.gov.cn/article/tjsj/tjgb/201709/20170902653690.shtml
Ministry of Commerce of China (2017) Report on development of China's outward investment and economic cooperation. (中国对外投资合作发展报告). http://fec.mofcom.gov.cn/article/tzhzcj/tzhz/upload/zgdwtzhzfzbg2017.pdf
Ministry of Commerce of China (2015). Introduction of the CDB special loans product for small and medium-sized African businesses. http://www.mofcom.gov.cn/aarticle/i/jshz/rlzykf/201204/20120408048826.html
Ministry of Foreign Affairs (2015) The forum on China-Africa cooperation Johannesburg action plan (2016–2018). http://www.fmprc.gov.cn/mfa_eng/zxxx_662805/t1323159.shtml
Ministry of Foreign Affairs of the Republic of Kenya. "5th Diplomatic Brief/2016–2017". http://www.mfa.go.ke/wp-content/uploads/2017/06/Diplomatic-briefing-Speech-by-Amb.-Monica-Juma-on-June-14-2017.pdf
Mohai P et al (2009) Environmental justice. Annu Rev Environ Resour 34:405–430
Moon J (2002) Business social responsibility and new governance. Govern Oppos 37(3):385–408
Mol A (2011) China's ascent and Africa's environment. Glob Environ Change 21(3):785–794
Moreta M, Liu B (2018) The challenge of bringing to justice transnational corporations for environmental damages: case of study Texaco Oil Company and Chevron vs Lago Agrio Plaintiffs. In: Christina V et al (eds) Courts and the environment. Edward Elgar, Cheltenham
Morgera E (2009) Corporate accountability in international environmental law. Oxford University Press, New York
Moss T, Rose S (2006) China Exim Bank and Africa: new lendings, new challenges. Centre for Global Development. https://www.cgdev.org/files/11116_file_China_and_Africa.pdf
Mohan G, Power M (2008) New African choices? The politics of Chinese engagement in Africa and the changing architecture of international development. Rev Afr Polit Econ 35(1):23–42
Morrock R (1973) Heritage of strife: the effect of colonialist 'divide and rule' strategy upon the colonized peoples. Sci Soc 37(2):129–151
Mungai M et al (eds) (2010) (Re)membering Kenya: identity, culture and freedom. Twaweza Communications Ltd.
Munson P, Zheng R (2011) Feeding the dragon: managing Chinese resource acquisition in Africa. Seattle J Environ Law 2:343–382
Murray J (2001) A new phase in the regulation of multinational enterprises: the role of the OECD. Ind Law J 30(3):255–270
Mulinge E (2012) An analysis of China-Kenya bilateral relations on infrastructure development. Kenya Institute for Public Policy Research and Analysis, KIPPRA Discussion Paper No. 134
Mwendwa M (2017) SGR will destroy the ecology of Nairobi National Park. http://www.talkafrica.co.ke/sgr-will-destroy-the-ecology-of-nairobi-national-park-experts-warn/

Ndulu B et al (2007) Challenges of African growth: opportunities, constrains and strategic directions. World Bank. http://siteresources.worldbank.org/AFRICAEXT/Resources/AFR_Growth_Advance_Edition.pdf

New Development Bank (2016) Environmental and social framework. https://www.ndb.int/wp-content/uploads/2017/02/ndb-environment-social-framework-20160330.pdf

Newig J, Fritsch O (2009) Environmental governance: participatory, multi-level-and effective? Environ Policy Govern 19(3):197–214

Nyassy D (2015) Hands off Railway Project, Company Tells County officials. Daily Nation. http://mobile.nation.co.ke/counties/Mombasa-Standard-Gauge-Railway-CRBC/-/1950480/2761446/-/format/xhtml/-/8y1o2bz/-/index.html

O'faircheallaigh C (2007) Environmental agreements, ESIA follow-up and aboriginal participation in environmental management: the Canadian experience. Environ Impact Assess Rev 27(4):319–342

Official Journal of the European Union (2024) Directive (EU) 2024/1760 of the European Parliament and of the Council of 13 June 2024 on corporate sustainability due diligence and amending Directive (EU) 2019/1937 and Regulation (EU) 2023/2859. https://eur-lex.europa.eu/legal-content/EN/TXT/PDF/?uri=OJ:L_202401760

Okeowo A (2013) China, Zambia, and a Clash in a Coal Mine. The New Yorker. https://www.newyorker.com/business/currency/china-zambia-and-a-clash-in-a-coal-mine

Ombaba K et al (2012) A study on the impact of China's investments in Africa: the case of Kenya. J Emerg Trends Econ Manag Sci 3(5):529–537

Omoruyi E (2018) Xi's visit Bolsters China-Africa relations. Belt and Road Portal. https://eng.yidaiyilu.gov.cn/home/rolling/60999.htm

Ong D (2001) The impact of environmental law on corporate governance: international and comparative perspectives. Eur J Int Law 12(4):685–726

Orlitzky M et al (2003) Corporate social and financial performance: a meta-analysis. Organ Stud 24:403–441

Owen JR, Kemp D (2024) Corporate responses to community grievance: voluntarism and pathologies of practice. J Bus Ethics 1:55–68

Paine J, Sheargold E (2023) A climate change carve-out for investment treaties. J Int Econ Law 26(2):285–304

Pandey E (2018) China's debt-trap diplomacy is spreading across Africa. Axios. https://www.axios.com/china-debt-africa-djibouti-kenya-angola-belt-and-road-initiative-c65b82fa-48a6-4140-bb01-bc19580a16c9.html

Parker C (2002) The open corporation: effective self-regulation and democracy. Cambridge University Press, Cambridge

Pearson MM (2019) China and global climate change governance. In: Zeng K (ed) Handbook on the international political economy of China. Edward Elgar, Cheltenham, pp 411–23

Peh K, Eyal J (2010) Unveiling China's impact on African environment. Energy Policy 38(8):4729–4730

Petrović-Ranđelović M (2011) Host country policy as a determinant of environmentally sustainable foreign direct investment inflows. Econ Org 8(2):235–246

Pellow D (2007) Resisting global toxics: transnational movements for environmental justice. The MIT Press, Cambridge

Pew Research Center (2017) Opinion of China, do you have a favorable or unfavorable view of China?". http://www.pewglobal.org/database/indicator/24/

People's Bank of China (2018) People's Bank of China Reponses to the BRI and Build Global First-Class Bank. http://www.boc.cn/aboutboc/bi1/201803/t20180312_11698999.html

People's Daily Online (2018) Together with South Africa's largest bank, industrial and commercial Bank of China Assists Africa Development. http://world.people.com.cn/n1/2018/0724/c1002-30165973.html

PRI (2021) Principles for Responsible Investment: Investor Initiative in Collaboration with the United Nations Environment Programme Finance Initiative and the United Nations Global Compact. https://www.unpri.org/download?ac=10968
Potter P (2011) Introduction: selective adaptation, institutional capacity, and the reception of international law under conditions. In: Potter P, Biuković L (eds) Globalization and local adaptation in international trade law. University of British Columbia Press, Vancouver, pp 3–20
Potter P (2009) Coordinating corporate governance and corporate social responsibility. Hong Kong Law J 39:675–695
Pike L (2017) Is the Belt and Road compatible with Paris?. China Dialogue. https://www.chinadialogue.org.cn/article/show/single/en/10284-Is-the-Belt-and-Road-compatible-with-Paris
Qi A (2019) Relationship between corporate manager compensation and corporate social responsibility. Front Theory 1:117–119
Qin T, Bingyu L (2024) China and global climate change governance: a union of top-down governance and multistakeholder engagement. In: De La Rasilla I, Cai CY (eds) The Cambridge Handbook of China and International Law. Cambridge University Press, Cambridge
Qingrong W et al (2013) The sustainable performance of chinese banking and international financial institutions comparative study. China Banking Regulatory Commission, WWF and PWC
Ratner SR (2020) International investment law and domestic investment rules: tracing the upstream and downstream flows. J World Invest Trade 21(7):32–33
Rees C, Vermijs D (2008) Mapping grievance mechanisms in the business and human rights arena. Corporate Social Responsibility Initiative Report
Richardson B (2019) Socially and environmentally responsible investment. In: Kate M (ed) Research handbook on environment and investment law. Edward Elgar, pp 504–524
Ruggie JG (2013) Just business: multinational corporations and human rights. W.W. Norton & Company, pp 87–89, 120
Richardson B (2002) Environmental regulation through financial organizations: comparative perspectives on the industrialized nations. Kluwer Law International
Ribstein L (2006) Accountability and responsibility in corporate governance. Notre Dame Law Rev 81:1444–1447
Rosnes O, Shkaratan M (2011) Africa's power infrastructure: investment, integration, efficiency. World Bank Publications, Washington
Roque P (2009) China in Mozambique: a cautious approach country case study. South African Institute of International Affairs, Occasional Paper No. 23. http://www.eisourcebook.org/cms/June%202013/China%20in%20Mozambique,%20A%20Cautious%20Approach.pdf
Rotberg R (ed) (2009) China into Africa: trade, aid, and influence. Brookings Institution Press
Ruchi A (2004) Global environmental justice: a North-South dimension. Ashgate, Hampshire
Sanghi A, Johnson D (2016) Deal or no deal: strictly business for China in Kenya?. World Bank Policy Research Working Paper 7614. http://documents.worldbank.org/curated/en/801581468195561492/pdf/WPS7614.pdf
Sautman B, Yan H (2015) Localizing Chinese enterprises in Africa: from myths to policies. Institute for emerging market studies, thought leadership Brief No.5. http://iems.ust.hk/assets/publications/thought-leadership-briefs/tlb05/hkust_iems_thought_leadership_brief_tlb05.pdf
Scherer M, Reichenbach C (2024) Climate-related counterclaims in international investment arbitration. In: Ipp A, Magnusson A (eds) Investment Arbitration and Climate Change. Wolters Kluwer, p 124
Schreurs M (2017) Multi-level climate governance in China. Environ Policy Govern 27(2):163–174
Schickerling E (2012) Foreign development aid in China's Foreign policy Africa: exploring the China-Africa development fund. University of Lovemore Chikova
Setzer J, Catherine H (2021) Global trends in climate change litigation: 2021 Snapshot, 5
Sun T (2021) How to deliver international aid to climate change: mitigation, adaptation and mainstreaming. low carbon world 12

Settle D (1996) The impact of colonialism on African economic development. University of Tennessee Honors Thesis Projects. http://trace.tennessee.edu/cgi/viewcontent.cgi?article=1182&context=utk_chanhonoproj

Schreuer C, Dolzer R (2008) Principles of international investment law, 1st edn. Oxford University Press, pp 352–385

Scherer A et al (2013) Democratizing corporate governance: compensating for the democratic deficit of corporate political activity and corporate citizenship. Bus Soc 52(3):473–514

Schiere R (2011) China and Africa: an emerging partnership for development? An overview of issues. African Development Bank Working Paper Series. https://www.afdb.org/fileadmin/uploads/afdb/Documents/Publications/WPS%20No%20125%20China%20and%20Africa%20%20An%20Emerging%20Partnership%20.pdf

Schiere R, Rugamba A (2011) Chinese infrastructure investments and African integration. African Development Bank Group, Working Paper Series. http://www.afdb.org/fileadmin/uploads/afdb/Documents/Publications/WPS%20No%20127%20Chinese%20Infrastructure%20Investments%20.pdf

Schiller B (2005) The China Model. https://www.opendemocracy.net/democracy-china/china_development_3136.jsp

Schickerling E (2012) Foreign development aid in China's Foreign Policy Africa: exploring the China-Africa development fund. University of Lovemore Chikova

Sharam B (2013) Contextualizing CSR in Asian: corporate social responsibility in asian economics and the drivers that influence its practices. http://ink.library.smu.edu.sg/cgi/viewcontent.cgi?article=1004&context=lien_reports

Scott D (2012) Do Chinese extraction (mining, oil & gas) activities in Africa overlap with areas of conservation value? Afr East-Asian Aff 68:11–16

Shanghai Stock Exchange (2008) Environmental information disclosure guidelines for listed companies of Shanghai Stock Exchange. http://www.sse.com.cn/lawandrules/sserules/listing/stock/c/c_20150912_3985851.shtml

Shinn D (2016) The environmental impact of China's investment in Africa. Cornell Int Law J 25:25–65

Silk Road Fund (2024) Silk road fund sustainability report. https://www.silkroadfund.com.cn/enweb/20241031/Silk%20Road%20Fund%20Sustainability%20Report.pdf

Silk Road Fund (2023) Silk road fund sustainable investment policy. https://www.silkroadfund.com.cn/uiFramework/js/pdfjs/web/viewer.html?file=/enweb/attachDir/2023/01/2023010400145011962.pdf

Spear T et al (eds) (1993) Being Maasai: ethnicity and identity in East Africa. Jame Currey Ltd, Oxford

Stefancic J (2002) Jurisprudence: classical and contemporary: from natural law to postmodernism. West Academic Publishing, pp 20–22

Sun Y (2014) Africa in China's Foreign Policy. John L. Thornton China Center and the Africa Growth Initiative at Brookings Institution. https://www.brookings.edu/wp-content/uploads/2016/06/Africa-in-China-web_CMG7.pdf

Tan-Mullins M, Mohan G (2013) The potential of corporate environmental responsibility of Chinese state-owned enterprises in Africa. Environ Dev Sustain 15(2):265–284

Tang X, Sun Y (2016) Social responsibility or development responsibility-what is the environmental impact of Chinese investments in Africa: what are its drivers, and what are the possibilities for action. Cornell Int Law J 49(1):69–99

Tang X (2022) Research on the considerations and typology of mandatory human rights due diligence legislation. Chin J Hum Rights 39:43

Teng F, Wang P (2021) The evolution of climate governance in China: drivers, features, and effectiveness. Environ Polit 30(1):141–61

Trombetta MJ (2019) Securitization of climate change in China: implications for global climate governance. China Q Int Strat Stud 5(1):97–116

Tarragona Centre for Environmental Law Studies (2016) Human rights in European business: a practical handbook for civil society organizations and human rights defenders. http://www.cedat.cat/publicacions/en_human-rights-in-european-business/

Taylor I (2007) China's environmental footprint in Africa. China Dialogue. https://www.ChinaDialogue.net/article/741-China-s-environmental-footprint-in-Africa

Toetzke M et al (2022) Consistent and replicable estimation of bilateral climate finance. Nat Clim Change 12:897

Tukic N, Yejoo K (2015) Paving the road ahead–China-Africa co-operation in the infrastructure sector. Center for Chinese Studies

Tian J (2016) One Belt and One Road': connecting China and the world. McKinsy &Co. https://www.mckinsey.com/industries/capital-projects-and-infrastructure/our-insights/one-belt-and-one-road-connecting-china-and-the-world

The Economic Times, "Definition of 'Investment Risk'". https://economictimes.indiatimes.com/definition/investment-risk

The Infrastructure Consortium for Africa (2015) Infrastructure financing trends in Africa. <https://www.icafrica.org/fileadmin/documents/Annual_Reports/ICA_2015_annual_report.pdf>.

The Investor Agenda (2021) Investor Climate Action Plan (ICAPS) Ladder of Expectations. https://www.aigcc.net/wp-content/uploads/2021/11/expectations-ladder-english-1.pdf

The State Council Information Office of China (2017) Industrial and Commercial Bank of China supported 212 BRI project in total of 67.4 billion dollars. http://www.scio.gov.cn/xwfbh/xwbfbh/wqfbh/35861/36645/zy36649/Document/1551520/1551520.htm

The State Council Information Office of China (2021) China's international development cooperation in the new era. People's Publishing House 45

The Stock Exchange of Hong Kong Ltd (2015) Environmental, social and governance reporting of the Hong Kong Stock Exchange. http://www.ngocn.net/column/2015-12-23-a3ec9ad0e79abf5b.html

Tian Z (2014) Chinese enterprises overseas investment risk assessment and early warning research. Science Press, Beijing

Transparency International (2018) Corruption perceptions index 2017. https://www.transparency.org/news/feature/corruption_perceptions_index_2017?gclid=CjwKCAiA24PVBRBvEiwAyBxf-S2YUEBHgUxMZNbVo-dOsRxyhgnDMixrqJ7Y7WFbC5mbOiW-gQ2eCxoCLVEQAvD_BwE

Tull D (2006) China's engagement in Africa: scope, significance and consequences. J Mod Afr Stud 44(3):459–479

Tukic N, Kim Y (2015) Paving the road ahead–China-Africa co-operation in the infrastructure sector. Center for Chinese Studies, Policy Briefing. http://scholar.sun.ac.za/handle/10019.1/98935

Urban F et al (2012) An analysis of China's investment in the hydropower sector in the greater mekong sub-region. Environ Dev Sustain 15(2):301–324

U.S. Chamber of Commerce (2012) Corporate responsibility and sustainable economic development in China: implications for business. https://www.uschamber.com/sites/default/files/legacy/international/files17296_China%20Corp%20Social%20Responsibility_Opt.pdf

Van Dijk M (2009) Introduction: objectives of and instruments for China's new presence in Africa. In: Van Dijk M (ed) The new presence of China in Africa. Amsterdam University Press, Amsterdam, pp 9–30

Van-Vliet G, Magrin G (2012) The environmental challenges facing a Chinese oil company in chad. Agence Française de Développement. https://portals.iucn.org/library/sites/library/files/documents/SPE-Int-674.3-001.pdf

Van de Ven A (2010) Risk management from an accounting perspective. In: Van Daelen M, Van Der Elst C (eds) Risk management and corporate governance: interconnections in law, accounting and tax. Edward Elgar, Cheltenham, pp 7–55

Van den Bersselaar D, Decker S (2017) No longer at ease: corruption as an institution in West Africa. Int J Public Adm 34(11):741–752

Verdier P-H (2009) Transnational regulatory networks and their limits. Yale J Int Law 34(1):114–171

Voegtlin C, Pless N. Global governance: CSR and the role of the UN global compact. J Bus Ethics 122(2):179–191

Visser W (2008) Corporate social responsibility in developing countries. In: Crane A, McWilliams A, Matten D, Moon J, Siegel DS (eds) The Oxford handbook of corporate social responsibility. Oxford University Press, Oxford, pp 473–499

Viñuales J (2013) The environmental regulation of foreign investment schemes under international law. In: Dupuy P-M, Viñuales J (eds) Harnessing foreign investment to promote environmental protection: incentives and safeguards. Cambridge University Press, Cambridge, pp 273–320

Warf B (2017) Geographies of African corruption. PSU Res Rev 1(1):20–38

Walsh C (2006) Is China the new colonial power in Africa. The Guardian. https://www.theguardian.com/business/2006/oct/29/china.theobserver

Wamotsa DS (2014) Implementation of the constitutional right of access to environmental information in Kenya. Appl Mater Interfaces 6(9):6098–6110

Wan Y, Li Z (2018) Sino-Congolese Bank for Africa building inaugurated in Congo. People's Daily. http://en.people.cn/n3/2018/0413/c90000-9448984.html

Wang B et al (2014) Overseas impact of China's outward direct investment: China's outward direct investment. Asian Econ Policy Rev 9(2):227–249

Wang-Kaeding H (2018) What does Xi Jinping's new phrase 'ecological civilization' mean?". The Diplomat. https://thediplomat.com/2018/03/what-does-xi-jinpings-new-phrase-ecological-civilization-mean/

Wang Y, Luo Y (2015) Business perception index Kenya 2014. Sino Africa Center of Excellence Foundation. http://www.focac.org/eng/xsjl/xzzs/P020150803357007793815.pdf

Watson A (2008) Civil Society in a transitional state: the rise of associations in China. In: Unger J (ed) Associations and the Chinese state: contested spaces. Routledge, Oxon, pp 14–47

Wawryk A (2002) Adoption of international environmental standards by rransnational oil companies: reducing the impact of oil operations in emerging economies. J Energ Nat Resour Law 20(4):402–434

Wan Y, Li Z (2018) Sino-Congolese Bank for Africa Building Inaugurated in Congo. People's Daily. http://en.people.cn/n3/2018/0413/c90000-9448984.html

Wang W, Zhang Y (2022) China-Africa green cooperation from the perspective of global ecological civilization construction. China Afr J 4:128–141

Wang H, Zhemeng L (2022) China-Africa cooperation on climate change: implications, challenges and strategies. J Zhejiang Normal Univ 6:37–43

Wang X et al (2020) Analysis and countermeasures for south-south cooperation on climate change in the 14th five-year plan. Environ Prot 16:65

Wagemans FAJ et al (2014) The effectiveness of socially responsible investment. J Integr Environ Sci 10:235–252

Weng X, Lila B (eds) (2016) Chinese businesses in Africa: perspectives on corporate social responsibility and the role of Chinese government policies (IIED)

Wei YR (2021) Climate governance from the perspective of international investment agreements. Jiangxi Soc Sci 41:193–194

Weller M-P, Mai-Lan T (2022) Climate litigation against companies. Clim Action 14(1):1

Weaver G et al (1999) Integrated and decoupled corporate social performance: management commitments, external pressures, and corporate ethics practices. Acad Manag J 42(5):539–552

Weissbrodt D, Kruger M (2003) Norms on the responsibilities of transnational corporations and other business enterprises with regard to human rights. Am J Int Law 97:901–922

Wissenbach U, Wang Y (2016) Local politics meets chinese engineers: a study of the Chinese-built standard Gauge railway project in Kenya. China Africa Research Initiative Policy Brief, No. 16. https://static1.squarespace.com/static/5652847de4b033f56d2bdc29/t/58136e42b3db2ba8eafb7cbb/1477668419649/kenya+v3.pdf

World Population Review (2018) Kenya Population 2018. http://worldpopulationreview.com/countries/kenya-population/

WWF (2016) Partnership approaches beginning to Bear Fruit in Gabon's Forest. http://wwf.zxzx.me/content/press/publication/2016/WWF英文版单页.pdf

WWF (2016) China's Belt and road initiative and its implications for Africa. http://assets.wwfke.panda.org/downloads/china_s_belt_and_road_initiative_and_its_implications_for_africa.pdf

Xi J (2018) Work together for common development and a shared future. Keynote Speech at the Opening Ceremony of the 2018 Beijing Summit Of the Forum on China-Africa Cooperation. http://www.gov.cn/xinwen/2018-09/03/content_5319004.htm

Xiao J (2015) How can a prospective China–EU BIT contribute to sustainable investment: in light of the UNCTAD investment policy framework for sustainable development. J World Energy Law Bus 8:521–523

Xinhua News (2018) The Export-Import Bank of China Financed US$67.2 Billion, Surpassing the World Bank. http://www.mofcom.gov.cn/aarticle/i/jyjl/k/201201/20120107913576.htm

Yan B (2017) Divergences and convergences between the EU and China on post-2020 global climate governance. In: Telò M et al (eds) Deepening the EU–China partnership in an unstable world. Routledge, Abingdon, pp 193–203

Yan M (2019) Corporate social responsibility versus shareholder value maximization: through the lens of hard and soft law. Northwest J Int Law Bus 40:76

Yan-ting D (2022) Addressing climate change: Africa's exploration and the significance of China-Africa cooperation. J Univ Chin Acad Soc Sci 10:117

Yu H, Wang W (2022) African issues and China-Africa cooperation in the context of climate geocompetition. West Asia Afr 1:93–110

Young I (2004) Responsibility and global labor justice. J Polit Philos 12:365–388

Young O (1994) International governance: protecting the environment in a stateless society. Cornell University Press, Ithaca

Yu L et al (eds) (2016) National strategy: policy and investment of "Belt and Road" initiative. Zhejiang University Press

Zadek S (2001) The civil corporation: the new economy of corporate citizenship. Earthscan, London

Zafar A (2007) The growing relationship between China and sub-saharan Africa: macroeconomic, trade, investment and aid links. World Bank Res Obs 22(1):103–130

Zerk J (2006) Multinationals and corporate social responsibility: limitations and opportunities in international law. Cambridge University Press, Cambridge, pp 104–196, 243–309

Zhan D (2014) Case study of social and environmental risk of chinese foreign investment. Peking University Press

Zhao B, Zhang Y (2021) China-Africa technical cooperation on climate change in the post-Paris era. China Afr J 3:80–97

Zhang R, Sun T (2023) China-Africa clean energy cooperation under the global development initiative. China Afr J 1:62–82

Zhao M (2024) What has the china export-import bank brought to Africa. Financial News. https://www.financialnews.com.cn/2024-09/03/content_407548.html

Zhang J (2016) Chinese foreign assistance explained. Brookings Institution. https://www.brookings.edu/blog/order-from-chaos/2016/07/19/chinese-foreign-assistance-explained/

Zhang Z et al (2022) Actively participating in and leading south-south cooperation on climate change: status quo, problems and countermeasures. Environ Econ Res 7:28

Zheng G et al (2016) Paris climate change conference: a fresh start of international climate governance in the new era. Chin J Urban Environ Stud 4(1)

Zhou Y (2023) China-Africa green development cooperation under the global development initiative. China Afr J 1:46–61

Zuo J et al (2021) A new model of global cooperation on climate change: an analysis of tripartite cooperation on climate change. Adv Clim Change Res 1:98

Zhang J (2016) Chinese foreign assistance explained. Brookings Institution

Zhao J (2014) Corporate Social Responsibility in Contemporary China. Edward Elgar, Cheltenham

Zheng J et al (2017) The construction of green finance to support green one belt one road investment. Environ Prot 19:23–35

Laws and Guidelines

Africa Energy Outlook 2021. https://energychamber.org/wp-content/uploads/AEC_Outlook_2021.pdf

Agenda 2063 of the African Union. https://au.int/en/agenda2063/overview

Act on Corporate Due Diligence in Supply Chains (2021) https://www.csr-in-deutschland.de/SharedDocs/Downloads/EN/act-corporate-due-diligence-obligations-supply-chains.pdf?__blob=publicationFile. section 5–8

Appendix 27 Environmental, Social and Governance Reporting Guide. http://en-rules.hkex.com.hk/node/3841

A Guide on Sustainable Management and Utilization of Overseas Forest by Chinese Enterprises (2009) (中国企业境外森林可持续经营利用指南). http://www.mofcom.gov.cn/aarticle/b/g/200904/20090406191363.html

China's Policies and Actions Addressing Climate Change (2024). https://english.mee.gov.cn/News_service/news_release/202501/P020250122370358250549.pdf

China's Second African Policy Paper (2015). http://www.china.org.cn/world/2015-12/05/content_37241677_5.htm

Constitution of Kenya. http://kenyalaw.org/kl/index.php?id=398

China-Africa Economic and Trade Cooperation (2013). http://english.gov.cn/archive/white_paper/2014/08/23/content_281474982986536.htm

Circular on Full Implementation of Green Credit Policies and Further Improvement of Information Sharing (2009) (关于全面落实绿色信贷政策进一步完善信息共享工作的通知). http://zfs.mep.gov.cn/hjjj/gjfbdjjzcx/lsxdzc/201507/t20150716_306758.shtml

Environmental Risk Management Initiative for China's Overseas Investment. http://www.greenfinance.org.cn/displaynews.php?id=1472

Environmental Management Coordination (EMCA) Amendment (2015). http://kenyalaw.org/kl/fileadmin/pdfdownloads/AmendmentActs/2015/EnvironmentalManagementandCo-ordination_Amendment_Act_2015_No5of2015_.pdf

"Environmental Risk Management Initiative for China's Overseas Investment (2017) (中国对外投资环境风险管理倡议). http://www.greenfinance.org.cn/displaynews.php?id=1472

FOCAC Beijing Action Plan (2019–2021). http://focacsummit.mfa.gov.cn/chn/hyqk/201809/t20180905_5859862.htm

FOCAC—Beijing Action Plan (2025–2027). https://www.gov.cn/yaowen/liebiao/202409/content_6972589.htm

Green Industry Guidance Catalogue. (绿色产业指导目录). http://www.ndrc.gov.cn/gzdt/201903/W020190306355285868217.pdf

Guidance on Environmental Protection in Foreign Investment and Cooperation (2013) (对外投资合作环境保护指南). http://www.mofcom.gov.cn/article/b/bf/201302/20130200039930.shtml

Guidance on Building Green Finance System (2016) (关于构建绿色金融体系的指导意见). http://www.mep.gov.cn/gkml/hbb/gwy/201611/t20161124_368163.htm

Guidelines to the State-owned Enterprises Directly under the Central Government on Fulfilling Corporate Social Responsibilities (2008) (关于中央企业履行社会责任的指导意见). http://www.sasac.gov.cn/n103/n85881/n85921/c969197/content.html

Guidelines for Environmental Information Disclosure of Listed Companies in Shanghai Stock Exchange (2008) (上海证券交易所上市公司环境信息披露指引). http://www.sse.com.cn/lawandrules/sserules/listing/stock/c/c_20150912_3985851.shtml

Guidelines for Social Responsibility in Outbound Mining Investments (2015) (中国对外矿业投资行业社会责任指引). http://www.csr.gov.cn/article/policies/ind/201709/20170902652964.shtml

Guidance on Safety Risk Prevention for Chinese Overseas Companies (2016) (中国企业海外安全风险防范指南). http://www.mofcom.gov.cn/article/i/dxfw/gzzd/201606/20160601345155.shtml

Guidance on Promoting Green One Belt One Road (2017) (关于推进绿色"一带一路"建设的指导意见). http://www.mep.gov.cn/gkml/hbb/bwj/201705/t20170505_413602.htm
Guidance on Green Loans (2012) (绿色信贷指引), 2012. http://www.cbrc.gov.cn/chinese/home/docView/127DE230BC31468B9329EFB01AF78BD4.html
Guidance on Social Responsibility of Chinese Banking Financial Institutions (2009) (中国银行业金融机构企业社会责任指引). http://www.china-cba.net/bencandy.php?fid=44&id=6901
Guidelines on Compliance Risk Management of Commercial Bank (2007) (商业银行合规风险管理指引). http://www.cbrc.gov.cn/chinese/home/docDOC_ReadView/2835.html
Guidance on Social Responsibility for Chinese International Contractors (2012) (对外承包工程行业社会责任指引). http://www.mofcom.gov.cn/article/b/bf/201302/20130200039930.shtml
Guiding Opinions on Promoting Investment and Financing in Response to Climate Change. (关于促进应对气候变化投融资的指导意见). https://www.mee.gov.cn/xxgk2018/xxgk/xxgk03/202010/t20201026_804792.html
Guidelines on Green Development in Overseas Investment Cooperation. (对外投资合作绿色发展工作指引). http://images.policy.mofcom.gov.cn/file/20220711/50791657527087450.pdf
Guidance on Promoting Green One Belt One Road. (关于推进绿色"一带一路"建设的指导意见). http://www.mep.gov.cn/gkml/hbb/bwj/201705/t20170505_413602.htm>
General Approach to Reform Central State-owned Enterprises during the 12th Five-Year Plan Period (2011) ("十二五"时期中央企业改革发展的总体思路). http://www.scio.gov.cn/xwfbh/yg/2/Document/860921/860921.htm
How Developing Countries Can Move Towards Modernization—Summary of the Fourth High-Level Think Tank Forum on National Governance for Developing Countries (2023) https://www.ccps.gov.cn/xyyw/202311/t20231112_159850.shtml
Integrated Reform Plan for Promoting Ecological Progress. http://english.www.gov.cn/policies/latest_releases/2015/09/22/content_281475195492066.htm
Interim Measure on Supervision and Administration of the Assets of Central State-Owned Overseas Companies (2011) (中央企业境外国有资产监督管理暂行办法).http://www.gov.cn/flfg/2011-06/24/content_1891821.htm
Kenya Vision 2030. http://www.vision2030.go.ke/
Kenya National Adaptation Plan (2015–2030). http://www4.unfccc.int/nap/Documents%20NAP/Kenya_NAP_Final.pdf
National Climate Change Response Strategy (2010) http://www.environment.go.ke/wp-content/documents/complete%20nccrs%20executive%20brief.pdf
National Climate Change Action Plan (2013–2017) https://cdkn.org/wp-content/uploads/2013/03/Kenya-National-Climate-Change-Action-Plan.pdf
National Environment Policy (2013). http://www.environment.go.ke/wp-content/uploads/2014/01/NATIONAL-ENVIRONMENT-POLICY-20131.pdf
Norms on Foreign Investment Cooperation in the Field of Competition (2013) (规范对外投资合作领域竞争行为的规定). <http://www.mofcom.gov.cn/article/b/g/201309/20130900322914.shtml
OFDI Project Verification and Registration Management Plan (2014) (境外投资项目核准和管理办法). http://www.sdpc.gov.cn/zcfb/zcfbl/201404/W020140410560098013507.pdf
Opinions on Implementing Environmental Protection Policies and Regulations to Prevent Credit Risks (2007) (关于落实环保政策法规防范信贷风险的意见). http://www.cbrc.gov.cn/chinese/home/docView/20080129C3FA6D993AC4AEF7FFE133D6E2AD0D00.html
Overall Reform Plan for Ecological Civilization (2015) (生态文明体质改革总体方案). http://www.gov.cn/guowuyuan/2015-09/21/content_2936327.htm
Public Private Partnerships Act (2013). http://www.kpda.or.ke/documents/Policies/Public%20Private%20Partnerships%20Act%20No.15,%202013.pdf
Programme for the Reform of the Legal Disclosure System for Environmental Information(环境信息依法披露制度改革方案). https://www.mee.gov.cn/xxgk2018/xxgk/xxgk03/202105/W020210525651775162451.pdf

Pilot Work Programme on Climate Investment and Finance (气候投融资试点工作方案). https://www.gov.cn/zhengce/zhengceku/2021-12/25/5664524/files/10bf58f69f4d40269e07f3b84a47bb78.pdf

Responding to Climate Change: China's Policies and Actions. global.chinadaily.com.cn/a/202110/28/WS6179dfdba310cdd39bc71b86.html

Regulation on Management of Foreign Contracted Projects (对外承包工程管理条例) (2012) http://www.gov.cn/gongbao/content/2017/content_5219165.htm

Respond to Climate Change: China's Policies and Actions (2021). cciced.net/ccicedPhoneEN/NewsCenter/LEaDN/202111/t20211104_130073.html

Several Important Resolutions on the Construction of Socialist Harmonious Society by the Central Commission of the Chinese Communist Party (2016) (中共中央关于构建社会主义和谐社会若干重大问题的决定). http://www.gov.cn/govweb/gongbao/content/2006/content_453176.htm

The Critical Assessment Criteria on Green Loan Implementation (2014) (绿色信贷实施情况关键评价指标). http://www.cbrc.gov.cn/chinese/home/docDOC_ReadView/FC5E38D62BE54E3D836E441D6FC2442F.html

The Prevention, Protection and Assistance to Internally Displaced Persons and Affected Communities Act (2012). http://www.refworld.org/docid/511219962.html

The 13th Five-year Plan for Economic and Social Development of the People's Republic of China (2016–2020). http://en.ndrc.gov.cn/newsrelease/201612/P020161207645765233498.pdf

The 2015 China Policy Paper on Africa. https://www.gov.cn/xinwen/2015-12/05/content_5020197.htm

The Vision 2035 for China-Africa Cooperation. https://www.yidaiyilu.gov.cn/p/293626.html

The Environment and Land Court Act (2011) § 18. http://extwprlegs1.fao.org/docs/pdf/ken112134.pdf

"The Land Act of Kenya", Part VIII. http://kenyalaw.org/kl/fileadmin/pdfdownloads/AmendmentActs/2016/LandLaws_Amendment_Act_28of2016.pdf

The National Land Commission Act (2012) § 3. https://www.ecolex.org/details/legislation/national-land-commission-act-2012-no-5-of-2012-lex-faoc112132/

The Interpretations of the Johannesburg Summit of the FOCAC and the Sixth Ministerial Conference on the 10 Major China-Africa Cooperation Plans in Economic and Trade Domains (2015). http://english.mofcom.gov.cn/article/policyrelease/Cocoon/201512/20151201219036.shtml

"The 13th five-year plan on eco-environmental protection" ("十三五"生态环境保护规划), 2016. http://www.gov.cn/zhengce/content/2016-12/05/content_5143290.htm

Vision and actions on jointly building silk road economic belt and 21st-century maritime silk road. 2015. http://en.ndrc.gov.cn/newsrelease/201503/t20150330_669367.html

White Paper on China's Policies and Actions on Climate Change. m.thepaper.cn/baijiahao_15094136

White Paper on China-Africa cooperation in the new era. https://www.gov.cn/zhengce/2021-11/26/content_5653540.htm

International Organization Documents

African Development Bank (2023) Electricity regulatory index for Africa 2022. https://africa-energy-portal.org/reports/electricity-regulatory-index-africa-2022-eri

OECD (2011) The OECD guidelines for multinational enterprises. http://www.oecd.org/daf/inv/mne/48004323.pdf

The United Nations Global Compact. https://www.unglobalcompact.org/

UNCTAD (2022) South–South cooperation for climate adaptation and sustainable development. unctad.org/system/files/official-document/tcsgdsinf2022d1_en.pdf

UNCTAD (2017) UNCTAD Methodological Note. http://unctad.org/en/PublicationChapters/wir2017chMethodNote_en.pdf

UNCTAD (2015) Investment policy framework for sustainable development. https://unctad.org/system/files/official-document/diaepcb2015d5_en.pdf. 77–78

UN Conference on Trade and Development (2016) Foreign direct investment to Africa fell by a moderate three per cent in 2016. http://unctad.org/en/pages/PressRelease.aspx?OriginalVersionID=408

UNDP China (2017) 2017 report on the sustainable development of chinese enterprises overseas supporting—the belt and road regions to achieve the 2030 agenda for sustainable development. http://www.cn.undp.org/content/china/en/home/library/south-south-cooperation/2017-report-on-the-sustainable-development-of-chinese-enterprise.html

UNDP (2016) The 2016 human development reports of UNDP. http://hdr.undp.org/sites/default/files/2016_human_development_report.pdf

UNDP (2016) China's climate change South–South cooperation: history and future trends. https://bit.ly/44ja0Zy

UNDP(2016) More money, more impact? China's climate change south–south cooperation to date and future trends. https://bit.ly/456PYCw

UNDP(2014) China-Zambia South-South cooperation on renewable energy technology transfer. https://www.undp.org/china/projects/china-zambia-south-south-cooperation-renewable-energy-technology-transfer

UN Economic Commission for Africa (2016) Measuring corruption in africa: the international dimension matters. https://repository.uneca.org/handle/10855/23012

UN Economic Commission for Africa (2016) Green Africa's industrialization, pp 54–58. http://repository.uneca.org/bitstream/handle/10855/23017/b11560861.pdf?sequence=1

UN Economic Commission for Africa (2014) Common African position on the post-2015 development agenda. https://sustainabledevelopment.un.org/index.php?page=view&type=400&nr=1329&menu=35

UNEP Financial Initiative (UNEP FI). https://www.unpri.org/

UNEP (2024) Emissions Gap Report 2024. <https://www.unep.org/resources/emissions-gap-report-2024

UNEP (2023) As climate impacts accelerate, finance gap for adaptation efforts at least 50% bigger than thought. https://www.unep.org/news-and-stories/press-release/climate-impacts-accelerate-finance-gap-adaptation-efforts-least-50

UNEP (2021) Adaptation Gap Report 2021: the Gathering Storm-Adapting to Climate Change in a Post-Pandemic World. https://www.unep.org/resources/adaptation-gap-report-2021

UNEP (2020) Emissions Gap Report 2020. https://www.unep.org/emissions-gap-report-2020

UNEP (2018) African Countries, China Launch Joint Environmental Effort with Plans for New Center Based in Nairobi. https://www.unenvironment.org/zh-hans/news-and-stories/xinwengao/zhongfeihuanjinghezuozhongxinlinshimishuchujiepaichengli

UNEP Inquiry (2016) Environmental risk analysis of financial institutions. unepinquiry.org/wpcontent/uploads/2016/09/2_Environment_Risk_Anlysis_by_Financial_Institutions.pdf

UNEP (2016) Green is Gold. The strategy and actions of China's ecological civilization. https://reliefweb.int/sites/reliefweb.int/files/resources/greenisgold_en_20160519.pdf

UNEP (2016) GEO-6: regional assessment for Africa. https://www.unep.org/resources/assessment/geo-6-regional-assessment-africa#:~:text=The%20GEO%2D6%20regional%20assessment,well%2Dbeing%20are%20continuously%20enhanced

UNEP. The Belt and Road Initiative International Green Development Coalition. unep.org/regions/asia-and-pacific/regional-initiatives/belt-and-road-initiative-international-green

UNEP (2016) Green is Gold. The strategy and actions of China's ecological civilization. https://reliefweb.int/sites/reliefweb.int/files/resources/greenisgold_en_20160519.pdf

UNEP (2014) Aligning the financial system with sustainable development. https://www.unep.org/resources/report/aligning-financial-system-sustainable-development-coming-financial-climate

UNEP Finance Initiative. Financial Institutions Taking Actions on Climate Change. unepfi.org/fileadmin/documents/FinancialInstitutionsTakingActionOnClimateChange.pdf

UNEP Finance Initiative (2019) Principles for Responsible Banking (PRB). https://www.unepfi.org/wordpress/wp-content/uploads/2019/07/FINAL-PRB-Signature-Document-2-Interactive-22-07-19.pdf

UNFCCC (2016) "The Paris Agreement". https://unfccc.int/sites/default/files/resource/parisagreement_publication.pdf

UNFCCC (2016) Decision 1/CP.21, Adoption of the Paris Agreement. UN Doc CCC/CP/2015/10/Add.1, paras 117, 133 and 134

UNFCCC (2022) China's achievements, new goals and new measures for nationally determined contributions. unfccc.int/sites/default/files/NDC/2022-06/中国落实国家自主贡献成效和新目标新举措.pdf

UNFCCC. China's long-term low greenhouse gas emissions development strategy for the mid-century. unfccc.int/documents/307766

IFC (2007) General environmental, health, and safety guidelines. https://www.ifc.org/wps/wcm/connect/topics_ext_content/ifc_external_corporate_site/sustainability-at-ifc/publications/publications_policy_ehs-general

IFC (2012) IFC sustainability framework. https://www.ifc.org/wps/wcm/connect/b9dacb004a73e7a8a273fff998895a12/IFC_Sustainability_+Framework.pdf?MOD=AJPERES

IFC (2012) IFC performance standards on environmental and social sustainability. https://www.ifc.org/wps/wcm/connect/c8f524004a73daeca09afdf998895a12/IFC_Performance_Standards.pdf?MOD=AJPERES

The UN Human Rights Council (2021) Legally Binding Instrument to Regulate, in International Human Rights Law, the activities of transnational companies and other business companies, OEIGWG Chairmanship Third Revised Draft 2021. preamble 6(4), 8(6)

World Bank, Environmental, Health, and Safety Guidelines. http://www.ifc.org/wps/wcm/connect/topics_ext_content/ifc_external_corporate_site/sustainability-at-ifc/policies-standards/ehs-guidelines

World Bank (2022) African governments urgently need to restore macro-economic stability and protect the poor in a context of slow growth. <https://www.worldbank.org/en/news/press-release/2022/10/04/african-governments-urgently-need-to-restore-macro-economic-stability-and-protect-the-poor-in-a-context-of-slow-growth

World Bank (2017) The World Bank in Kenya. http://www.worldbank.org/en/country/kenya/overview

World Bank (2016) World Bank Group climate change action plan. http://pubdocs.worldbank.org/en/677331460056382875/WBG-Climate-Change-Action-Plan-public-version.pdf

World Bank (2016) World Bank Group sets new course to help countries meet urgent climate challenges. http://www.worldbank.org/en/news/feature/2016/04/07/world-bank-group-sets-new-course-to-help-countries-meet-urgent-climate-challenges

World Bank (2015) Africa climate business plan: accelerating climate-resilient and low-carbon development. Working Paper. http://documents.worldbank.org/curated/en/401711468185370301/pdf/101130-REPLACEMENT-FILE-SAME-BOX-PUBLIC-K8545.pdf

World Bank (2002) The World Bank Policy on Disclosure of Information. http://siteresources.worldbank.org/OPSMANUAL/Resources/DisclosurePolicy.pdf

World Bank (2013) World Bank Safeguard Policies. http://web.worldbank.org/WBSITE/EXTERNAL/PROJECTS/EXTPOLICIES/EXTSAFEPOL/0

MIX
Papier aus verantwortungsvollen Quellen
Paper from responsible sources
FSC® C105338

If you have any concerns about our products,
you can contact us on
ProductSafety@springernature.com

In case Publisher is established outside the EU,
the EU authorized representative is:
Springer Nature Customer Service Center GmbH
Europaplatz 3, 69115 Heidelberg, Germany

Printed by Libri Plureos GmbH
in Hamburg, Germany